We Believe—Therefore We Speak

The Theology and Practice of Evangelism

WE BELIEVE— THEREFORE WE SPEAK

The Theology and Practice of Evangelism

David J. Valleskey

NORTHWESTERN PUBLISHING HOUSE
Milwaukee, Wisconsin

Third printing, 2004
Second printing, 1997

Library of Congress Card 94-69559
Northwestern Publishing House
1250 N. 113th St., Milwaukee, WI 53226-3284

Published 1995
Printed in the United States of America
Paperback ISBN 0-8100-0539-5
Hardbound ISBN 0-8100-0540-9

TABLE OF CONTENTS

Part Two: Therefore We Speak— The Practice of Evangelism in the Congregation

Study Questions for We Believe—Therefore We Speak

Preface

Purpose

This book, God willing, will serve a twofold purpose: It is first of all meant to be a classroom text for a course I am presently teaching at Wisconsin Lutheran Seminary on the theology and practice of evangelism. We pray that this text will help to fill a significant gap. Though there is no lack of books on evangelism in the marketplace, there are very few books that treat this subject from an evangelical Lutheran perspective. Among the texts that do this is *Speaking the Gospel Today,*[1] by Robert Kolb. This volume, however, is somewhat theoretical, covering only the theology of evangelism. A second book, *The Church in the Community*, by Arthur E. Graf, former professor of practical theology at Concordia Theological Seminary, Springfield, Illinois, deals with both the theology and practice of evangelism, but is rather brief on the theology side. Originally published by Eerdmans in 1965, *The Church in the Community* has been reprinted by Concordia Theological Seminary, Fort Wayne, Indiana.

It is also my hope that this volume may serve as a resource for pastors and others working in the area of outreach in their congregations. Since it is anticipated that lay leaders will also be utilizing the book, I have kept the use of technical terminology, e.g., Greek words, to a minimum.

In Part Two of this book especially, I will be referring to a number of evangelism resources produced under the auspices of the Commission on Evangelism of the Wisconsin Evangelical Lutheran Synod. The initials NPH will indicate that these materials are available from Northwestern Publishing House, 1250 N. 113th St., Milwaukee, WI 53226-3284 (Phone: 800-662-6022 or 414-475-6600). A WELS Parish Services Catalog that describes and gives the NPH order number of all WELS-produced evangelism materials may be obtained from the WELS Board for Parish Services, 2929 N. Mayfair Rd., Milwaukee, WI 53222-4398.

---

[1]Robert Kolb, *Speaking the Gospel Today* (St. Louis: Concordia, 1984).

Acknowledgments

We Believe—Therefore We Speak is the outgrowth of practical experience—22 years in the parish ministry—and of teaching a course in evangelism at Wisconsin Lutheran Seminary from 1984 to the present. Actually, it goes back farther than that. The author traces his zeal for outreach with the gospel to his father, Wilmer M. Valleskey, who throughout his ministry modeled a passionate concern for carrying out the Great Commission. This book is dedicated to him.

I cannot help but mention others who have helped to shape my attitude toward the ministry: Edgar Hoenecke, a man with an unflagging zeal for missions; E. Arnold Sitz, and his evangelical approach to ministry; Robert Hochmuth, who throughout his ministry worked with untiring, loving efforts to reach out to the lost and to nurture the believer; the members of Apostles Lutheran Church, San Jose, California, who for 20 years shared with their pastor the vision of a Christian congregation as the people of God on a mission to go out into the highways and byways with the gospel.

I would like to express my thanks to Richard Balge, Joel Gerlach, and Paul Kelm, who carefully reviewed my manuscript and offered many helpful suggestions. Thanks also to my colleagues in the New Testament department of Wisconsin Lutheran Seminary, with whom I consulted on certain portions of the manuscript. Also, a word of thanks to James Tiefel, professor of worship at Wisconsin Lutheran Seminary, for his considerable assistance with the section on worship and evangelism in chapter four.

Above all, thanks and praise to a gracious God. Through baptism he incorporated me into his family. Through the Word and the Holy Supper he has kept me his own. And through his church, he has permitted me to proclaim the gospel in the parish and the seminary classroom for more than 30 years.

David J. Valleskey
Fall 1994

Introduction

Title

The title of this book, *We Believe—Therefore We Speak,* tells the story of what the reader will find within. As the subtitle indicates, it is intended to cover both the theology and the practice of evangelism. The order is significant. Theology—*We Believe*—precedes proclamation—*Therefore We Speak.* Theology also propels proclamation. What we believe, the content of our faith, will direct and inspire what we say.

So it was when the apostle Paul wrote the words that have provided the title for this book: "It is written: 'I believed; therefore I have spoken.' With that same spirit of faith we also believe and therefore speak" (2 Corinthians 4:13). "I believed; therefore I have spoken" is a quotation of Psalm 116:10 in the Septuagint translation. This psalm focuses on three things: great affliction, deliverance from affliction, and gratitude for deliverance.

The psalmist had endured a time of great affliction: "The cords of death entangled me, the anguish of the grave came upon me; I was overcome by trouble and sorrow" (116:3). But then the Lord had rescued him: "When I was in great need, he saved me" (116:6). "You, O LORD, have delivered my soul from death, my eyes from tears, my feet from stumbling" (116:8).

Now he is grateful for that deliverance: "How can I repay the LORD for all his goodness to me?" (116:12). "I will sacrifice a thank offering to you," he says, "and call on the name of the LORD" (116:17).

The psalmist summarizes his grateful response with the words Paul quotes: "I believed; therefore I have spoken." Paul applies these words to himself: "With that same spirit of faith we also believe and therefore speak." Paul had been rescued from the greatest affliction of all, the wages of his sin, eternal death. His grateful heart, convinced by the gospel that "Christ Jesus came into the world to save sinners," of whom he was "the worst" (1 Timothy 1:15), cannot help but speak.

So it is with Christians today. We believe; therefore we speak. In this book we intend to demonstrate in particular that Christians who have and hold to the teachings of the evangelical Lutheran church, drawn solely from the Scriptures and summarized in the confessional writings of the church as contained in the Book of Concord (1580), have every reason to be leaders in outreach with the gospel. F. Bente, author of the historical introduction to the Concordia Triglotta, which contains the confessional writings ("symbols") of the Lutheran Church, writes:

"Not the great number of her adherents, not her organization, not her charitable and other institutions, not her beautiful customs and liturgical forms, etc., but the precious truths confessed by her symbols in perfect agreement with the Holy Scriptures constitute the true beauty and rich treasures of our Church as well as the never-failing source of her vitality and power."[2]

As Lutheran Christians we do have a beautiful and rich treasure to share with the world. Francis Pieper properly asserts that "the Lutheran Church in its original, unchangeable form of doctrine should therefore not act timidly among men, as though it had to apologize for still existing, but it should by God's grace step before the Church and the world with that confidence which the knowledge of the divine truth flowing from the continuance in the Word of the Apostles and Prophets inspires."[3] What we believe provides a solid foundation and a compelling motive for speaking.

Structure

The outline for Part One, *We Believe,* will follow two of the ancient confessions of Christendom, the Apostles' and Nicene Creeds. The chapter headings will use the wording of the Nicene Creed:

We Believe in One God, the Father, the Almighty, Maker of Heaven and Earth.

We Believe in One Lord, Jesus Christ, the Only Son of God.

We Believe in the Holy Spirit, the Lord, the Giver of Life.

Part Two, *Therefore We Speak,* will apply the doctrines discussed in Part One. It will center on the practice of evangelism, especially as carried out by the congregation.

Definition

Before moving into Part One, we should take a few moments to clarify how we will be using the word "evangelism" in this book. The

---

[2]Quoted in *Popular Symbolics,* Th. Engelder, W. Arndt, Th. Graebner, F. E. Mayer (St. Louis: Concordia, 1934), pp. 24,25.

[3]Francis Pieper, *Christian Dogmatics,* Vol. 1 (St. Louis: Concordia, 1950), p. 184.

Greek word from which it comes (*euangelion*) means "good news." The verb "to evangelize" (*euangelizomai*) means "to announce, to tell, to be a messenger of good news."

In the Greek translation of the Old Testament, the Septuagint, *euangelizomai* is used for the Hebrew word *bisser,* which means "to make one cheerful with, to bring, to announce glad tidings." It is used in the Old Testament especially to announce the glad tidings of God's salvation through his promised Messiah. The verb *euangelizomai,* to tell or proclaim good news, is used in each of the following passages:

> Sing to the LORD, praise his name; *proclaim* his salvation day after day. Declare his glory among the nations, his marvelous deeds among all peoples. (Psalm 96:2,3)
>
> You who *bring good tidings* to Zion, go up on a high mountain. You who *bring good tidings* to Jerusalem, lift up your voice with a shout, lift it up, do not be afraid; say to the towns of Judah, "Here is your God!" (Isaiah 40:9)
>
> How beautiful on the mountains are the feet of those who *bring good news,* who proclaim peace, who *bring good tidings,* who proclaim salvation, who say to Zion, "Your God reigns!" (Isaiah 52:7)
>
> All from Sheba will come, bearing gold and incense and *proclaiming* the praise of the LORD. (Isaiah 60:6)
>
> The Spirit of the Sovereign LORD is on me, because the LORD has anointed me to *preach good news* to the poor. He has sent me to bind up the brokenhearted, to proclaim freedom for the captives and release from darkness for the prisoners. (Isaiah 61:1)

In the New Testament, likewise, the emphasis is on verbal proclamation. Evangelism is:

- the angel announcing to the shepherds, "Do not be afraid. I bring you good news of great joy that will be for all the people. Today in the town of David a Savior has been born to you; he is Christ the Lord" (Luke 2:10,11)
- Peter in the house of Cornelius "telling the good news of peace through Jesus Christ" (Acts 10:36)
- the disciples, following their release from prison, "proclaiming the good news that Jesus is the Christ" (Acts 5:42)

- the evangelist Philip preaching "the good news of the kingdom of God" to the people of Samaria and telling the eunuch of Ethiopia "the good news about Jesus" (Acts 8:12,35)
- Paul in Athens "preaching the good news about Jesus and the resurrection" (Acts 17:18)

The evangel, the gospel, is a message. A message needs to be communicated—either by voice or printed page. In either case the emphasis is on verbal proclamation.

Some include under the term evangelism "the total work of the church as it relates to the proclamation of the gospel."[4] This would embrace not just verbal but non-verbal witness, e.g., the appearance of a church's property or a Christian letting the light of his faith shine by his deeds. While one could conceivably call this evangelism in a very broad sense, it appears to be better to use some other term, e.g., pre-evangelism, to describe such non-verbal witness and to reserve the word evangelism for the verbal proclamation of the good news of salvation. It is the message and the message alone which is "the power of God for the salvation of everyone who believes" (Romans 1:16).

That message, properly speaking, is the gospel only, not the law. It is through the gospel that the Holy Spirit calls one to faith (2 Thessalonians 2:14). This does not discount the need for the law, however. When Peter told the people gathered at Solomon's Colonnade, "You killed the author of life" (Acts 3:15), he was using the law. But he followed with the comforting gospel promise, "Repent, then, and turn to God, so that your sins may be wiped out, that times of refreshing may come from the Lord" (Acts 3:19).

In a wide sense we can say that Peter's entire message at Solomon's Colonnade, law and gospel, was evangelizing, or preaching the gospel. The Lutheran Confessions remind us that

> the little word "Gospel" does not always have one and the same meaning but is used in a twofold way in the Holy Scripture of God and by ancient and modern theologians. In the one case the word is used in such a way that we understand by it the entire teaching of Christ, our Lord. . . . Here the term includes both the exposition of the law and the proclamation of the mercy and grace of God [the gospel]. . . . In addition, however, the word

---

[4]Armin W. Schuetze and Irwin J. Habeck, *The Shepherd under Christ,* 2nd ed. (Milwaukee: Northwestern Publishing House, 1981), p. 228.

> "Gospel" is also used in another (that is, in a strict) sense. Here it does not include the proclamation of repentance [the law] but solely the preaching of God's grace [the gospel].[5]

When Christians tell others of their sins (law) and then tell them of their Savior (gospel), it can therefore properly be said that they are evangelizing them. In its wide sense, evangelism is the verbal proclamation of sin and grace, law and gospel.

Strictly speaking, though, the evangel, the gospel, has to do with God's gracious action on behalf of mankind. It is the good news that in Christ God has reconciled the world to himself, not counting people's sins against them (cf. 2 Corinthians 5:19). Above all, therefore, the evangelist's message will center on the finished work of Jesus Christ.

Part One

We Believe—

The Theology of Evangelism

Chapter One:
We Believe in One God, the Father, the Almighty, Maker of Heaven and Earth

1—Natural Knowledge of God

What natural knowledge is

On their first missionary journey, Paul and Barnabas visited the city of Lystra in Asia Minor. There Paul came upon a man who had been lame from birth. To this man who had never walked, Paul said, "Stand up on your feet." The man jumped up and began to walk. A crowd of people quickly gathered. They concluded, "The gods have come down to us in human form." They called Barnabas "Zeus," the chief of the gods, and Paul "Hermes," the messenger god, since Paul was the one doing the speaking. They tried to offer sacrifices to these "gods" in human form.

Paul attempted to prevent this idolatrous worship. He rushed into the midst of the crowd, shouting, "Men, why are you doing this? We too are only men, human like you" (cf. Acts 14:8-15).

Paul did more than that, however. He used the occasion to try to turn the Lystrans' thinking from false gods to the one true God. He told them:

> We are bringing you good news, telling you to turn from these worthless things to the living God, who made heaven and earth and sea and everything in them. In the past, he let all nations go their own way. Yet he has not left himself without testimony: He has shown kindness by giving you rain from heaven and crops in their seasons; he provides you with plenty of food and fills your hearts with joy. (Acts 14:15-17)

Paul did not have to prove the existence of a god to the people of Lystra. The testimony of God's existence surrounded them: the heavens, the earth, the seas, the rain, the sunshine, the crops that had sprouted from seed and grown into mature grain. The people knew that they themselves could not have made the heavens. They could not have formed the earth and the seas. They were incapable of making it rain or causing the sun to shine. They did not possess the power to create a plant from a seed. Someone beyond them, some power higher than they, a god, or gods, must have done it.

The people of Lystra knew that there was a god. For them that was a given. Their thinking had to be elevated, though, from god to God. Paul used their "natural" knowledge that there is a god as a point of contact. His next step, had his enemies not stirred up the crowd to stone him and drag him out of the city, would have been to tell them more about the one true God and what he had done to bring them into a right relationship with him.

On his second missionary journey, a few years after the incident in Lystra, Paul arrived in Athens. While waiting for Silas and Timothy to catch up with him, he did some sight-seeing in that historic city, the ancient Greek center of learning and philosophy. Unlike the people of Lystra, none of the Athenians mistook him for a god. There was no lack of other gods, however, in Athens. We are told that Paul "was greatly distressed to see that the city was full of idols" (Acts 17:16).

There were some big differences between the people in Lystra and the citizens of Athens. The Lystrans were a relatively unlearned and unsophisticated people; the Athenians prided themselves on their wisdom and sophistication. Both, however, had this in common: they took for granted the existence of a god.

As in Lystra, so in Athens, Paul used this "natural" knowledge of God as a point of contact to try to turn the Athenians' thinking toward the one true God. Listen to Paul as he addresses a meeting of the Areopagus. He introduced his message by referring to what he had seen in Athens. Then he continued:

> The God who made the world and everything in it is the Lord of heaven and earth and does not live in temples built by hands. And he is not served by human hands, as if he needed anything, because he himself gives all men life and breath and everything else. From one man he made every nation of men, that they should inhabit the whole earth; and he determined the times set for them and the exact places where they should live. God did this so that men would seek him and perhaps reach out for him and find him, though he is not far from each one of us. (Acts 17:24-27)

The true God, says Paul, is far above any statue or temple made by man. The true God is the one who made man and everything else. Paul concludes with a call to repentance:

> Therefore since we are God's offspring, we should not think that the divine being is like gold or silver or stone—an image made

> by man's design and skill. In the past God overlooked such ignorance, but now he commands all people everywhere to repent. For he has set a day when he will judge the world with justice by the man he has appointed. He has given proof of this to all men by raising him from the dead. (Acts 17:29-31)

The creature is accountable to the Creator. One day he will judge all people by the man he has appointed according to the standards he has established.

In both Lystra and Athens, Paul's initial point of contact with those who did not know Christ was their natural knowledge of the existence of some kind of higher being. It was on his third missionary journey that Paul, under inspiration of the Holy Spirit, set forth the doctrine of the natural knowledge of God most thoroughly. Writing from Corinth to the church at Rome, Paul brings out two points that are applicable to the church's work of evangelizing the unbeliever.

First, as Paul had made clear at both Lystra and Athens, God has not left himself without testimony of his existence, testimony that even the heathen can easily recognize. One clear indication of the existence of God is the created universe:

> What may be known about God is plain to them, because God has made it plain to them. For since the creation of the world God's invisible qualities—his eternal power and divine nature—have been clearly seen, being understood from what has been made, so that men are without excuse. (Romans 1:19,20)

The existence of the universe not only tells people there is a god, but makes it clear that he is a powerful being.

A second equally clear evidence of God's existence is an internal one—the voice of conscience, which acknowledges the existence of a law higher than itself, and hence also the existence of a law-giver:

> When Gentiles, who do not have the law, do by nature things required by the law, they are a law for themselves, even though they do not have the law, since they show that the requirements of the law are written on their hearts, their consciences also bearing witness, and their thoughts now accusing, now even defending them. (Romans 2:14,15)

Limitations of natural knowledge

The second point that Paul makes clear about the natural knowledge of God through nature and conscience is that such knowledge is insufficient for salvation. Natural knowledge tells only that there is a god; it does not reveal the one true God. It tells that there is a law, but it does not give one the power or, for that matter, even the inclination, to keep it.

Natural knowledge of the law produces rebellion, not obedience—and guilt. Paul writes that unbelievers, who know that there is a god who made the heavens and inscribed his law on their hearts, "suppress the truth by their wickedness. . . . They exchanged the truth of God for a lie, and worshiped and served created things rather than the Creator" (Romans 1:18,25).

"They have become filled with every kind of wickedness, evil, greed and depravity," Paul writes. "They are full of envy, murder, strife, deceit and malice. They are gossips, slanderers, God-haters, insolent, arrogant and boastful; they invent ways of doing evil; they disobey their parents; they are senseless, faithless, heartless, ruthless. Although they know God's righteous decree that those who do such things deserve death, they not only continue to do these very things but also approve of those who practice them" (Romans 1:29-32).

The use of natural knowledge in evangelism

It is clear from the above that the task of evangelism involves much more than appealing to what people innately know about God. Natural knowledge cannot save. Both of these evidences of God's existence, the universe without and the voice of conscience within, however, provide an excellent point of contact for the evangelist. Luther, for example, writes about the law of God implanted in everyone's heart:

> If the Natural Law had not been inscribed and placed by God into the heart, one would have to preach a long time before the consciences are touched; to a donkey, horse, ox, cow one would have to preach 100,000 years before they would accept the Law in spite of the fact that they have ears, eyes, and heart, as man has; they can also hear it, but it does not touch their heart. Why? What is at fault? Their soul is not so constituted and formed that this preaching would take hold. But when the Law is propounded to man, he soon says: Yes, it is so; I cannot deny it. Of this validity he could not be convinced so quickly were it not for the fact that the Law is written in his heart. Since, however, it is already in his heart, although completely blurred, it is aroused by the preaching of the Word.[1]

[1]*St. Louis Edition,* III:1053, quoted in Francis Pieper, *Christian Dogmatics,* Vol. 1 (St. Louis: Concordia, 1950), p. 374.

That is true today also. In general, people accept the existence of God. As the Scriptures say, only a fool maintains that there is no god (cf. Psalm 14:1). In most cases people also recognize that all is not completely right with their lives and, as a result, suffer a certain vague sense of guilt. That remains true even in a society such as ours, which seeks to write off the idea of guilt.

Though some claim we are living in a post-Christian era, that does not mean this is a post-natural knowledge of God era. People can and do seek to suppress their knowledge of God's existence. They cannot, however, completely eradicate it.

A survey taken by the Barna Research Group indicates that 74% of Americans agree strongly (and another 12% agree somewhat) that there is only one true God, who is holy and perfect, who created the world and rules today.[2] The survey respondents were asked to comment on the statement: There is a God who watches over you and answers your prayers. Almost three-fourths of those polled (73%) agreed strongly with the statement and another 16% agreed somewhat.[3] It should not come as a surprise, however, recognizing the limitations of the natural knowledge of God, that 64% either strongly or somewhat agreed that Christians, Jews, Muslims, Buddhists, and others all pray to the same God.[4]

The statistics gathered by George Gallup corroborate those of Barna:

- 98% of Americans believe there is a god of some kind
- 90% pray
- 88% say they have never doubted the existence of God
- 81% believe they will face God at Judgment Day to answer for their sins
- 71% believe in life after death[5]

Judging from statistics such as these, Paul's natural knowledge of God approach to the unbelievers in Lystra and Athens is not at all irrelevant to our times. People today are also "religious," as were the

---

[2]George Barna, *What Americans Believe—An Annual Survey of Values and Religious Views in the United States* (Ventura: Regal Books, 1991), p. 203.

[3]*Ibid.*, p. 209.

[4]*Ibid.*, p. 212.

[5]George Gallup Jr. and Jim Castelli, *The People's Religion—American Faith in the Nineties* (New York: Macmillan, 1989), pp. 45,51,56,58.

citizens of Athens (cf. Acts 17:22). That is true even in a "sophisticated" society such as the one in which we live. The popularity of various forms of "New Age" religion in our time is vivid testimony to that fact.

To ask people how they feel about their relationship with God; to inquire of them where they think they stand with God; to explore where they envision they will spend eternity; to ask people, "If you were to die tonight and stand before God and he were to ask you, 'Why should I let you into my heaven?' what would you say?"—is to be putting one's finger on matters which people know they should be thinking about, whether due to prior religious training,[6] or natural knowledge, or a combination of the two. They may be trying to suppress the truth that there is a god, that there are certain standards he has set, and that they are accountable to their Maker, but deep within they know all these things and in most cases (cf. the statistics above) readily admit them to be true.

To touch on people's feelings of guilt, anxiety, loneliness, emptiness, depression, and worthlessness, their relentless and never successful pursuit of happiness and fulfillment through hedonistic and materialistic means, and to show how all these things have a spiritual basis—this is also possible because of people's innate knowledge of God.

People can be shown that, as St. Augustine put it in his *Confessions,* "Thou, O God, hast made us for Thyself; and our heart is restless until it rests in Thee." They can be led to see that when they are separated from God they have to fill this "God-void" with something. And, since whatever they fill their lives with ultimately does not satisfy, the result is a troubled, frustrated, empty existence. With that they are at a point where the evangelist can proceed to the message God has revealed to solve such problems, a message that centers on the real problem, sin, and the real solution, God's grace in Christ.

2—Revealed Knowledge of God

The Holy Scriptures

In his address to the Areopagus, Paul expressed a key purpose of the natural knowledge of God: "God did this so that men would seek him and perhaps reach out for him and find him" (Acts 17:27). On their own, though, people will never find God, not the God they need, the one God who saves the sinner. "No eye has seen, no ear has heard, no mind has conceived what God has prepared for those who

---

[6]"Eighty-two percent of [American] adults had some religious education as children" (Gallup, *ibid.,* p. 67.)

love him" (1 Corinthians 2:9). Knowledge of "what God has prepared," salvation through Jesus Christ, must come through a revelation of God beyond nature and conscience.

God has graciously given such a revelation. "God has revealed it to us by his Spirit," says Paul (1 Corinthians 2:10). The Spirit works through the "words taught by the Spirit" (1 Corinthians 2:13), the Holy Scriptures. "Men spoke from God as they were carried along by the Holy Spirit" (2 Peter 1:21).

It is in the Scriptures that people are introduced to "the only true God, and Jesus Christ, whom you [God] have sent" (John 17:3). To know the only true God, and Jesus Christ, that, says Jesus, is "eternal life" (John 17:3).

This underscores the importance of the Scriptures to the evangelist. Only the Scriptures reveal the true God who saves the sinner. Essentially, then, the work of the evangelist is to bring the message of the Scriptures to the sinner in need of salvation.

There are a number of reasons why one can do this with absolute confidence.

The Scriptures are the inspired, inerrant Word of God

"All Scripture is God-breathed" (2 Timothy 3:16), writes Paul. God himself breathed into the writers the very words he wanted them to write. Since the Scriptures were written under inspiration of the Holy Spirit, it should come as no surprise that Jesus himself speaks of their inerrancy. "The Scripture cannot be broken," he declares (John 10:35).

While the Lutheran Confessions do not have a separate article on the inspiration and inerrancy of Scripture (that was not a matter under debate at the time), it is clear that they do assume Scripture's inspiration and inerrancy. The Confessions use phrases such as "the Holy Spirit through the mouth of the holy apostle"[7] and "the clear Scripture of the Holy Spirit."[8] The Formula of Concord asserts: "God's Word is not false nor does it lie."[9] In his Large Catechism Luther says, "God's Word cannot err."[10]

The implication for evangelism is clear. In using the message of the Scriptures to speak to people, an evangelist can have complete confidence in his message. What he or she tells them about sin and

---

[7]Formula of Concord, Solid Declaration, Article X, 15.

[8]Apology of the Augsburg Confession, Preface, 9.

[9]Epitome, Article VII, 13.

[10]Large Catechism, Baptism, 57.

grace, law and gospel, is the truth. God, whose Word it is, cannot lie. To ask a person, "May I share with you what the Bible says about the way to a right relationship with God?" turns the individual away from the evangelist's personal, subjective feelings about religion and leads the person into the very presence of God.

Because their message is that of the inspired, inerrant Word, evangelists do not have to say, "I think," or "It could be." With St. Paul, present-day evangelists can say, "I know" (2 Timothy 1:12). The Scriptures have been written "so that you may know that you have eternal life" (1 John 5:13).

The Scriptures are sufficient

This does not mean that the Scriptures tell us everything we may want to know; but they do reveal everything we need to know. What we need most is found in the statement with which John summarized his Gospel: "These [things] are written that you may believe that Jesus is the Christ, the Son of God, and that by believing you may have life in his name" (John 20:31).

Recall the parable of the rich man and Lazarus. The rich man in hell begged Abraham to permit Lazarus to return from the dead and warn the rich man's brothers of the eternal consequences of unbelief. "They have Moses and the Prophets," Abraham replied. "Let them listen to them." The Rich Man was not convinced that would work. It would take something more. He said, "If someone from the dead goes to them, they will repent." In no uncertain terms Abraham responded, "If they do not listen to Moses and the Prophets, they will not be convinced even if someone rises from the dead" (cf. Luke 16:27-31).

The Word is sufficient. This, too, has implications for evangelism. People need nothing more than the message of the Word, sin and grace, law and gospel. The evangelist's tool is not the Word plus something else; it is the Word alone.

This is not meant to imply that there is no evangelistic value, for example, in a godly personal lifestyle (cf. 1 Peter 3:1-7) or in a warm and welcoming congregational atmosphere. We will talk about a number of such things in Part Two of this book. It does mean, though, that the Word alone is all we need for what evangelism is all about—proclaiming the way to life with God now and forever. Only the Scriptures contain that message.

The Scriptures are powerful

Not only do the Scriptures authoritatively and sufficiently reveal everything necessary for salvation, they also have within them the power to lead people to accept what they authoritatively and sufficiently teach.

"The word of God is living and active," the writer of Hebrews says (4:12). Peter tells us, "You have been born again . . . through the living and enduring word of God" (1 Peter 1:23). "The gospel . . . is the power of God for the salvation of everyone who believes," writes Paul to the Romans (1:16). "Our gospel came to you," Paul reminds the Thessalonians, "not simply with words, but also with power, with the Holy Spirit" (1 Thessalonians 1:5).

Again, the implications for evangelism are significant. The Christian needs only to get the Word out, to unsheath its power. Knowing this helps to overcome timidity and feelings of inadequacy. The Word will produce its own results. The Word is the seed sown in the soil which springs up and sprouts of its own accord (Mark 4:26-29). It is the net cast into the sea by fishers of men (Luke 5:1-11). Evangelists are seed-sowers. Evangelists are net-casters. God makes the seed grow. God fills the net.

Evangelists are witnesses telling the truth about what they have seen and heard (cf. Acts 1:8; 4:20). They are not lawyers who have to convince a jury. God does that. Christ's witnesses have a simple commission: Unsheath the powerful Word of truth.

The Scriptures are clear

The psalmist says to the Lord, "Your word is a lamp to my feet and a light for my path" (Psalm 119:105). The purpose of a lamp and a light is to illuminate, to show the way. So, says the psalmist, God's Word is like a lamp and a light. It clearly shows the way to salvation. It is so clear that even a child can understand what it is saying, as the psalmist declares, "The entrance of your words gives light; it gives understanding to the simple" (Psalm 119:130). Writing to Timothy, Paul reminds him, "From infancy you have known the holy Scriptures" (2 Timothy 3:15).

God's purpose in giving the Scriptures was not to obscure whatever pertains to the world's salvation, but to reveal these truths. That is why he chose to address us in human language rather than in the kind of "inexpressible" words St. Paul heard when he "was caught up to Paradise" (2 Corinthians 12:4). Since we cannot rise to his level, in love he chose to descend to ours and to speak to us in words we can understand.

While it is true there are "some things that are hard to understand" in the Scriptures, as the apostle Peter says in his second epistle (2 Peter 3:16), this does not deny the clarity of the Scriptures but simply points to our human weakness to grasp all that God has clearly revealed to us. "Everything that was written in the past," writes Paul to the Romans, "was written to teach us" (Romans 15:4). That which is not clear cannot teach; that which is clear can teach. And that is why God has given us the Scriptures and made sure that, objectively, externally, its message is clear: so that through it he might teach us, especially the way of salvation (cf. 2 Timothy 3:15).

There are implications for evangelism here also. The clear message of the Scriptures, which God has used to teach us through parents, pastors, and teachers, is the same tool he puts into the mouths of those who have learned and believed its message. Evangelists do not go out armed with a complex, convoluted philosophical system that no one, not even they, really understands. They do not present some vague, indefinable "new age" system of religious thought. The message of the Christian evangelist is very simple, very clear. It can even be summed up in a sentence:

- The wages of sin is death, but the gift of God is eternal life in Christ Jesus our Lord (Romans 6:23); or
- God so loved the world that he gave his one and only Son, that whoever believes in him shall not perish but have eternal life (John 3:16); or
- God made him who had no sin to be sin for us, so that in him we might become the righteousness of God (2 Corinthians 5:21).

The familiar children's song puts it this way: "Jesus loves me, this I know; for the Bible tells me so." There is hardly a simpler, clearer, more straightforward declarative sentence than that. Even a child can grasp it.

This is not to say that, just because this message is clear and simple, it will therefore instantly be understood and accepted by everyone. Sinful humanity is blind and dead to things spiritual, an enemy of God, as we will remind ourselves in more detail later. It is to say, though, that the message the evangelist brings to people is, in and of itself, clear and, by the operation of the Holy Spirit, will become clear to the hearer.

The only thing evangelists will want to do is to take care to present this clear message in a way that does not obscure its clarity. We can learn from the way Jesus addressed the people of his day. He laced his discourses with word pictures. He didn't simply say, "Do not worry. Trust God." To illustrate the truth that God provides, he pointed his hearers to the birds of the air and the lilies of the field.

He made frequent use of metaphors and similes to get his point across. He described himself as the Door, the Bread of Life, the Good Shepherd. He began many a discourse with, "The kingdom of heaven is like. . . ."

All of this served the purpose of helping his hearers grasp and appreciate various abstract spiritual concepts. Evangelists today will find the use of illustrations and picturesque speech to be no less helpful as they seek to present God's plan of salvation as clearly as possible.

Sola Scriptura is one of the three solas of the church of the Reformation. The Holy Scriptures—inspired, inerrant, sufficient, powerful, clear—are the tool of the evangelist. Evangelism, in fact, stripped to its bare essentials, is not very complex at all. One needs just three things: the gospel, someone to communicate the gospel, and someone to whom to communicate the gospel. When a Christian brings to a non-Christian the good news of what God has done to rescue the world from condemnation, that's evangelism.

The doctrine of inspiration and the evangelism message

Before moving on, we should explore one further issue: What place does the doctrine of inspiration have in the message the evangelist brings? The Bible, as the inspired, inerrant Word of God, is the sure source of the evangelist's message. It is the power behind his message. It is not the message itself, however.

The purpose of the evangelist is not to convince a person that the Bible is the inspired, inerrant Word of God. The purpose of the evangelist is to tell the good news that the inspired Scriptures reveal. When the Holy Spirit through the evangelist's message of sin and grace, law and gospel, brings a person to repentance and faith in Jesus Christ, one of the results of this faith will be an acceptance of the Bible as the inspired, inerrant Word of God.

If one approaches the doctrine of inspiration before one brings the message of sin and grace, he can do so only on the basis of rational arguments, e.g., the extraordinary preservation of the biblical manuscripts, the remarkable fulfillment of prophecy, the striking effects the Scriptures have had on people over the ages, the way archeology continues to confirm the historical details of the Scriptures.

Such rational arguments do have their place, especially if the person to whom one is speaking objects to hearing anything from the

Bible because he has heard that the Bible has been changed so much over the years, that it has all kinds of errors and contradictory interpretations. The presentation of some rational arguments for the Bible's trustworthiness may result in the person being willing to give its message a hearing.

In the final analysis, though, inspiration can never be proved to an unbeliever. It is an article of faith. Faith in the atoning blood of Christ, produced by the Spirit through the proclamation of law and gospel, is the starting point. That faith will lead one to accept the inspiration of the book from which came the message that saved him. Spurgeon's counsel to a young pastor who inquired how best to defend the Bible is good advice yet today: "How would you defend a lion? Let it loose. It will defend itself."

Pieper summarizes well what we have been discussing here:

> Our missionaries in heathen countries, our home missionaries, and our institutional workers do not therefore begin with rational arguments for the divinity of Holy Scripture, but they preach to one and all repentance and remission of sins. And when faith in *Christum crucifixum* [Christ crucified] has once been created, there is no need to worry about securing faith in the divinity of Holy Scripture.[11]

The same holds true on the congregational level. A congregation that hopes to gain a hearing with *unbelievers* through an advertising strategy that centers on its adherence to inspiration and inerrancy will find few takers. Such a strategy may appeal to some conservative Christians who are disenchanted with what is happening in their congregation or church body, but it is not likely to attract non-Christians. It is more likely, in fact, to keep them at arm's length and thus make it more difficult for the congregation to bring them the message of sin and grace.

The Triune God

Natural knowledge reveals the existence of a god. Revealed knowledge, the Holy Scriptures, reveals the true God, the God whom the church has come to know as the triune God. The triune God, one God in three distinct persons, is the *who* of what "no eye has seen, no ear has heard, no mind has conceived" (1 Corinthians 2:9), while the salvation planned and carried out by the triune God is the *what*.

---

[11]Francis Pieper, *Christian Dogmatics,* Vol. 1 (St. Louis: Concordia, 1950), p. 313.

On their own, people can and will recognize that there must be a god of some sort. They might identify the created world itself with God (pantheism). They might conclude that there are many gods, each with a specific role to play (polytheism). Or, they might become convinced that there is only one god (monotheism).

No one, however, will be able, by a process of observation and reasoning, to come up with the Bible's teaching that God is one (Deuteronomy 6:4) and that this one God has revealed himself to the world in three distinct persons—Father, Son, and Holy Spirit—each of whom is fully God (Matthew 28:19; 2 Corinthians 13:14; Matthew 3:16,17). That is why we confess in the Apostles' Creed, "I *believe* in God the Father. . . . I *believe* in Jesus Christ. . . . I *believe* in the Holy Spirit." The doctrine of the Trinity is an article of faith that is engendered by God's revelation of himself in the Holy Scriptures.

The Bible's teaching about the triune God has many implications for the church's work of evangelism.

The triune God is the only saving God

The Old Testament prophets are scathing in their denunciation of idolatry (cf., Isaiah 44:9-20). They repeatedly declare the exclusivity of the God they represent. Through the prophet Isaiah the Lord says of himself: "I am the first and I am the last; apart from me there is no God. . . . Is there any God besides me? No, there is no other Rock; I know not one" (Isaiah 44:6,8).

Again through Isaiah, the Lord's call to repentance goes out to the whole world, since there is no other saving God in the world: "Turn to me and be saved, all you ends of the earth; for I am God, and there is no other" (Isaiah 45:22).

The New Testament speaks in no less definite a fashion. Jesus addresses his Father as "the only true God" (John 17:3). He claims for himself, "I am the way and the truth and the life. No one comes to the Father except through me" (John 14:6). Peter tells the members of the Sanhedrin, "Salvation is found in no one else, for there is no other name under heaven given to men by which we must be saved" (Acts 4:12). Paul clearly states that "there is one God and one mediator between God and men, the man Christ Jesus" (1 Timothy 2:5). And again in 1 Corinthians:

> We know that an idol is nothing at all in the world and that there is no God but one. For even if there are so-called gods, whether in heaven or on earth (as indeed there are many "gods" and many "lords"), yet for us there is but one God, the Father,

> from whom all things came and for whom we live; and there is but one Lord, Jesus Christ, through whom all things came and through whom we live. (8:4-6)

This one true God is clearly revealed and defined in the Scriptures and in the Scriptures alone. The deities worshiped by the Hindus, Buddhists, Muslims, Jews, as well as the non-Trinitarian sects or cults are not various manifestations of the same God. They are among the "other gods" which the First Commandment forbids. Only those who have no grasp of or who have rejected the essentials of the Christian message could presume to equate, in even a vague way, any other gods with the triune God. The triune God reveals himself in the Scriptures as the God who saves. All other gods challenge their adherents to save themselves. Paul's exhortation to the idolatrous people of Lystra still applies today: "Turn from these worthless things to the living God" (Acts 14:15).

To be saved people must hear about the one true God

In contrast to what the Scriptures clearly teach about the one true God and the one way of salvation, Roman Catholicism and much of modern Protestantism teach to the contrary.

Roman Catholicism teaches:

> Those also can attain to everlasting salvation who through no fault of their own do not know the gospel of Christ or his church, yet sincerely seek God and, moved by grace, strive by their deeds to do his will as it is known to them through the dictates of conscience. Nor does divine Providence deny the help necessary for salvation to those who, without blame on their part, have not yet arrived at an explicit knowledge of God, but who strive to live a good life, thanks to his grace.[12]

John Shelby Spong, a bishop in the Episcopal church, writes in an article entitled, "Evangelism When Certainty Is an Illusion":

> Evangelism as an activity of the church seems to require for its very existence a sense that those who evangelize possess certainty. Its vital nerve is cut by relativity. . . . [But] first of all, the proclamation of the gospel must be honest. . . . Christianity itself does not and cannot embrace the whole truth of God. So I

---

[12]Dogmatic Constitution of the Church, 16. *The Documents of Vatican II* (New York: Guild Press, 1966), p. 35.

can make no claims for God that are ultimate, and if I do, am dishonest. I cannot limit God to my understanding of God. I cannot limit salvation to those who share my vision. . . . To be honest in our day is to embrace relativity as a virtue and to recognize that absolutism is a vice. . . . We cannot give what we do not have. Certainty has never been our possession, but rather our illusion.[13]

A study volume prepared for an assembly of the World Council of Churches states that it is *unlikely* that "only those calling upon Jesus as their personal Savior can be saved, the rest of humanity being assigned to eternal perdition."[14]

Although Carl Braaten, a seminary professor in the Evangelical Lutheran Church of America, speaks of "one salvation and one way of salvation" and the "exclusive uniqueness of Jesus," it is hardly the Jesus of the Scriptures he is describing when he writes:

His [Jesus'] true identity is still being disclosed in the encounter of the gospel with the world religions. The gospel does not meet the world religions on a one-way street, giving them the traditional symbols of christology and receiving nothing back. The dialogue will be a two-way street, in which the condition of openness to the *other religions* will be motivated by knowledge that they *also somehow speak of Jesus Christ*. . . . If the apostles and the church fathers could find anticipations of Christ in the Old Testament, we have a right to expect a similar thing in the texts and traditions of other religions [italics added].[15]

Even some within the more conservative Evangelical camp are questioning the biblical restriction of salvation to those who have heard and believed the gospel. A brief article in *Christianity Today* entitled "The Perennial Debate" brings out that, though the dominant view among Evangelicals is that "no unevangelized person will be saved," some Evangelicals espouse the position "that if any un-

---

[13]John Shelby Spong, "Evangelism When Certainty Is an Illusion," *The Christian Century* (January 6-13, 1982), pp. 12,14.

[14]*Christianity Today,* April 20, 1984, p. 12.

[15]Carl E. Braaten and Robert W. Jenson, ed., *Christian Dogmatics,* Vol. 1 (Philadelphia: Fortress Press, 1984), pp. 567,568. The reader will quickly discover that this book bears little resemblance to Francis Pieper's earlier work of the same name.

evangelized person repents and desires God's mercy, he will be saved by the work of Christ even though ignorant of that work."[16]

If it were true that somehow, someway, God will save all people, or at least more people than have heard the Scripture's message about the one true God and his work of redemption through Jesus, there would be no need for evangelism.

The truth, however, is clearly stated by the apostle Paul:

> "Everyone who calls on the name of the Lord will be saved." How, then, can they call on the one they have not believed in? And how can they believe in the one of whom they have not heard? And how can they hear without someone preaching to them? . . . Consequently, faith comes from hearing the message, and the message is heard through the word of Christ. (Romans 10:13,14,17)

Why evangelize? One answer for the Christian certainly will be, "Because there is only one true God, who has revealed himself in the Holy Scriptures, and people need to hear about him to be saved."

People hear about the triune God through the preaching of sin and grace, law and gospel

Of the three ecumenical creeds of Christendom, the Athanasian Creed presents the most in-depth exposition of the doctrine of the Trinity. That is understandable, given the reason for its formation. It combats errors that, in one way or another, denied the full deity of Christ and of the Holy Spirit. Accordingly, it states in a forceful way:

> Whoever wishes to be saved must, above all else, hold to the true Christian faith. Whoever does not keep this faith pure in all points will certainly perish forever.
>
> Now this is the true Christian faith: We worship one God in three persons and three persons in one God, without mixing the persons or dividing the divine Being. . . .
>
> The Father is God, the Son is God, the Holy Spirit is God; yet they are not three Gods, but one God. . . .
>
> Just as Christian truth compels us to confess each person individually to be God and Lord, so the true Christian faith forbids us to speak of three Gods or three Lords. . . .

---

[16]*Christianity Today,* May 14, 1990, p. 21.

> All three persons are to be worshiped as one God and one God worshiped as three persons. Whoever wishes to be saved must have this conviction of the Trinity. . . .
>
> This is the true Christian faith. Whoever does not faithfully and firmly believe this cannot be saved.

Strong words indeed! How does one reconcile them with the evangelistic message recorded in the book of Acts? To what degree did the apostles explicitly teach the doctrine of the Trinity when they evangelized those who had no or very little knowledge of the one true God?

In Samaria Philip "preached the good news of the kingdom of God and the name of Jesus Christ" (Acts 8:12). On the road to Gaza he told the Eunuch of Ethiopia "the good news about Jesus" (Acts 8:35). Peter announced to the group gathered at the home of Cornelius "how God anointed Jesus of Nazareth with the Holy Spirit and power, and how he went around doing good and healing all who were under the power of the devil, because God was with him" (Acts 10:38). Then, after relating that Jesus died and rose and would be coming again as Judge, Peter repeated the promise of the Old Testament prophets, "Everyone who believes in him receives forgiveness of sins through his name" (Acts 10:43). The Christians who evangelized the Gentiles in Antioch of Syria are described as "telling them the good news about the Lord Jesus" (Acts 11:20).

Let this brief look at the earliest days of the expansion of the church into the world of the Gentiles suffice to show that the way the early Christians introduced the one true God to those who did not know him was to tell what he had done for them. God's name is not just his titles but "everything God has revealed to us about himself in his Word."[17] To tell people what the God of the Bible had done for them and their salvation was to proclaim the name of the Triune God. We can properly assume that in time the relationship of the three persons in the one God would also have been taught. That would be a part of "teaching them to obey everything I have commanded you" (Matthew 28:20).

Today, too, what is essential in the basic message of evangelism is not an exposition of the doctrine of the Trinity, but an unfolding of what the triune God has done for the world's redemption, i.e., the message of sin and grace, law and gospel. Those who "call on the

---

[17]David P. Kuske, *Luther's Catechism—The Small Catechism of Dr. Martin Luther and an Exposition for Children and Adults Written in Contemporary English* (Milwaukee: WELS Board for Parish Education, 1982), p. 59.

name of the Lord" and thus are saved will be those whom the Holy Spirit has led to accept what the one true God, the triune God of the Bible, has done for them.

This is also the way to deal with anti-Trinitarian cults. Rather than arguing the doctrine of the Trinity with a Jehovah's Witness or a Mormon, it is best, if possible, to focus the discussion on humanity's problem and God's solution in Christ. Give the Holy Spirit an opportunity to convict people of sin and to convince them that Jesus Christ is God's answer to the dilemma caused by sin. Then delve into the mystery of the Trinity—the one God who could and did rescue all people from sin and damnation.

The triune God earnestly desires the world's salvation

This is clearly stated in the Scriptures regarding each person of the Trinity:

"God [the Father] so loved the world that he gave his one and only Son, that whoever believes in him shall not perish but have eternal life" (John 3:16).

Jesus says, "The Son of Man came to seek and to save what was lost" (Luke 19:10).

It was the Holy Spirit who told the church at Antioch, "Set apart for me Barnabas and Saul for the work to which I have called them" (Acts 13:2) and with that set in motion the expansion of the saving gospel to all the world.

This is a further encouragement for evangelism. When Christians go out to people with the message of salvation, they do so in full harmony with the gracious will of the one true God "who wants all men to be saved and to come to a knowledge of the truth" (1 Timothy 2:4).

Creation

God, the Father, the Almighty, Maker of heaven and earth

In both the Nicene and Apostles' Creeds, we confess that the one true God is the "Maker of heaven and earth." Though the entire Godhead was involved in the act of creation, the Scriptures ascribe this work especially to the Father. The natural knowledge of God makes it clear that the world has been made by someone. Revealed knowledge tells who that Someone is and how he did it: "In six days the LORD made the heavens and the earth, the sea, and all that is in them" (Exodus 20:11). He made it all, out of nothing, through the power of his creative Word. In the beginning there was just God. Then God spoke: "Let there be." "And there was."

On the sixth day God molded man from the dust of the ground and formed woman from the rib of man to be "a helper suitable for him" (Genesis 2:18). The first human beings—so carefully crafted by God—were clearly the crown of God's creation. Only of man and woman is it said that they were created in the image of God (Genesis 1:27), which the Scriptures elsewhere describe as "true righteousness and holiness" (Ephesians 4:24), coupled with a true knowledge of God (Colossians 3:10). The intellect, will, and emotions of Adam and Eve were in perfect harmony with the good and holy will of God.

The Scriptures throughout assume the historicity of the creation account in Genesis 1 and 2, including the creation of man and woman. The psalmist writes, "By the word of the LORD were the heavens made, their starry host by the breath of his mouth" (Psalm 33:6). Paul tells the Athenians, "From one man he [God] made every nation of men" (Acts 17:26).

Paul speaks of the creation of a real Adam and then a real Eve: "Adam was formed first, then Eve" (1 Timothy 2:13). He points to a real fall into sin by a real person and contrasts this with a real redemption accomplished by a real Christ. "As in Adam all die," he writes, "so in Christ all will be made alive" (1 Corinthians 15:22). And again:

> Just as the result of one trespass [Adam's] was condemnation for all men, so also the result of one act of righteousness [Christ's] was justification that brings life for all men. For just as through the disobedience of the one man [Adam] the many were made sinners, so also through the obedience of the one man [Christ] the many will be made righteous. (Romans 5:18,19)

The basic message of evangelism can, in fact, be arranged around the concept of the image of God: Given at creation, lost in the fall, restored through Christ.

Creation, evolution, and evangelism

The current theory of the world's origins, the theory of evolution, which maintains that the present world is the result of a gradual development from the inanimate to the animate, from lower to higher forms, denies the existence of a personal God as Creator. Or, at the very most, it consigns to him the single role of creating matter and energy, after which he backed away to let natural forces take over.

Some, in an unsuccessful attempt to harmonize the Scriptures with the theory of evolution, suggest lengthening the six days of the creation week into periods of indefinite length to give time for the world to evolve to its present state (theistic evolution). Even with that, however, man and woman do not stand out as the special creation of God, created in his image, created to give special glory to their Creator (cf. Isaiah 43:21). Our first parents are rather pictured as descended from the animal kingdom, with no more moral responsibility to their Creator than any other creature.

The evangelist needs to be aware that many, probably most, of the people he encounters will have drunk deeply from the poisoned well of evolutionary thought, since they are likely to be products of an educational system that assumes the theory of evolution to be a fact.

This has a number of implications. For one thing, the person who has been taught that he is simply part of an evolutionary process will find it easier to suppress an accusing conscience. Right and wrong become blurred when there is no personal Creator to whom the creature is answerable. What is right is what is right to me, or what society by consensus considers to be right.

Secondly, if people consider themselves to be products of evolution, it makes it easier to shift the blame away from themselves for whatever may be wrong in their lives. They are not responsible. They cannot help it. They are what they are because they are merely part of a continuous evolutionary process.

When there is no personal Creator to whom the creature is personally accountable, the concept of sin is lost. This has serious consequences. Where there is no consciousness of sin, there will be no contrition. Where there is no contrition, there will be no repentance and trust in a Savior. Where there is no repentance and trust in a Savior, there is no salvation, but only condemnation.

The solution to this problem, it might appear, would be for the evangelist to prove to a person that evolution is false and the Bible's teaching about creation is true. There is a difficulty here, however. The doctrine of creation is an article of faith. It is not scientifically verifiable. One can present good, logical arguments against evolution and likewise good, logical arguments for the doctrine of creation as recorded in Genesis 1 and 2. They remain just that, however—logical arguments, but not scientific proof.

In 1 Corinthians the apostle Paul writes, "The man without the Spirit does not accept the things that come from the Spirit of God, for they are foolishness to him, and he cannot understand them, because they are spiritually discerned" (2:14). Acceptance of the Bible's teaching about a divine, six-day, Word-generated creation is one of those things "that come from the Spirit of God." To the believer it is an article of Spirit-engendered faith (Hebrews 11:3). To the unbeliever, the "man without the Spirit," such teaching is "foolishness."

The key, then, is to begin with what the Holy Spirit uses to turn an unbeliever into a believer. That brings us back to what we have been emphasizing repeatedly. When we evangelize an unbeliever, we need to begin at the beginning. Preaching "repentance and forgiveness of sins" (Luke 24:47) is the way Jesus described what his disciples would do as they moved out as Christ's spokesmen from Jerusalem to all nations. They would put first things first.

Our Lutheran dogmaticians differentiate between fundamental and non-fundamental doctrines. This is not to say that some of the doctrines in the Scripture are important and some unimportant. It is to say, though, that there are certain truths taught in Scripture that are absolutely essential for salvation, truths that constitute the foundation of the Christian faith. These truths revolve around the article of justification by grace through faith, which the Lutheran dogmaticians rightly term the most fundamental doctrine of all. We will spend some time in the next two chapters discussing this doctrine and its significance for evangelism.

The issue, then, revolves around the question, "What must people know and believe in order to be declared not guilty in God's eyes?" They must be convinced they cannot hope to hear a "not guilty" verdict through their own efforts. They, therefore, need to hear the law, whose purpose is to show people's sin and condemnation. And they need to be convinced that God has done all that is needed for them to be able to stand as innocent people before their Maker. They therefore need to be pointed to the person and saving work of Jesus Christ as revealed in the Holy Scriptures. This is the gospel.

The primary task of the evangelist, then, is to preach the law to point out to people what is wrong with their lives and why this is so and what the consequences are, and then to preach the gospel to reveal how God has solved their spiritual dilemma.

Evangelism training manuals sometimes use the term "majoring on the minors" to describe spending time with unbelievers on such subjects as a literal six-day creation, the doctrine of the antichrist, the practice of close communion, or the role of women in the church. These doctrines are not "minor" (or non-fundamental) in the sense that they are inconsequential. Every word of God is important. The appropriate time for dealing with such issues, however, is after the "majors," law and gospel, sin and grace, have been shared and the

Holy Spirit has worked a conviction of sin and a turning to Jesus in faith for forgiveness and a right standing with God.

The Fall

A real creation was followed by a real fall. The details—the doubt, the denial, the defiance, the disobedience—as recorded in Genesis 3, are familiar. To carry out the work of evangelism properly, we need to have a clear understanding of the consequences of the fall.

Consequences for Adam and Eve

The immediate consequence for Adam and Eve was the loss of God's image. No longer was their will in perfect harmony with God's will. Their perfect, loving fellowship with God was shattered. A calm conscience was replaced by a guilty one; joy in the presence of God gave way to fear. No longer could they comfortably walk with God, as is seen by their frantic and futile effort to hide from him in the Garden and by the excuses they offered for what they had done. Such was the effect of their sin.

Loss of God's image also adversely affected Adam and Eve's relationship with each other. When one no longer loves God perfectly, one can no longer love one's neighbor as oneself. The latter is dependent on the former. Broken fellowship on the vertical plane (fellowship with God) makes impossible a genuine, loving fellowship on the horizontal plane (fellowship with other people).

This truth is graphically displayed in the Garden following the Fall. Adam tried to shift the whole burden of blame on the one whom God had made as a perfect partner for him: "The woman you put here with me—she gave me some fruit from the tree, and I ate it" (Genesis 3:12). Instead of treating each other with mutual love and respect, Adam and Eve now began to manipulate and use each other for their own selfish advantage. Such were the repercussions of the Fall.

The ultimate consequence was death. "You will surely die," God had warned them, if they ate the fruit of the tree of the knowledge of good and evil (Genesis 2:17).

They would experience death in three dimensions. First, and immediately, with the loss of God's image they began to experience spiritual death, the breaking off of their perfect fellowship with God.

Secondly, they would undergo physical death, "the unnatural disruption of the union of soul and body which have been created by God to be one."[18] This did not happen immediately, but in time the hearts of Adam and Eve, which were meant to go on ticking forever, stopped beating. And they died.

The third dimension of death is the most fearsome—an eternal separation of soul and body from God in hell. Jesus warns about that eternal death when he says, "Do not be afraid of those who kill the body but cannot kill the soul. Rather, be afraid of the One [God] who can destroy both soul and body in hell" (Matthew 10:28). An eternal destruction, not annihilation, but ongoing punishment in hell—that is the ultimate death-wage that sin pays.

Consequences for all—original sin

All this would affect all people. "Through the disobedience of the one man the many were made sinners. . . . The result of one trespass was condemnation for all men" (Romans 5:19,18). "In Adam all die" (1 Corinthians 15:22).

Loss of the image of God, death in all three of its dimensions—that is the birthright of everyone descended from Adam and Eve. "Flesh gives birth to flesh" (John 3:6). Sinners beget sinners. A stream does not rise higher than its source. All people share Adam's nature. All share Adam's guilt. All share Adam's condemnation.

The Scriptures describe the descendants of Adam and Eve as *dead.* Paul reminds the believers in Ephesus and us as well: "As for you, you were dead in your transgressions and sins" (Ephesians 2:1).

Adam and Eve's descendants are characterized as *enemies* of God: "The sinful mind is hostile to God. It does not submit to God's law, nor can it do so. Those controlled by the sinful nature [which is 100% true of every unbeliever] cannot please God" (Romans 8:7,8). Not only are they opposed to God, but they are unable to change their disposition toward him. The "things that come from the Spirit of God," that is, all the things God reveals in his Word, "are *foolishness* to him, and he *cannot* understand them" (1 Corinthians 2:14).

This, then, is the nature of those descended from Adam: They are blind to things spiritual; they are enemies of God and everything that stands for God; they are dead spiritually; they call God's message foolishness; they are helpless and unwilling to change their condition.

This condition, this spiritual disease, usually called original, or inherited, sin, is referred to frequently in the Lutheran Confessions. The Augsburg Confession, for example, puts it this way:

---

[18]Francis Pieper, *Christian Dogmatics,* Vol. 1 (St. Louis: Concordia, 1950), p. 536.

> Since the fall of Adam all men who are born according to the course of nature are conceived and born in sin. That is, all men are full of evil lust and inclinations from their mothers' wombs and are unable by nature to have true fear of God and true faith in God. Moreover, this inborn sickness and hereditary sin is truly sin and condemns to the eternal wrath of God all those who are not born again through Baptism and the Holy Spirit.[19]

Note here the two sides of original sin. Negatively, it is a lack of something: "Since the fall of Adam all men . . . are unable by nature to have true fear of God and true faith in God." Positively, it is a propensity to evil: "Since the fall of Adam, all men . . . are full of evil lust and inclinations from their mothers' wombs."

The Formula of Concord states, "Original sin is not a slight corruption of human nature, but . . . is so deep a corruption that nothing sound or uncorrupted has survived in man's body or soul, in his inward or outward powers."[20] St. Paul summarizes mankind's sorry condition in very simple fashion: "I know that nothing good lives in me, that is, in my sinful nature" (Romans 7:18).

Consequences for all—actual sin

Original sin manifests itself in thoughts, speech, and actions that reveal the depravity of those descended from Adam (actual sin). Jesus speaks of the kinds of thoughts and words and actions that flow out of the heart of those who inherited Adam's sin: "Out of the heart come evil thoughts, murder, adultery, sexual immorality, theft, false testimony, slander" (Matthew 15:19). Writing to the Romans, Paul describes all unregenerated people, Jew and Gentile alike. He does not paint a pretty picture:

> "There is no one righteous, not even one; there is no one who understands, no one who seeks God. All have turned away, they have together become worthless; there is no one who does good, not even one." "Their throats are open graves; their tongues practice deceit." "The poison of vipers is on their lips." "Their mouths are full of cursing and bitterness." "Their feet are swift to shed blood; ruin and misery mark their ways, and the way of peace they do not know." "There is no fear of God before their eyes." (Romans 3:10-18)

---

[19]Augsburg Confession, Article II, 1,2.

[20]Formula of Concord, Epitome, Article I, 8.

Implications for evangelism

The Bible's teaching about the Fall and its consequences has some major implications for evangelism. For one thing, knowledge of this doctrine should help the evangelist understand the spiritual mindset of the unbeliever. One should not expect proper spiritual responses from a person who does not have the Spirit. The picture the Scripture paints prepares us to expect just the opposite.

What this means in a practical way for the evangelist can perhaps best be brought out through a few illustrations. A congregation is trying to decide whether to conduct a vacation Bible school and, if so, what its emphasis should be. Someone suggests, "I think we should use it, at least in part, as an outreach tool. There are many unchurched families in the vicinity of the church who may be willing to send their children to a vacation Bible school."

Another member of the committee responds, "I don't think we should do that. All these people want is some free baby-sitting for a week or two." That could well be, though probably they are looking for more than that. Common sense (prompted by the natural knowledge of God) and the general opinion of society is that it is good for children to receive moral training of some sort. A week at vacation Bible school might help.

Even such a motive, however, falls far short of proper spiritual motivation. But—and this is the point we should not ignore—what kind of motivation can one expect from an unbeliever? Unbelievers cannot possibly send their children to vacation Bible school or Sunday school or even attend a church service themselves for proper spiritual reasons. They are blind, dead, enemies of God. They call God's message foolishness. What will motivate them is self-interest of some sort. One needs to realize—and accept—this fact. You will look in vain for living fruit on dead trees.

The same would apply if an unbelieving family wants to enroll their children in the congregation's Lutheran elementary school. Someone might object: "All they want to do is get out of the public school. They're just looking for better discipline, for more personal attention on the part of the teacher. They're not coming for 'the one thing needed'" (Luke 10:42). That, of course, is correct. They are not coming for the right reason. What unbeliever would, or could, do that?

The point is that we should not be determining whether or not to conduct an outreach-oriented vacation Bible school or to open the doors of the Lutheran elementary school to the unchurched on the basis of their desire to make use of such services for the right reasons. That will never happen.

Both the vacation Bible school and the Lutheran elementary school, however, may well be avenues through which the Lord can touch families with his life-giving, life-changing Word. The following scenario was repeated often during my years in the parish ministry: Parents enrolled their children in the Lutheran elementary school and then attended the Bible information class. By the end of the class they told me, "We had one reason for wanting our children to be in your school to begin with. Now we have an entirely different, and far more important, reason." With a Spirit-generated faith in their hearts, they now desired for their children what God desired for them.

The doctrine of the Fall and its consequences has a second major implication for evangelism: It tells us that when we seek to evangelize the unbeliever we involve ourselves in a battle of cosmic proportions.

There are some who maintain with Donald McGavran that "the greatest obstacles to conversion are social not theological,"[21] that "in most cases of arrested growth of the church, men are deterred not so much by the offense of the cross as non-biblical offenses."[22]

As an example of non-biblical offense, McGavran cites forcing people to cross linguistic, class, or racial barriers in order to hear the gospel. He speculates that in the early Christian church the Jews, who "liked to become Christian without crossing racial barriers," stopped becoming Christians once Gentiles predominated and they had to join a "house church full of Gentiles"; so they "turned sorrowfully away." He further surmises that "in the initial turnings to the Christian faith in northern Europe, the principle that men like to become Christian without crossing barriers kept whole countries out of eternal life for centuries."[23]

The solution, McGavran claims, is to work among homogeneous units—Anglo to Anglo, Hispanic to Hispanic, Black to Black, Asian to Asian—because "men like to become Christians without crossing racial, linguistic, or class barriers."[24]

---

[21]Donald A. McGavran, *Understanding Church Growth,* 2nd ed. (Grand Rapids: Eerdmans, 1980), p. 215.

[22]*Ibid.*, p. 230.

[23]*Ibid.*, pp. 230-232.

[24]*Ibid.*, p. 223.

While there is undoubtedly some value in evangelizing people of one's own culture, the truth of the matter is that no unbeliever, whether of one's own or another culture, likes to become a Christian. Evangelism is not just a simple matter of removing a few external social barriers that are holding a person back from the Christian faith he would otherwise gladly embrace.

We need to remember who the unbeliever is. He is born in sin. He is living in sin. He is actively opposed to God. Writing to the Christians in Ephesus, Paul urges them to arm themselves spiritually against Satan. He says, "Our struggle is not against flesh and blood, but against the rulers, against the authorities, against the powers of this dark world and against the spiritual forces of evil in the heavenly realms" (Ephesians 6:12). Those evil forces that rage against the Christian totally control the non-Christian. Every unbeliever is a part of Satan's "dominion of darkness" (Colossians 1:13).

That is the battleground the Christian enters when he or she seeks to evangelize the unbeliever. On the Damascus Road the Lord Jesus commissioned Saul of Tarsus to go to people and "turn them from darkness to light, and from the power of Satan to God" (Acts 26:18). He was sent to do battle with the prince of darkness, Satan. Every soul won to Christ would have to be wrested from Satan's grasp.

The evangelist today faces the same battle. He is not going to be dealing with one who is morally neutral. He will look in vain for some little spark of goodness to fan into a glowing flame of faith. It is not reform that is needed, but rebirth.

To be forewarned is to be forearmed. If we underestimate the magnitude of the battle, we will not be properly equipped for it. We are entering the devil's stronghold. We need to be armed, then, with something, or Someone, stronger than Satan.

The Promise

That is exactly what God promised to our first parents in the Garden when, speaking to Satan, the instigator of the Fall, he said, "I will put enmity between you and the woman, and between your offspring and hers; he will crush your head, and you will strike his heel" (Genesis 3:15). An Offspring of the woman would enter the world and crush the serpent's head.

That gracious promise of the Lord in the Garden, the gospel, the good news of rescue from the power of sin and Satan and death, fulfilled at Calvary, is what gave hope to Adam and Eve. It is likewise the weapon evangelists need to bring into the battle for people's souls. Rescuing people from Satan's clutches and restoring them to their place in God's family—that is God's business. Evangelists are his agents, using his means—law and gospel, the message of sin and grace—to convict people of sin and to bring about repentance, faith, and a new life.

Through this message people once again will be able to call God their "Father."

Chapter Two: We Believe in One Lord, Jesus Christ, the Only Son of God

The second stanza of Christian Scheidt's hymn, "By Grace I'm Saved," summarizes quite well what follows in this chapter:

By grace God's Son, our only Savior,
Came down to earth to bear our sin.
Was it because of your own merit
That Jesus died your soul to win?
No, it was grace, and grace alone,
That brought him from his heavenly throne.[1]

Sola gratia, grace alone, is the second of the three mottoes of the Lutheran Church. Grace is first of all an attitude, a disposition of God. It means, as Luther puts it in his Preface to the Epistle of Paul to the Romans, "God's favor, or the good will which in *himself* [emphasis added] he bears toward us, by which he is disposed to give us Christ and to pour into us the Holy Spirit with his gifts."[2] Pieper puts it this way: "The term 'grace' (*charis*) denotes God's gracious disposition, which for Christ's sake he cherishes in himself toward sinful mankind and by which he in his heart, 'before his inner forum,' does not charge men with their sins, but forgives them."[3]

That is the subject of this chapter, the grace of God toward all as revealed in the redemptive work of Christ Jesus, the result being the forgiveness of sins and justification of all. Quite obviously this has deep implications for evangelism. Telling others that God, in his grace, has redeemed the world through Christ, with the result that all people are now not guilty (justified) in his eyes—that is what evangelism is all about.

St. Paul put the message of God's grace in Christ this way: "There is no difference, for all have sinned and fall short of the glory of God,

---

[1]Hymn 384, stanza 2, in *Christian Worship* (Milwaukee: Northwestern Publishing House, 1993).

[2]*American Edition,* Vol. 35 (Philadelphia: Muhlenberg Press, 1960), p. 369.

[3]Francis Pieper, *Christian Dogmatics,* Vol. 2 (St. Louis: Concordia, 1951), p. 7.

and are justified freely by his grace through the redemption that came by Christ Jesus" (Romans 3:22-24).

"All have sinned and fall short of the glory of God." Because of sin, inherited from our first parents and exhibited in our lives, no one comes close to the splendor and majesty of the holiness of God. The penalty? A deserved death: "The wages of sin is death" (Romans 6:23). God's response? Undeserved love, grace, that centers in "the redemption that came by Christ Jesus."

This chapter will focus on Jesus Christ, the one through whom God the Father graciously effected the redemption and justification of the world. We will consider the person of Christ, his work, and the result of his work, exploring along the way what this means for evangelism.

1—The Person of Christ

The God-man

The Lutheran Confessions, especially the Formula of Concord, devote much space to the doctrine of the person of Christ.[4] Our Lutheran dogmaticians likewise spend a considerable amount of time discussing this doctrine. Pieper's *Christian Dogmatics,* volume 2, for example, takes 215 pages to cover this subject. Pieper dedicates more than two-thirds of the space he reserves for the whole doctrine of Christ (which includes Christ's two states, his three-fold office, and his work of atonement) to a treatment of who Christ is.

Is 215 pages on the person of Christ overdoing a good thing? Not when we realize that our certainty of a right standing with God is based not just on *what* God did for us but on *who* did it. It would take a unique person to serve as the instrument through whom God would rescue the world from the fate it had earned for itself. That becomes clear when, on the one hand, we examine the predicament of the whole human race since the Fall and, on the other, we consider the nature of God.

The predicament of the human race since the Fall is clear, as was brought out in the previous chapter. The human race has fallen from fellowship with God, and it cannot, in fact, it does not even desire to return to the warm relationship with God our first parents enjoyed. Enmity against God, rather than friendship with him, and death, rather than life, are the distinguishing marks of fallen humanity. And eternal death is its fate.

---

[4]Article VIII in the Epitome and Solid Declaration.

Then there is the nature of God. The Bible describes him as absolute holiness: "I, the LORD your God, am holy," he declares (Leviticus 19:2). He is also absolute love. So says the Word, clearly and unequivocally: "God is love" (1 John 4:16). God is also eternal and changeless. This means that holiness and love always have been and always will be his attributes.

From our human point of view, the God of holiness and love faced a dilemma when his perfect creatures fell. With the fall mankind no longer was what it had been intended to be: holy as God is holy (cf. Leviticus 19:2). Instead mankind now was what it had not been intended to be: sinful, actively opposed to God's will.

In his changeless *love* God still longed for fellowship with his highest creation. What he said regarding the sinful house of Israel through his prophet Ezekiel, he still says about all: "'As surely as I live, declares the Sovereign LORD, I take no pleasure in the death of the wicked'" (Ezekiel 33:11). Yet at the same time, in his changeless *holiness* he is a just and righteous God who states, "The soul who sins is the one who will die" (Ezekiel 18:4).

How can a loving God, who does not want to see the sinner die remain at one and the same time a holy God who punishes sin and unholiness with death? The way human beings apart from divine revelation attempt to solve this dilemma is to remake God. They inevitably water down his attributes in one way or another.

Some will stress God's holiness and justice and will minimize, if not completely eradicate, his love. By so doing they create a stern, unyielding tyrant of a God whose wrath they must appease in some way. Missionaries soon discover that most of the people to whom they bring the gospel have such a perception of God. People who hold to such a view of God can look only to themselves as "savior."

Others will stress God's love and minimize his holiness and justice. By so doing they create a kindly, benevolent grandfather-like God who makes liberal allowances for our weaknesses, as long as they are not too much out of line. This is the kind of "god" those engaged in evangelism in our country will most often encounter. People who have such a perception of God feel they do not need a Savior, for their "loving god" will overlook their human failings.

Neither of these "gods," however, is the God who reveals himself in the Scriptures. The God who always has been and always will be absolute holiness and absolute love in one indivisible being could not and would not resolve the predicament of the human race by diminishing either of these attributes. If he did that, he would no longer be God.

But what if God himself would step into the picture? What if God would so totally identify himself with the human race that he would become fully human, yet without ceasing to be God? What if this God and man in one person would place himself under the same holy will of God to which every other human being is subject? But what if he, unlike every other human being, would obey that holy will perfectly?

Furthermore, what if this God-man would so fully identify himself with the human race that he would suffer the wages of sin, which includes not only temporal death but the punishment of hell? And then what if God would say, "I will consider everything done by the God-man to have been done by every single member of the human race. His obedience was the obedience of everyone. His death, his suffering of hell, was the death, the suffering of hell, of everyone"?

That would fully satisfy God's holiness and justice, would it not? In this God-man the sin of the whole human race would be punished. It would also in no way tarnish the brilliance of God's love. It would, in fact, magnify it. To take upon oneself the punishment another deserved, there can hardly be greater love than that.

The above scenario, of course, is not a "what if" at all. It is a "has been done." God himself has done what it took to rescue the world from its self-inflicted predicament. And he has done it through the unique person described above. St. Paul speaks of him in this way: "In Christ all the fullness of the Deity lives in bodily form" (Colossians 2:9).

From what we have sketched briefly above, it becomes clear that only such a person, who was both fully God and fully human at one and the same time, perfectly fit what was required to accomplish God's divine rescue operation. On the one hand, a human being was needed. Only a human being could be placed under the demands of the law of God and be given the charge to be a second Adam who would undo by his obedience what Adam had done by his disobedience. St. Paul writes, "Just as through the disobedience of the one man the many were made sinners, so also through the obedience of the one man the many will be made righteous" (Romans 5:19).

Likewise only a human being could be on the receiving end of God's righteous wrath against sin and pay the death penalty for sin. The writer of the letter to the Hebrews says, "Since the children have flesh and blood, he too shared in their humanity. . . . He had to be made like his brothers in every way . . . that he might make atonement for the sins of the people" (Hebrews 2:14,17).

God, therefore, became incarnate. He who was the Son of God from all eternity took on human flesh: "When the time had fully come, God sent his Son, born of a woman, born under law, to redeem those under law, that we might receive the full rights of sons" (Galatians 4:4,5). This happened "when the time had fully come," says Paul. It was, however, far from a spur of the moment action on the part of God. God had this solution in mind before the problem that necessitated it occurred, before creation, in fact. Peter writes: "You were redeemed from the empty way of life handed down to you from your forefathers . . .with the precious blood of Christ, a lamb without blemish or defect. He was *chosen before the creation of the world,* but was revealed in these last times for your sake" (1 Peter 1:18-20).

If the predicament of the human race were to be resolved, however, something more was needed than a man who lived a perfect life and who then died. The psalmist tells us, "No man can redeem the life of another or give to God a ransom for him—the ransom for a life is costly, no payment is ever enough—that he should live on forever and not see decay" (Psalm 49:7-9).

How could *all people* be called righteous in God's eyes through the *obedience* of just *one* man (Romans 5:19)? It was because the one "born of a woman, born under law" was none other than God's *"Son"* (Galatians 4:4). The obedience of the Son of God, and his obedience alone, could and did count for all.

How could God have reconciled *the whole world* to himself through the *death* of only *one* person (2 Corinthians 5:19)? It was because "we were reconciled to him through the death of his *Son"* (Romans 5:10). The death of the Son of God, and his death alone, could and did count for all.

The Formula of Concord quotes Luther on this subject:

> We Christians must know that unless God is in the balance and throws in weight as a counterbalance, we shall sink to the bottom with our scale. I mean that this way: If it is not true that God died for us, but only a man died, we are lost. But if God's death and God dead lie in the opposite scale, then his side goes down and we go upward like a light and empty pan. . . . But he could never have sat in the pan unless he had become a man like us, so that it could be said: God dead, God's passion, God's blood, God's death. According to his nature God cannot die, but since God and man are united in one person, it is correct to talk about God's death when that man dies who is . . . one person with God.[5]

[5]Formula of Concord, Solid Declaration, Article VIII, 44.

In Christ, God is man and man is God. The Scriptures put it this way: "The Word [the eternal God, cf. John 1:1] became flesh" (John 1:14). "In Christ all the fullness of the Deity lives in bodily form" (Colossians 2:9).

It was this unique person, fully God and fully human in one indivisible person, who lived and died. The possession of both divine and human natures does not make of Christ two persons, as though only the human nature of Christ was placed under the law and suffered and died, and only the divine nature performed miracles, rose from the dead, and now is with us always. Because Christ was truly human, he could be made subject to the law and could suffer and die. But it was the whole Christ, God and man, who was "born of a woman, born under law" (Galatians 4:4). And it was the whole Christ, God and man, who suffered and died, as one of our hymns properly puts it, "O sorrow dread! God's Son is dead!" (The original German version says, even more strongly, "God himself is dead"). Anything less than the perfect life of the God-man and the death of the God-man would have been an insufficient atonement for sin.

We could spend much more time on this subject. The doctrine of the person of Christ occupied the attention of most of the early councils of the church, and rightly so. Only the Christ of the Scriptures is the world's hope for life now and forever. It was not theological nit-picking, therefore, for the early church to insist that we must not divide Christ as though he were two separate persons, a divine Christ and a human Christ.[6] Nor was it splitting theological hairs when the early church condemned the teaching that Christ's human nature was somehow absorbed into the divine so that the human nature no longer existed.[7]

It is no insignificant thing to hold to what the Scriptures say about the person of Christ. Though we cannot understand how it can be, the Scriptures clearly teach that in the one person, Christ, are two distinct natures, divine and human, each of which contributes to the world's salvation according to its specific attributes. That is the Savior the world needed, God and man in one indivisible person.

Virgin-born

God brought this unique person into the world through the incarnation. The angel Gabriel, quoting from the prophet Isaiah, told

---

[6]Called Nestorianism, after Nestorius who espoused that error in the 5th century A.D.

[7]Called Eutychianism, after Eutyches who championed that error, also in the 5th century A.D.

Joseph, "'The virgin will be with child and will give birth to a son, and they will call him Immanuel'—which means, 'God with us'" (Matthew 1:23). Earlier the same angel had informed the virgin Mary, "The Holy Spirit will come upon you, and the power of the Most High will overshadow you. So the holy one to be born will be called the Son of God" (Luke 1:35).

That is the way God would get into the world the Savior it needed. He would be "conceived by the Holy Spirit, born of the virgin Mary."

The doctrine of the virgin birth of Christ has been assailed throughout the ages and continues to be attacked today. For example, Carl Braaten writes in *Christian Dogmatics:*

> The primary interest of dogmatics is to interpret the virgin birth as a symbol and not as a freakish intervention in the course of nature. . . . The exclusion of a human father in the birth of Jesus has become more problematic to modern Christians than it was in ancient times. . . . Why should the absence of human paternity make the truth of God's presence in the incarnation more apparent? Is God the Father in competition with the role of our human father? Did not God create fatherhood and look upon it as "very good"? Why then should human fatherhood be eliminated in the work of salvation?[8]

It should not surprise us that Satan has directed attacks against the doctrine of the virgin birth. If there is no virgin birth, Jesus is robbed of his divine nature. The angel Gabriel in his message to Mary clearly connects the coming of the Holy Spirit upon the virgin Mary with the divinity of her Son. "So" (Greek, *dio,* "therefore"), he says, because the Holy Spirit would come upon her and the power of the Most High would overshadow her, "the holy one to be born will be called the Son of God" (Luke 1:35).

Without the virgin birth Jesus is but a man, born of a normal union of a man and a woman. Even if he had grown up to be a perfect man and ended his life at Calvary, he could not have served as the sinner's Substitute, and the wrath of a holy God would still rest upon every person in the world.

Implications for evangelism

What does all this have to do with evangelism? For one thing, the doctrine of the person of Christ gives *confidence* to the evangelist.

---

[8]Carl E. Braaten and Robert W. Jenson, ed., *Christian Dogmatics,* Vol. 1 (Philadelphia: Fortress Press, 1984), pp. 546,547.

The Christ we share is not a vague, ill-defined, or perhaps totally undefined entity. The Scriptures reveal Jesus Christ as a unique person—two natures, divine and human, yet only one person in whom all the attributes of his divine and human nature reside and work together to carry out our salvation. The Scriptures make it amply clear that in the God-man Jesus Christ is to be found everything we need and everything all people need for a right standing with God. Evangelists therefore do not have to be timid or apologetic when they speak to others about Jesus Christ.

The doctrine of the person of Christ not only gives confidence to the evangelist, but also shapes the *content* of his message. A true proclamation of Christ means proclaiming the Christ of the Scriptures. I have found it helpful to begin the gospel portion of an evangelism presentation by speaking of the person of Christ before proceeding to a discussion of his work. The presentation of the law has made it clear that the human race is in a predicament no human being is able to rectify. What, then, can be done?

"God's solution is a person," we can say, "but not any person. This is a special, unique person, the only one qualified to resolve the terrible dilemma mankind is in. His name is Jesus Christ.

"Who is Jesus Christ? The Bible says that he is true God from all eternity. He always has been and always will be God. But 2,000 years ago he was born of the virgin Mary and became a man. Jesus Christ is God's gift of love to the world. The Bible says, 'God so *loved* the world that he *gave* his one and only Son' (John 3:16). In another place it says, '[God] did not spare his own Son, but gave him up for us all' (Romans 8:32). God gave the very best, his own dear Son, to rescue you and me. It is this special, God-sent Savior—God and man in one person—who is the answer, the only answer, to your problem. Let me tell you about him."

His person, who he is, then leads into a discussion of his work, what he has done.

2—The Work of Christ

Vicarious satisfaction

Let us return to the passage we looked at briefly as we began this chapter:

> There is no difference, for all have sinned and fall short of the glory of God, and are justified freely by his grace through the redemption that came by Christ Jesus (Romans 3:22-24).

We have reminded ourselves of the consequences of sin. We have marveled over the "grace" of God, his loving kindness and mercy toward undeserving sinners. We have seen how God lavished his grace on the world in the gift of his Son, Christ Jesus, who assumed our humanity without forfeiting his deity to become the Savior the world needed.

Now we want to explore another key concept in the passage, that of redemption: "justified freely by his grace *through the redemption* that came by Christ Jesus." The word translated "redemption" comes from a Greek verb that has the idea of "to let one go free on receiving the price." The noun (Greek: *apolutrosis*) means "a releasing effected by payment of ransom."

The Scriptures do not leave us in doubt as to what the release consisted of. They tell us that in Christ "we have redemption, the forgiveness of sins" (Colossians 1:14). The releasing effected by the payment of a ransom is the releasing, the being set free, from sin.

Nor do the Scriptures force us to speculate as to what the ransom price was: "In him [Christ] we have redemption *through his blood,* the forgiveness of sins, in accordance with the riches of God's grace" (Ephesians 1:7). Using a different form of the same verb, Peter points us to the same ransom price: "You were redeemed . . . with the precious blood of Christ, a lamb without blemish or defect" (1 Peter 1:18,19).

The picture is clearly one of substitution. This is accentuated in Paul's first letter to Timothy: "There is one God and one mediator between God and men, the man Christ Jesus, who gave himself as a ransom for all men" (1 Timothy 2:5,6). In the original Greek, Paul adds a preposition which means "instead of, in place of" (*anti*) to the word for "ransom" (*lutron*). In addition he uses another preposition with the meaning of "on behalf of" (*huper*) with "all" (*panton*). To put it more literally, Paul says that Christ Jesus "gave himself as a ransom instead of and on behalf of all."

This action on the part of Christ in which he willingly went to the cross as the sinners' Substitute is often termed his *passive obedience.* It is what he permitted himself to endure to pay the just penalty for sin on behalf of the human race. By allowing the full thunder and lightning of God's wrath against sin to strike him he served as the Substitute for all of humanity.

Luther never tired of speaking of the substitutionary, or vicarious, character of the work of Christ. In his commentary on Galatians, for example, he writes in his exposition of chapter 3, verse 13:

> [Paul] does not say that Christ became a curse on his own account, but that he became a curse "for us." Thus the whole emphasis is on the phrase "for us." For Christ is innocent so far as his own person is concerned; therefore he should not have been hanged from the tree. But because, according to the Law, every thief should have been hanged, therefore, according to the Law of Moses, Christ himself should have been hanged; for he bore the person of a sinner and a thief—and not of one but of all sinners and thieves. For we are sinners and thieves, and therefore we are worthy of death and eternal damnation. But Christ took all our sins upon himself, and for them he died on the cross. Therefore it was appropriate for him to become a thief and, as Isaiah says (53:12), to be "numbered among the thieves."
>
> And all the prophets saw this, that Christ was to become the greatest thief, murderer, adulterer, robber, desecrater, blasphemer, etc., there has ever been anywhere in the world. . . . He is a sinner, who has and bears the sin of Paul, the former blasphemer, persecutor, and assaulter; of Peter, who denied Christ; of David, who was an adulterer and a murderer. . . . In short, he has and bears all the sins of all men in his body—not in the sense that he has committed them but in the sense that he took these sins, committed by us, upon his own body, in order to make satisfaction for them with his own blood.[9]

St. John puts it this way in his epistle: "He is the atoning sacrifice for our sins, and not only for ours but also for the sins of the whole world" (1 John 2:2). The King James Version translates "atoning sacrifice" with "propitiation." To "propitiate" is to "appease." Christ became sin for us to bear its curse and thus appease the wrath of God against "all the godlessness and wickedness of men" (Romans 1:18).

That is one side of the vicarious, substitutionary work of Christ. The other side is what dogmaticians call his *active obedience*. That, too, St. Paul speaks of in his letter to the Galatians: "When the time had fully come, God sent his Son, born of a woman, born under law, to redeem those under law, that we might receive the full rights of sons" (Galatians 4:4,5).

He was "born under law" that he might obey the law in our place, and that his obedience might be credited to our account in God's divine ledger. Paul brings this out clearly in his letter to the congrega-

[9]*American Edition,* Vol. 26 (St. Louis: Concordia, 1963), p. 277.

tion at Rome: "Just as through the disobedience of the one man the many were made sinners, so also through the obedience of the one man the many will be made righteous" (Romans 5:19).

Christ's obedience on behalf of all people is also, as Pieper states, "an integral part of the payment which Christ, as our Substitute, made to the just God for the reconciliation of men."[10] Luther puts it this way:

> He satisfied the Law; he fulfilled the Law perfectly, for he loved God with all his heart, and with all his soul, and with all his strength, and with all his mind, and he loved his neighbor as himself. Therefore, when the Law comes and accuses you of not having kept it, bid it go to Christ. Say, There is the Man who has kept it; to him I cling; he fulfilled it for me and gave his fulfillment to me. Thus the Law is silenced.[11]

Our Lutheran Confessions, likewise, point to the substitutionary character of the active obedience of Christ:

> His obedience consists not only in his suffering and dying, but also in his spontaneous subjection to the law *in our stead* and his keeping of the law in so perfect a fashion that, reckoning it to us as righteousness, God forgives us our sins, accounts us holy and righteous, and saves us forever on account of this entire obedience which, by doing and suffering, in life and in death, Christ rendered *for us* to his heavenly Father [emphasis added].[12]

In that way—through his active and passive obedience in the place of all—Christ, as the Substitute for all, paid the price to fully satisfy the justice of the holy God on behalf of all.

Implications for evangelism

In speaking of the work of Christ, we have taken time to review familiar ground. We have done this for three reasons. First, whenever we return to the Scriptures and meditate on Christ's work on our behalf the Holy Spirit is at work, strengthening our faith in the Christ whose substitutionary work counted for us. A strengthened faith, in

---

[10]Francis Pieper, *Christian Dogmatics,* Vol. 2 (St. Louis: Concordia, 1951), p. 374.

[11]*Erlangen Edition,* XV, 61,63, quoted in Pieper's *Christian Dogmatics,* Vol. 2, p. 375.

[12]Formula of Concord, Solid Declaration, Article III, 15.

turn, results in an increased zeal to give to others what Christ has given to us.

Second, we always need to return to the Scriptures and our Lutheran Confessions, which we recognize as a faithful exposition of the Scriptures, to be sure of where we stand and thus be equipped to combat teachings that run contrary to the Scriptures.

There have been and still are those who say that the Bible's teaching of the vicarious atonement is merely one of many theories of the atonement, none of which describes adequately the work he did. They maintain that there are a number of atonement motifs, or strands, in the Scriptures, each of which only partially portrays Christ's work.

It is true that the Scriptures use various pictures to describe the redemptive work of Christ. He is portrayed as the victor, for example, the one who came to this world "to destroy the devil's work" (1 John 3:8). He is also pictured as the victim in the sense of being the willing sacrifice for sin, the Lamb of God who goes uncomplaining forth and "takes away the sin of the world" (John 1:29).

Both of these portrayals, however, simply serve to illustrate the vicarious atonement. As the sinner's substitute, by his perfect life and his death in payment for sin, Jesus is the victor over Satan who held the threat of death over every human being. Again, it was as the sinner's substitute that Jesus, as hymn 309 in *Christian Worship* puts it, was "offered . . . for greatest and for least, / Himself the victim and himself the priest."

The vicarious atonement, Christ our Substitute, is not just one of many atonement motifs which one can pick or choose according to personal preferences. Christ for us, Christ our Substitute—living in our place, dying in our place—this is the gospel. If one loses the vicarious atonement, he loses the gospel.

It is sad to see how this doctrine has been mutilated in a book that likely is in use in many of the seminaries of the Evangelical Lutheran Church in America (ELCA) today.[13] Gerhard Forde writes regarding the doctrine of the vicarious atonement:

> This view would hold that Jesus' death is a sacrifice in which he is a substitute for us who pays the divine justice what is due for human sin and/or appeases the divine wrath. . . . There seems to be a virtual consensus among contemporary biblical scholars, however, that this tradition finds little support in the Scrip-

---

[13]Carl E. Braaten and Robert W. Jenson, ed., *Christian Dogmatics,* Vol. 2 (Philadelphia: Fortress Press, 1984).

> tures, either in the Old or New Testament. . . . At the most it could claim to be only one of the ways the early Christians sought to come to terms with Jesus' death. . . . Paul does not seem to speak so much of Jesus' death as a sacrifice for sin or a ransom. Nor does he dwell on the concept of guilt and forgiveness coming from the cross. . . . Rather for him the cross is total crisis, the end of the old, the breaking of the demonic powers and the opening of something new, the life of love and freedom. . . . It has to do with the future, the new age.[14]

What, then, is Christ's work? How shall it be described? Forde asserts that a careful study of Luther will give this picture of the atonement:

> Atonement occurs when God gives himself in such fashion as to create a people pleasing to God, a people no longer under law or wrath, a people who love and trust God. When God succeeds in that, God is "satisfied". . . . [God's] wrath cannot be placated in the abstract by heavenly transactions between Jesus and God [i.e, through Jesus' perfect obedience and sacrificial death as the sinner's Substitute]. Nothing is accomplished for us by that. God's wrath is placated only when God's self-giving makes us his own, when God succeeds in creating faith, love, and hope.[15]

That this is not the way the Scriptures or Luther or the Lutheran Confessions speak hardly needs to be said. Luther writes, as we quoted earlier: "He [Christ] has and bears all the sins of all men. . . . He took these sins, committed by us, upon his own body, in order to make satisfaction for them with his own blood."[16] God is satisfied, his wrath is appeased, when the death penalty for sin has been paid. To maintain, as Forde does, that "God's wrath is placated only when God's self-giving makes us his own, when God succeeds in creating faith, love, and hope," is a repudiation of the objective character of the work of Christ. It is a denial that his work was valid and efficacious in and of itself apart from our response. It is to say that Christ had no right to cry out from Calvary, "It is finished."

What place, then, does the death of Jesus have in Forde's theological system? Here is his response: "Jesus had to die because God is

---

[14]*Ibid.*, pp. 15,16,17,18.

[15]*Ibid.*, pp. 50,51.

[16]*American Edition,* Vol. 26 (St. Louis: Concordia, 1963), p. 277.

forgiving and because God insists on being so. Jesus died precisely because he said, 'I forgive you in God's name.' He died because we would not have it."[17] It is difficult to interpret what the above is meant to say. Imagine trying to share the content of one's faith with an unbeliever on the basis of such a statement! It is not difficult at all, though, to interpret the following: "He was delivered over to death for our sins" (Romans 4:25). On the cross he was "the Lamb of God, who takes away the sin of the world" (John 1:29). That kind of a message can, and should, be communicated to others.

That brings us to the third reason we have spent some time reviewing what the Scriptures say about the work of Christ. We need to be clear about his work not only for our own sakes, not only to be able to detect error, but also to be able to share the message of Christ's work with others.

To be properly doing the work of an evangelist we must be telling what Christ has done. To speak of Christ without telling about his work of vicarious atonement—his obedience, his cross—is not the gospel. The gospel has content and not just any content. The gospel is not "God succeeding in creating faith, love, and hope," as Forde seems to imply. Nor is the gospel the bare message, "Whoever believes on the Son will have everlasting life."[18] This is defining the gospel in terms of people's response to it rather than in terms of what it is. Nor is the gospel a message such as, "Jesus makes me feel good. Jesus gives me peace. Jesus gives me happiness." Peace and happiness, an inner joy that outer circumstances cannot destroy, are the fruit of the gospel, but not the gospel itself.

The gospel is the good news of a Substitute, God and man in one indivisible person, who took the place of the human race under the law and then hung in place of the human race on the cross. The gospel is our Substitute's cry of triumph from the cross, "It is finished! Complete! Paid in full!" It is the good news that no matter how far we have strayed from the path, no matter how far short we have fallen of God's standard of perfection, through Christ the way back to God has been thrown wide open. His life and his death count for us—and for all.

A bare Jesus without his work of satisfying the demands and punishment of the holy God in our place is not the Jesus of the Scriptures

---

[17]Carl E. Braaten and Robert W. Jenson, ed., *Christian Dogmatics,* Vol. 2 (Philadelphia: Fortress Press, 1984), p. 92.

[18]As maintained by Donald A. McGavran and Win Arn in *Ten Steps for Church Growth* (San Francisco: Harper and Row, 1977), p. 28.

and cannot produce real and enduring peace and happiness. Valid Christian witness centers around what the Scriptures reveal about the person and work of Christ.

The two states and their implication for evangelism

Humiliation

It was a real historical figure who engaged in real activities to carry out his work of redemption. As we trace the path he followed to do this, it soon becomes apparent that, though the Scriptures clearly declare Christ to be God himself in human flesh, he did not always fully use his divine attributes, e.g., his omnipresence, omniscience, and omnipotence. While on earth he chose to be bound for the most part by the same natural "laws" that govern everyone else. He "grew in wisdom and stature" (Luke 2:52). He tired (Mark 4:38). He wept (John 11:35). He thirsted (John 19:28). He suffered (Matthew 27:46). He died (Luke 23:46).

The Lutheran Confessions speak of this in the following way:

> According to the personal union he [Christ] always possessed this [divine] majesty. But in the state of humiliation he dispensed with it and could therefore truly increase in age, wisdom, and favor with God and men, for he did not always disclose this majesty, but only when it pleased him.[19]

The Confessions make reference to Philippians 2:6ff., the key passage on what Christians have come to call Christ's states of humiliation and exaltation. His humiliation is described in these words:

> Christ Jesus, . . . being in very nature God, did not consider equality with God something to be grasped, but made himself nothing, taking the very nature of a servant, being made in human likeness. And being found in appearance as a man, he humbled himself and became obedient to death—even death on a cross! (Philippians 2:5-8)

"Christ made himself nothing," says Paul, literally, "emptied himself." How did he do that? By not insisting that he hang on to the "equality with God" that was his. Instead, he took the "very nature of a servant," literally, "slave." These words are a brief summary of his whole earthly life as prophesied by Isaiah: "He had no beauty or majesty to attract us to him, nothing in his appearance that we should

---

[19]Formula of Concord, Epitome, Article VIII, 16.

desire him. He was despised and rejected by men, a man of sorrows, and familiar with suffering. Like one from whom men hide their faces he was despised, and we esteemed him not" (Isaiah 53:2,3).

"He humbled himself," Paul tells the Philippians. That self-humbling extended even to death, "death on a cross."

What makes this such an amazing display of love is the fact that none of it had to happen, in this sense: Jesus was not the helpless victim of circumstances. He was not without his divine nature during his 33 years on earth. He continued to be God. "I and the Father are one" (John 10:30), he declared. "No one takes [my life] from me," he says, "but I lay it down of my own accord. I have authority to lay it down and authority to take it up again." (John 10:18). The emptying of Jesus, his state of humiliation, consisted in this: during his earthly life and all the way through his death and burial, he voluntarily refrained from the full use of the divine glory that was always his. He chose to do so, since that was the only way he could live under the law for us (active obedience) and die the death we deserved (passive obedience).

The way the Apostles' Creed summarizes Christ's state of humiliation is a helpful outline for the evangelist in presenting what the Bible says about the work of Christ:

[He] was conceived by the Holy Spirit,
born of the virgin Mary,
suffered under Pontius Pilate,
was crucified, died, and was buried.

Having made it clear that "no one will be declared righteous in [God's] sight by observing the law," but "rather, through the law we become conscious of sin," and that "the wages of sin is death" (Romans 3:20; 6:23), the evangelist might then say, "God has the solution to your problem. The solution is a person." Then he or she can talk about Jesus in the way the Creed presents him: his conception and birth as God incarnate; his suffering, including his lowly life of obedience under the law; and his crucifixion, death, and burial. The evangelist might also bring out that, since Jesus never ceased to be God even in his state of humiliation, his obedience and his death counted for everyone.

Exaltation

We will not want to stop with Christ's death, however. The evangelist will want to go on to the resurrection, just as Paul did in his evangelistic work. He tells the Corinthians, "Brothers, I want to remind you of the gospel I preached to you, which you received and on which you have taken your stand." What was the gospel he had preached? A few verses later he answers this question: "that Christ died for our sins according to the Scriptures, that he was buried, that he was raised on the third day according to the Scriptures" (1 Corinthians 15:1,3,4).

The resurrection is a part of the gospel and a major part of what has come to be known as Christ's state of exaltation. St. Paul, having spoken of Christ's humiliation in verses 6-8 of Philippians, then says:

> Therefore God exalted him to the highest place and gave him the name that is above every name, that at the name of Jesus every knee should bow, in heaven and on earth and under the earth, and every tongue confess that Jesus Christ is Lord, to the glory of God the Father. (Philippians 2:9-11)

After his death and burial, Christ once again assumed the full use of the divine majesty that had always been his but that, as the Formula of Concord puts it, "he kept . . . hidden during the state of his humiliation and did not use . . . at all times, but only when he wanted to."[20] In full agreement with the Scriptures, the Confessions say that

> after his resurrection he laid aside completely the form of a slave (not the human nature) and was established in the full use, revelation, and manifestation of his divine majesty. Thus he entered into his glory in such a way that now not only as God, but also as man, he knows all things, can do all things, is present to all creatures, and has all things in heaven and on earth and under the earth beneath his feet and in his hands.[21]

The Apostles' Creed also gives the evangelist a helpful outline of Christ's state of exaltation, beginning with the words:

He descended into hell.

The Formula of Concord, on the basis of 1 Peter 3:18,19, asserts regarding Christ's descent into hell "that after the burial the entire person, God and man, descended into hell, conquered the devil, destroyed hell's power, and took from the devil all his might." It also cautions us that "we are not to concern ourselves with exalted and

---

[20]Formula of Concord, Solid Declaration, Article VIII, 26.

[21]*Ibid.*, Epitome, Article VIII, 16.

acute speculations about how this occurred. . . . We must only believe and cling to the Word."[22]

It is questionable that the teaching of Christ's descent into hell should be a part of a basic evangelism presentation. This would follow in later instruction. The truth the descent into hell emphasizes, that the devil has been totally defeated and that hell need no longer terrify us, will be brought out by the evangelist when he speaks of the resurrection.

If the descent into hell is brought up, however, it needs to be presented as something that actually happened, not merely as a "symbol," as Braaten calls it.[23] Nor dare we make the fact that Christ "went and preached to the spirits in prison who disobeyed long ago when God waited patiently in the days of Noah while the ark was being built" (1 Peter 3:19,20) to say, as Braaten maintains, that

> nations and generations of people who lived before the coming of Christ and who have never been confronted with the preaching of salvation in his name are not eternally lost. Christ goes even to the dead, so that he might be acclaimed the Lord of the living and the dead.[24]

The "preaching" mentioned in the passage from 1 Peter (from the verb *kerusso*) simply means "to make an announcement as a herald." It does not tell what kind of an announcement. The context must decide that. Here the context is that the victorious Christ made an announcement to those who had persistently rejected the gospel in the days of Noah. They already had been "confronted with the preaching of salvation" and had rejected the message. Christ's announcement, therefore, could have been nothing other than that of judgment, not salvation.

The third day he rose again from the dead.

In his letter to the Romans, Paul presents a most compelling reason for including the resurrection in the basic evangelism message. The translation of the New American Standard Bible (NASB) stays the closest to the original Greek: "[Christ] was delivered up because of our transgressions, and was raised because of our justification"

---

[22]*Ibid.*, Solid Declaration, Article IX, 2,3.

[23]Carl E. Braaten and Robert W. Jenson, ed., *Christian Dogmatics,* Vol. 1 (Philadelphia: Fortress Press), p. 548.

[24]*Ibid.*, p. 549.

(Romans 4:25). Raising Christ from the dead was the Father's way of saying that he was fully satisfied with his Son's work, that the sins of all people have been paid for in full. Conversely, as Paul says, "If Christ has not been raised, your faith is futile; you are still in your sins" (1 Corinthians 15:17).

Christ's victory over death also assures believers that they too will overcome death. If Christ had remained in the grave, there would be no resurrection. But, as St. Paul brings out so beautifully in 1 Corinthians 15, "Christ has indeed been raised from the dead." The risen Christ, says Paul, is "the firstfruits of those who have fallen asleep. For since death came through a man, the resurrection of the dead comes also through a man. For as in Adam all die, so in Christ all will be made alive" (verses 20-22).

Given the critical importance of the resurrection, it is disturbing, to say the least, to hear Braaten say, "The question has become acute in modern theology whether in the resurrection we are dealing only with a myth or with a truly historical event."[25] He goes on:

> The nature of the reality that appeared to the witnesses was more than historical. . . . Immediately they interpreted this event as the first instance of the widely anticipated eschatological event of resurrection from the dead. . . . This dual character of the resurrection—that it is at once an event within the horizon of history and an eschatological event—accounts for the fact that some theologians are willing, others unwilling, to call the resurrection an historical event.[26]

Braaten never does clearly state on which side of the fence he stands. St. Paul displays no such ambivalence. He says, "Christ died for our sins according to the Scriptures. . . . [Christ] was raised on the third day according to the Scriptures" (1 Corinthians 15:3,4). Christ really died; he really rose from the dead. God the Father has really accepted his Son's work. Our sins are really atoned for in full. A real heaven awaits us. That is the message the Christian evangelist is privileged to share with others.

He ascended into heaven
and
is seated at the right hand of God the Father almighty.

---

[25]*Ibid.*, p. 551.

[26]*Ibid.*

In speaking of Christ's ascension, the Creed again is speaking of something that actually occurred. The disciples watched as their Lord ascended and disappeared from sight. There is no need to "demythologize" "the mythical features of this trajectory,"[27] for there was nothing mythological about it.

Christ's ascension and his sitting at God's right hand give special comfort and confidence to the evangelist as he or she goes out with the gospel. It serves as a reminder that Christ continues to function in the three-fold office he filled while here on earth.

As our *High Priest* he not only sacrificed himself once and for all (Hebrews 9:12,26,28), but he continues to intercede for his Church. The writer of the letter to the Hebrews reminds us:

> We do not have a high priest who is unable to sympathize with our weaknesses, but we have one who has been tempted in every way, just as we are—yet was without sin. Let us then approach the throne of grace with confidence, so that we may receive mercy and find grace to help us in our time of need. (Hebrews 4:15,16)

When the evangelist is tempted to fear, to doubt, to lose confidence, to give up, he or she is invited to "take it to the Lord in prayer." He is there on our behalf "to help us in our time of need."

Christ also still functions as *Prophet.* He proclaimed the gospel personally while on earth (Luke 4:18-22). He continues in his prophetic office through his church. What he told the 72 when he commissioned them, he says yet today to everyone who goes with the gospel in his name: "He who listens to you listens to me" (Luke 10:16). Those who truly represent him in the world, that is, those whose message is Christ's Word, not their own ideas, have the promise:

> As the rain and the snow come down from heaven, and do not return to it without watering the earth and making it bud and flourish, so that it yields seed for the sower and bread for the eater, so is my word that goes out from my mouth: It will not return to me empty, but will accomplish what I desire and achieve the purpose for which I sent it. (Isaiah 55:10,11)

And Christ is also still active as *King.* In fact, his kingly office is much more evident now than when he walked the earth, during

---

[27]*Ibid.*, p. 552.

which time he concealed his divine nature for the most part. As King, he rules all things for the benefit of his Church:

> [God] raised him from the dead and seated him at his right hand in the heavenly realms, far above all rule and authority, power and dominion, and every title that can be given. . . . And God placed all things under his feet and appointed him to be head over everything for the church, which is his body, the fullness of him who fills everything in every way. (Ephesians 1:20-23)

That exalted, ruling Christ the King is the one who promises his witnessing church, "Surely I am with you always, to the very end of the age" (Matthew 28:20). What more does the evangelist need? We have a risen, ruling Christ who hears our prayers, who gives us a message that cannot fail, and who promises his personal presence wherever we go with the gospel.

From there he will come to judge the living and the dead.

It should come as no surprise that the same critics who dismiss a real ascension deny a real return. They maintain that "the picture of Jesus returning in the clouds of heaven through which he left the earth in his ascension cannot be taken literally."[28] The Scriptures say just the opposite. They tell us to expect a literal, bodily final return.

Jesus says, "All the nations of the earth . . . will see the Son of Man coming on the clouds of the sky, with power and great glory" (Matthew 24:30).

The apostle John, likewise, states at the beginning of Revelation, "Look, he is coming with the clouds, and every eye will see him, even those who pierced him" (1:7).

The same Jesus, the God-man, who went up will "come back in the same way you have seen him go into heaven" (Acts 1:11), the angel told the disciples. The Greek word translated "in the same way" (*houtos*), has in it the idea of "the exact same way." A visible, bodily ascension means a visible, bodily return.

A study of Matthew 24, Mark 13, and Luke 21 with their "signs of the times" leads to the unmistakable conclusion that, as we sing in hymn 207 of *Christian Worship,* "The day is surely drawing near / When God's Son, the Anointed, / Shall with great majesty appear / As judge of all appointed."

---

[28]*Ibid.*, p. 555.

The certainty and imminence of Christ's final coming as Judge adds an element of urgency to the work of evangelism. Jesus speaks of this in the Gospel of John: "As long as it is day, we must do the work of him who sent me. Night is coming, when no one can work" (John 9:4). Certainly those who know and believe what the Scriptures teach about the person and work of Christ have every reason to be in the forefront of the work of evangelism, especially as they see "the Day" approaching.

3—The Result of Christ's Work: Justification

The evangelist tells who Jesus Christ is. The evangelist speaks of the work that Jesus Christ carried out. We need to add yet one more important element to the evangelist's message: The evangelist will want to make known the result of Christ's work. That brings us to the heart and center of the gospel, the message of justification.

We look again to the words of Paul in Romans 3, "All have sinned and fall short of the glory of God, and are justified freely by his grace through the redemption that came by Christ Jesus" (23,24).

"Justified" is a translation of a Greek word (*dikaioo*) which means "to declare righteous." A legal, forensic term, justification is the act of a judge pronouncing a "not guilty" verdict upon a defendant. It is sin that makes people guilty in God's eyes. Justification, therefore, can be equated with the removal, the forgiveness, of sin. That is what Paul did in the synagogue of Antioch in Pisidia, where he spoke of forgiveness and justification in almost the same breath: "Through Jesus the *forgiveness of sins* is proclaimed to you. Through him everyone who believes is *justified* from everything you could not be justified from by the law of Moses" (Acts 13:38,39).

Justification is God declaring, "Your sins are forgiven; therefore you are no longer guilty, but righteous, in my eyes."

We note three aspects of the Bible's teaching about justification, each of which has considerable implications for evangelism.

Sola Gratia justification

First, the Scriptures make it clear that justification is *sola gratia,* by grace alone. The sinner's justification in the eyes of God is in no way a cooperative effort. Paul says that we are justified "freely." The original Greek word (*dorean*) means "as a gift, without payment, gratis."

This does not mean that no payment was made. This same verse brings out, in fact, that payment was made, but by another. It was "through the redemption that came by Christ Jesus." God himself took the initiative. In Christ he did everything that had to be done so that he could call the sinner "not guilty." The sinner's justification is free, gratis, to him. The sinner is justified "apart from observing the law" (Romans 3:28). But his justification was not cheap. The price was the humbling and sacrifice of the Son of God.

There cannot be any more positive, any more certain a message one can give to another person. The evangelist brings a conditionless, no strings attached message. The sinner's prior or subsequent lifestyle has nothing to do with his or her justification. Even faith, which we will consider in more detail in the next chapter, is not in any way a cause of the sinner's justification. Faith accepts God's verdict of "not guilty"; it does not bring it about.

Justification is free—by grace alone.

Universal justification

Secondly, Scriptures reveal that God's verdict of "not guilty" because of the redemption that came by Christ Jesus extends to all people of all time. The construction in the original Greek text of the passage cited above, Romans 3:23,24, makes it clear that as many as have sinned and thus fall short of the glory of God are also "justified." "All" (Greek: *pantes*) have sinned; "all," therefore, are also justified.

Writing to the Corinthians, St. Paul, while using a different term, makes the same point: "God was reconciling the *world* to himself in Christ, not counting men's sins against them" (2 Corinthians 5:19).

In his first letter to Timothy, Paul uses yet another term, but stresses the same truth: "There is one God and one mediator between God and men, the man Christ Jesus, who gave himself as a ransom for *all* men" (1 Timothy 2:5,6).

The apostle John emphasizes the same truth: "He is the atoning sacrifice for our sins, and not only for ours but also for the sins of the *whole world"* (1 John 2:2).

In Christ, God has effected a universal justification, a universal reconciliation, a universal ransom, a universal atonement. Different terms, but all communicating the same message: God in Christ has declared the whole world to be not guilty. God in Christ has won forgiveness of sins for the whole world. God in Christ has paid the ransom that has set the entire world free. God in Christ has atoned for the sins of the whole world.

What this means for the evangelist is not difficult to ascertain. As we go out into our communities with the good news of Jesus' finished work, we can do so in the confidence that there is not a single individual to whom this message does not apply. We do not have to qualify our testimony with such doubt-inducers as, "Perhaps you are among those whom God has declared 'not guilty' through Christ's redemption"; "Perhaps you are numbered among the ransomed of God"; "Perhaps God has reconciled you to himself in Christ"; "Perhaps Christ's atoning sacrifice counted for you."

We do not have to limit the good news of justification as the Reformed counselor, Jay Adams, feels constrained to do. Adams properly states that "to be true to God's commission and thus offer an adequate solution to man's need, evangelism is absolutely essential to counseling."[29] But then he says, "As a Reformed Christian, the writer believes that counselors must not tell any unsaved counselee that Christ died for him, for they cannot say that. No man knows except Christ himself who are his elect for whom he died."[30] The truth is that all have sinned and all have been justified. Since that is the case, all have a right to hear that fact. A universal truth deserves a universal dissemination.

Objective justification

Thirdly, and closely connected with both of the above, the Scriptures teach what has come to be known as objective justification. God's verdict of acquittal, his "not guilty" declaration regarding the whole world, is "objective" in this sense: it operates independent of any response on the part of the individual.

The resurrection of Jesus is the sign and seal of the objective character of justification. Paul writes to the Christians at Rome: "He [Christ] was delivered over to death for our sins and was raised to life for our justification" (Romans 4:25).

The Greek word (*dia*) translated as "for" in this verse ("for our sins"; "for our justification") literally means "on account of, because of." The first half of the verse states the reason for Christ's death: Because of the world's sins, which merit the death penalty, Christ was handed over to death as the Substitute for everyone in the world.

The second half of the verse tells of a primary reason for the resurrection: Christ was raised because of our justification. Paul does not say Christ was raised so we could be justified. He was raised because through his death we have been justified. Pieper puts it this way: "If

---

[29]Jay E. Adams, *Competent to Counsel* (Grand Rapids: Baker, 1970), p. 69.

[30]*Ibid.*, p. 70.

the Father raised Christ from the dead, He, by this glorious resurrection act, declared that the sins of the whole world are fully expiated, or atoned for, and that all mankind is now regarded as righteous before His divine tribunal."[31]

The objective fact of justification, apart from any human response, emphasizes its *sola gratia* character. When Christ said, "It is finished" (John 19:30) and died, at that very moment the world was acquitted. The world was no longer guilty, and that solely through what Christ had done.

By raising Christ from the dead, God the Father publicly declared that truth. It was God's way of saying, "I have accepted in full my Son's payment for sin. World, you are no longer guilty in my eyes. Your sins are forgiven."

In a treatise entitled *The Keys,* Martin Luther pointed to the objective character of the justification won at Calvary and proclaimed through the empty tomb. He wrote:

> Even he who does not believe that he is free and his sins forgiven shall also learn, in due time, how assuredly his sins were forgiven, even though he did not believe it. St. Paul says in Rom. 3[:3]: "Their faithlessness does not nullify the faithfulness of God.". . . Many do not believe the gospel, but this does not mean that the gospel is not true or effective. A king gives you a castle. If you do not accept it, then it is not the king's fault, nor is he guilty of a lie. But you have deceived yourself and the fault is yours. The king certainly gave it.[32]

The doctrine of objective justification distinctly flavors the message of evangelism. It strongly reminds us that our responsibility as evangelists is simply to get the Good News out. Everything necessary for rescue from death and assurance of life has been accomplished for every person. Our message is simple: "Your sins have been forgiven. Now God promises you: Believe in the Lord Jesus, the one who took your sins on himself and gave you his holiness, and you will be saved."

Distortions of the doctrine of justification

The doctrine of universal, objective, *sola gratia* justification is *the* message Christ has entrusted to his church. It is the gospel. It

---

[31]Francis Pieper, *Christian Dogmatics,* Vol. 2 (St. Louis: Concordia, 1951), p. 321.

[32]*American Edition,* Vol. 40 (Philadelphia: Fortress Press, 1958), pp. 366,367.

is the only message that can give the assurance of forgiveness and thus comfort and peace to the troubled conscience. It is the only message that makes one certain of his standing with God now and throughout eternity. It is to be expected, therefore, that Satan would do his utmost to distort and destroy this teaching.

The Calvinist, with his contention that Christ died, not for all, but only for the elect, denies the universality of justification. The Arminian, with his "decision theology," denies both the objective and the *sola gratia* character of justification. Justification becomes something that must be completed by one's decision to become a Christian. The Roman Catholic, with his teaching of "infused grace," likewise denies both the *sola gratia* and objective character of justification. Justification becomes a process of becoming righteous rather than God's decisive declaration of righteousness through Christ. Justification by "infused grace" becomes a cooperative affair, with people assisting in their justification by a life of love through the grace God implants in them.

All such aberrations rob people of the certainty of where they stand with God. The Calvinist can look only to his *faith* for the assurance that he is one of God's elect rather than to such beautiful promises as, "God was reconciling the *world* to himself in Christ" (2 Corinthians 5:19). The Arminian also looks to his faith but as a *cause* of his salvation ("I accepted Christ; therefore I am saved"). The Roman Catholic looks to his grace-assisted life of love.

But how can one be sure that his faith is genuine, that his love is sincere? If the assurance of my justification is not rooted solely in the external, objective Word and promise of God, which cannot change, then it is going to be based on inner, subjective feelings, which can change, even from minute to minute. The Calvinist's way of gaining assurance, for example, is described in the Westminster Confession (XVIII, 4):

> True believers may have the assurance of their salvation in diverse ways shaken, diminished, and intermitted . . . yet they are never utterly destitute of that seed of God, and life of faith, that love of Christ and the brethren, that sincerity of heart and conscience of duty, out of which, by the operation of the Spirit, the assurance may in due time be revived, and by the which, in the meantime, they are supported from utter despair.[33]

---

[33]Quoted in Philip Schaff, *The Creeds of Christendom,* Vol. 3 (New York: Harper, 1919), p. 639.

For assurance, says the Calvinist, look within yourself, to your new life of faith, to your love for Christ and the brethren. Such thinking can easily lead to religious activism, a restless, ceaseless effort to do more and more of the Lord's work in order to gain greater assurance that one really is a true believer. But how can you ever know if your faith is sincere enough or your love is deep enough? To look within does not create certainty, but doubt.

Those who hold, with Luther, to the Scripture's teaching on justification, will look, not within, but up and out to God's faithful Word. It tells us that 2,000 years ago God declared the whole world "not guilty" through the redemption that came by Christ Jesus. Justification is an accomplished fact. This is the message of the evangelist, as Siegbert Becker brought out nicely in a short treatise on the work of the Holy Spirit:

> It is the will of the Savior that we should go to all men (Matthew 28:20; Mark 16:15) and tell them the good news that their sins are all forgiven. We are not to tell them merely that they "can be" forgiven. We are certainly not to tell them that they "will be" forgiven, provided they on their part will meet certain conditions, such as contrition, or faith or amendment of life. We are simply and plainly to tell them that because of what Christ has done their sins are forgiven.[34]

Such a statement does not discount the need for faith, of course. The Bible says, "Believe in the Lord Jesus, and you will be saved" (Acts 16:31). Nor does it depreciate the value of a Christian's life of love. The first fruit the Spirit produces in the believer is love (cf. Galatians 5:22). It does, however, clearly remind us that what Christ has done for us is the sole cause of our justification. What Christ has done remains steady and immovable, even in those times when our faith may falter somewhat or our love does not shine as brightly as it could.

The evangelist has the happy privilege of telling people that God, for Christ's sake, has called them "not guilty," of announcing the good news that in Christ their sins have been forgiven. Some in our day are asking whether such a message is relevant to our times. People today, some maintain, are not plagued by guilt and fear of an angry God as Luther was. People, therefore, will not be interested in a message that centers on forgiveness and a right standing with God.

---

[34]Siegbert W. Becker, *The Holy Ghost and His Work* (Milwaukee: Northwestern Publishing House, 1977), p. 30.

Whether or not such a contention is true (I am not at all sure it is), what do people need more than to hear that which confessional Lutherans see as "the central message of Scripture upon which the very existence of the church depends"?[35]

> It is a message relevant to people of all times and places, of all races and social strata, for "the result of one trespass was condemnation for all men" (Romans 5:18). All need justification before God, and Scripture proclaims that all are justified, for "the result of one act of righteousness was justification that brings life for all men" (Romans 5:18).[36]

All need justification before God. All have been justified by God's grace through the redemption that came by Christ Jesus—this is still what people need to hear whether they realize it or not. The challenge for the evangelist is not to come up with a new message, but to find new and creative ways, if the situation so requires, of approaching people with the old message.

We have what people need. Somehow they have to be brought to the point where they are made aware of that need. They have to feel the crushing weight of the condemning law of God. And then God himself will lift them up when we, speaking on his behalf, pronounce the absolution, "Son, daughter, be of good cheer. Through Jesus Christ your sins are forgiven." Evangelical Lutherans, who know and treasure the doctrine of *sola gratia*, universal, objective justification, can hardly keep quiet about it.

---

[35]*This We Believe: A Statement of Belief of the Wisconsin Evangelical Lutheran Synod* (Milwaukee: Northwestern Publishing House, 1980), p. 11.

[36]*Ibid.*

Chapter Three: We Believe in the Holy Spirit, the Lord, the Giver of Life

With this chapter we come to the personal appropriation of the salvation won for the world through Christ. We will touch on such subjects as faith and conversion, the means of grace, and law and gospel. We will also discuss what the Scriptures say about the church and the ministry of the church.

A proper knowledge of all this is critical to the work of evangelism. We need to have a correct understanding of the place of faith in God's plan of salvation. We have to comprehend the function of the means of grace. We need to know what the term "church" denotes, and we need to understand the mission Christ has assigned to it. We also need to have a good grasp of the biblical concept of the ministry. If our understanding and application of any of these doctrines is faulty, it will adversely affect the way we carry out the work of evangelism. Each of these areas, therefore, is deserving of some careful scrutiny.

1—Justification by Faith

In the previous chapter we quoted several times Paul's words in Romans 3:23,24, which emphasize the *sola gratia*, universal, objective character of justification: "All have sinned and fall short of the glory of God, and are justified freely by his grace through the redemption that came by Christ Jesus." Objectively, apart from any response on the part of man, God has justified, declared "not guilty," the whole world. The Lutheran dogmaticians call this *objective* justification.

Just a few verses later, St. Paul adds another element that must also be considered when talking about justification: faith. He writes, "We maintain that a man is justified *by faith* apart from observing the law" (Romans 3:28).

Though in an objective sense God has declared every single person in the world to be not guilty through Christ's redemptive work, that verdict does not become one's personal possession apart from faith. The dogmaticians call this *subjective* justification. The Lutheran Confessions speak frequently about justification by faith. Article IV of the Augsburg Confession reads:

> Also they [our churches] teach that men cannot be justified before God by their own strength, merits, or works, but are freely justified for Christ's sake, through faith, when they believe that they are received into favor, and that their sins are forgiven for Christ's sake, who, by his death, has made satisfaction for our sins. This faith God imputes for righteousness in his sight. Romans 3 and 4.

The Formula of Concord, quoting the Apology to the Augsburg Confession and Luther, emphatically states:

> This article of justification by faith is "the chief article of the entire Christian doctrine," "without which no poor conscience can have any abiding comfort or rightly understand the riches of the grace of Christ." In the same vein Dr. Luther declared: "Where this single article remains pure, Christendom will remain pure, in beautiful harmony, and without any schisms. But where it does not remain pure, it is impossible to repel any error or heretical spirit."[1]

Justification by God's grace through the redemption that came by Christ Jesus, received by faith—this is the *articulus stantis et cadentis ecclesiae,* the article by which the church stands and falls.

Definition

It is important for the evangelist to understand what faith is. Perhaps the simplest definition is that faith is the hand that receives the benefits of the finished work of Christ. It is the hand into which God places the forgiveness of sins and justification won by Christ.

Faith is not the cause of justification. To say, "A person is declared righteous in the sight of God . . . because of having believed,"[2] is to fail to distinguish properly the relationship between faith and justification. Faith is not in any way that which brings about the sinner's justification. The cause of justification is the perfect life and sacrificial death of Christ. Faith is simply the way by which the individual sinner apprehends the salvation won by Christ.

---

[1]Solid Declaration, Article III, 6.

[2]Millard J. Erickson, *Christian Theology,* Vol. 3 (Grand Rapids: Baker, 1985), p. 1012.

The Confessions put it this way:

> Faith's sole office and property is to serve as the only and exclusive means and instrument with and through which we receive, grasp, accept, apply to ourselves, and appropriate the grace and merit of Christ in the promise of the Gospel.[3]

The Lutheran Confessions speak of faith as knowledge, assent, and trust. Faith is *knowledge*. "How can they believe in the one of whom they have not heard?" (Romans 10:14). This knowledge, however, is not merely knowing certain historical facts about Jesus. The Scriptures say, "Even the demons believe . . . —and shudder" (James 2:19).

Faith certainly involves knowing who Jesus Christ is and what he has done for our salvation. But when Jesus says, "This is eternal life: that they may know you, the only true God, and Jesus Christ, whom you have sent" (John 17:3), he is speaking about more than knowing the facts. The Confessions speak of faith as "freely accepting the forgiveness of sins." "This faith," the Confessions say, "is the true knowledge of Christ."[4]

Faith is *assent*. But as with knowledge, assent is not merely concurring with some historical facts. "The faith which justifies," the Confessions state, "is . . . the firm acceptance (Latin: *assentiri*) of God's offer promising forgiveness of sins and justification."[5]

And faith is *trust*. The Confessions speak of faith as "trust in God's promise and in his mercy."[6]

We can speak of faith, then, as knowledge. We can depict it as assent. We can define it as trust. We should not, however, use the terminology "knowledge, assent, and trust" to mechanically divide faith into three separate components. Pieper states correctly, "Each one presents, from different angles, the same thing, the same Spirit-wrought faith."[7] One who knows Christ in the biblical sense is one who has assented to what the Scriptures say of him and his work and who trusts in him for the forgiveness of sins. One who assents to what the Scriptures say of Christ is one who has come to know him and trust in him as Savior. One who trusts in Christ for forgive-

---

[3]Formula of Concord, Solid Declaration, Article III, 38.

[4]Apology of the Augsburg Confession, Article IV, 46.

[5]*Ibid.*, 48.

[6]*Ibid.*, 337 (III, 216 in the *Concordia Triglotta* [Minneapolis: The Mott Press, 1955]).

[7]Francis Pieper, *Christian Dogmatics,* Vol. 2 (St. Louis: Concordia, 1951), p. 430.

ness and justification is one who has come to know him as Savior and has assented to the promises the Scriptures make in connection with him.

A gift of God

In a certain sense we can speak of faith as an activity. Knowing, assenting, and trusting involve the intellect and will of a person. At the same time the Scriptures make it clear that faith is not a self-determined, self-willed activity. It is not a work performed by man, as Paul makes clear in the passage cited above: "A man is justified by faith *apart from observing the law*" (literally, "without the works of the law"). To say to a person, "All you have to do is believe in Jesus," is to make of faith a work of the law. The Scriptures say, "To the man who does not work but trusts God who justifies the wicked, his faith is credited as righteousness" (Romans 4:5).

Faith in Christ is not something a person would or could choose through his own volition. Luther emphasizes this in the first sentence of his explanation to the Third Article of the Apostles' Creed: "I believe that I cannot by my own thinking or choosing believe in Jesus Christ, my Lord, or come to him."

To be able to believe in Jesus Christ through one's own efforts would be inconsistent with the Bible's teaching about the nature of man. Recall the way the Bible describes mankind since the fall into sin. "As for you," Paul writes to the Ephesians, "you were *dead* in your transgressions and sins" (Ephesians 2:1). A dead person is unable to lift so much as a finger in the direction of God. Paul reminds the Romans, "The sinful mind is *hostile* to God" (Romans 8:7). One who hates God (and everyone does by nature) is unwilling to come to him. Paul tells the Corinthians, "The man without the Spirit does not accept the things that come from the Spirit of God, for they are *foolishness* to him, and he cannot understand them, because they are spiritually discerned" (1 Corinthians 2:14). The person without the Spirit of God, which is a description of every unbeliever, has neither the inclination nor the ability to "accept the things that come from the Spirit of God," in particular, the message of "Jesus Christ and him crucified" (1 Corinthians 2:2).

On the basis of Scripture passages such as quoted above, the Formula of Concord makes this strong statement on the will of unregenerate mankind:

> We believe that in spiritual and divine things the intellect, heart, and will of unregenerated man cannot by any native or

natural powers in any way understand, believe, accept, imagine, will, begin, accomplish, do, effect, or cooperate, but that man is entirely and completely dead and corrupted as far as anything good is concerned. Accordingly, we believe that after the Fall and prior to his conversion not a spark of spiritual powers has remained or exists in man by which he could make himself ready for the grace of God or to accept the proffered grace, nor that he has any capacity for grace by and for himself or can apply himself to it or prepare himself for it, or help, do, effect, or cooperate toward his conversion by his own powers, either altogether or half-way or in the tiniest or smallest degree, "of himself as coming from himself," but is a slave of sin (John 8:34), the captive of the devil who drives him (Eph. 2:2; 2 Tim. 2:26). Hence according to its perverse disposition and nature the natural free will is mighty and active only in the direction of that which is displeasing and contrary to God.[8]

Faith is not something man *does*. Faith, rather, is something God *gives*. Paul tells the Ephesians:

> It is by grace you have been saved, through faith—and this is not from yourselves, it is the gift of God—not by works, so that no one can boast. (Ephesians 2:8,9)

Salvation and the faith to accept that salvation—the source of neither of these is ourselves, says Paul. Both are the gift of God. In his first letter to the Corinthians, Paul tells us that it is the third person of the Trinity, the Holy Spirit, who brings us to faith in Jesus Christ: "No one can say, 'Jesus is Lord,' except by the Holy Spirit" (1 Corinthians 12:3).

It is unscriptural, therefore—and pointless—to ask a non-Christian to make a decision to believe in Jesus Christ. An unbeliever will not and cannot do this.

It is also unscriptural to assert that some people are more receptive to the gospel than others, and that the task of the evangelist is to seek out such receptive people. No people are by nature "friendly to the idea of becoming Christian," as Donald McGavran maintains.[9] Such thinking is based on a faulty idea of the nature of man. It assumes the presence of at least a little spark of inherent goodness that

---

[8]Solid Declaration, Article II, 7.

[9]Donald A. McGavran, *Understanding Church Growth* (Grand Rapids: Eerdmans, 1980), p. 170.

the evangelist can fan into flame, with the result that the person is now ready to choose Christ for himself or herself.

The evangelist, Billy Graham, for example, writes:

> As you stand at the foot of the cross, the Holy Spirit makes you realize that you are a sinner. He directs your faith to the Christ who died in your place. *You must open your heart and let him come in* [emphasis added]. . . . There are three things that are involved in faith. First, there must be a *knowledge* of what God has said. . . . Secondly, the *emotions* . . . are involved. . . . There is going to be a tug at the heart. Emotion may vary in religious experience. Some people are stoical and others are demonstrative, but the feeling will be there. . . . Third, and most important of all, is the *will.* It's like three little men—one is named "Intellect," the second is named "Emotion," and the third is named "Will." Intellect says that the gospel is logical. Emotion puts pressure upon Will and says, "I feel love for Christ," or "I feel fear of judgment." And then the middleman, called Will, is the referee. He sits there with his hand on his chin, in deep thought, trying to make up his mind. It is actually the will that makes the final and lasting decision.[10]

Jesus, though, says, "You did not choose me, but I chose you" (John 15:16). Decision theology, as Robert Kolb, aptly puts it, is "a theology which proclaims salvation by grace, but then undercuts it by insisting that a human act of will is necessary before divine grace can become operative."[11]

How, then, does one interpret passages such as Romans 10:9, "If you confess with your mouth, 'Jesus is Lord,' and believe in your heart that God raised him from the dead, you will be saved"? Or John 1:12, "To all who received him . . . he gave the right to become children of God"? Do they not indicate that a person must do something to be saved and enjoy a place in the family of God? Do they not say that an act of human will is involved, that one must confess, believe, receive?

When we look at these passages in the light of other verses that also speak of faith, then we see that words such as, "If you confess . . .

---

[10]Billy Graham, *Peace with God* (Westwood, NJ: Fleming H. Revell, 1968), pp. 137-139.

[11]Robert Kolb, *Speaking the Gospel Today: A Theology for Evangelism* (St. Louis: Concordia, 1984), p. 171.

and believe," and "To all who received him," are telling what must occur if the individual sinner is to personally share in the blessings of Christ's finished work. What Christ has done must be received by faith. In that sense faith is a condition of a person's salvation.

These verses, however, do not reveal how faith, how acceptance of Christ comes into existence. To discover that, we need to look to other passages, such as the ones quoted previously, e.g., Ephesians 2:8,9 and 1 Corinthians 12:3, which reveal that faith is a gift of God the Holy Spirit and not at all a matter of one's own doing.

Faith alone

Faith is knowing Jesus as my Savior. It is assenting to what the Scriptures say of his person and work. It is trusting in him for the forgiveness of sins and a "not guilty" verdict in the eyes of God. It is a gift of God, not of works. It is not a cause of justification, but the hand which receives the justification won by Christ.

To this we need to add one further point: It is by faith *alone* that one is justified. This is the third of the three Reformation mottoes: *sola fide*, faith alone.

Luther drew some sharp criticism when he translated Romans 3:28, "A man is justified by faith alone." In his "On Translating: An Open Letter" Luther answered his critics. Though he was well aware that the word "alone" (Latin: *solum*) did not appear in the Greek text of Romans 3:28, he defended its inclusion in his translation on two grounds. First, it was linguistically proper to do so. He writes:

> I knew very well that the word *solum* is not in the Greek or Latin text; the papists did not have to teach me that. . . . I wanted to speak German, not Latin or Greek, since it was German I had undertaken to speak in the translation. But it is the nature of our German language that in speaking of two things, one of which is affirmed and the other denied, we use the word *solum* *(allein)* along with the word *nicht* [not] or *kein* [no].[12]

We do the same thing in English. To say, "A man is justified by faith alone, apart from observing the law," is simply emphasizing positively in the first half of the verse what the second half is saying negatively: faith alone, not works.

Luther, however, had a deeper reason for translating "faith *alone*." He writes:

---

[12]*American Edition,* Vol. 35 (St. Louis: Concordia, 1960), pp. 188,189.

> The text itself and the meaning of St. Paul urgently require and demand it. For in that very passage he is dealing with the main point of Christian doctrine, namely, that we are justified by faith in Christ without any works of the law. . . . If a man is going to read St. Paul and understand him, he will have to say the same thing; he can say nothing else. Paul's words are too strong; they admit of no works, none at all. Now if it is not a work, then it must be faith alone. . . . The matter itself in its very core, then, demands that we say, "Faith alone justifies". . . . And the danger of the people also compels it, so that they may not continue to hang upon works and wander away from faith and lose Christ. . . . For these reasons it is not only right but also highly necessary to speak it out as plainly and fully as possible, "Faith alone saves, without works."[13]

In short, to translate, as Luther did, "A man is justified by faith *alone,*" is to say nothing more and nothing less than the Scriptures say.

To be justified by faith alone means that nothing that *precedes* faith and nothing that *follows* after faith is a part of a person's justification. Contrition, or sorrow over sin, will precede faith, and a new life of love will follow after faith. But faith is not contrition, and faith is not love.

The Lutheran Confessions speak directly to this matter. On the one hand they declare that contrition is necessary: "There cannot be genuine saving faith in those who live without contrition and sorrow and have a wicked intention to remain and abide in sin."[14] They speak in a similar way of the new life of love that will follow faith: "Love is a fruit which certainly and necessarily follows true faith. For if a person does not love, this indicates certainly that he is not justified but is still in death, or that he has again lost the righteousness of faith."[15]

"But," the Confessions maintain, "when Paul says, '*We are justified by faith apart from works,*' he indicates thereby that neither the preceding contrition, nor the subsequent works belong in the article or matter of justification by faith."[16]

If contrition were a part of justifying faith, a person could never be sure of his or her standing with God. One would constantly be won-

---

[13]*Ibid.*, pp. 195,197,198.

[14]Formula of Concord, Solid Declaration, Article III, 26.

[15]*Ibid.*, 27.

[16]*Ibid.*

dering, as Luther did in his early years, "Am I sorry *enough* for my sins? Have I done enough fasting and praying; have I practiced sufficient self-denial to show that I am truly contrite?"

C. F. W. Walther, a later champion of justification by faith alone, went through such a period of spiritual turmoil in his student days. He was deeply affected by the devotional writings of some of the Pietists who insisted that certainty of forgiveness could be gained only by a high degree of remorse and putting down of the flesh. Through excessive fasting and other forms of self-denial Walther harmed his physical health, requiring him to drop out of school for a time. And he fell into deep spiritual depression. He was lifted out of this depression only when he was offered "counsel and comfort from the Word of God which put aside all his useless struggling to become repentant enough to merit grace and directed him to accept forgiveness and salvation as a complete gift of God."[17]

The evangelist will use the law to reveal sin. He will look for a recognition of and a sorrow over sin. He will not, however, require a certain level of contrition before he speaks the word of absolution. One is justified by faith *alone.* He is justified by trusting the promise of God, "Your sins are forgiven," not by leaning on the depth or the sincerity of his contrition.

The contrition that precedes does not belong in the article of justification; nor do the works that follow. One is justified by faith *alone.* The Roman Catholic Church vehemently denies this teaching, as is clearly brought out in the decrees of the Council of Trent:

> If anyone says that justifying faith is nothing else than confidence in divine mercy, which remits sins for Christ's sake, or that it is this confidence alone that justifies us, let him be anathema.[18]

> If anyone says that . . . works are merely the fruits and signs of justification obtained, but not the cause of its increase, let him be anathema.[19]

> To those who work well unto the end and trust in God, eternal life is to be offered, both as a grace mercifully promised to the sons of

---

[17]Martin O. Westerhaus, "The Confessional Lutheran Emigrations from Prussia and Saxony around 1839," *Wisconsin Lutheran Quarterly,* 87:3, Summer 1990, p. 202.

[18]H. J. Schroeder, transl., *Canons and Decrees of the Council of Trent,* Sess. 6, can. 12 (St. Louis: B. Herder Book Co., 1941), p. 43.

[19]*Ibid.*, Sess. 6, can. 24, p. 45.

God through Christ Jesus, and as a reward promised by God himself, to be faithfully given to their good works and merits.[20]

With such statements Roman Catholic theology denies *sola fide* justification. It makes of justification a cooperative affair: faith plus grace-assisted works. If the works that follow faith are a part of justification, a person can be no more sure of salvation than if justification included the contrition that precedes faith. One would again constantly be in doubt: "Have I done enough good works? Have I been sufficiently sincere in what I have done?"

It is not difficult to recognize that adding works to faith to produce justification is contrary to passages such as the one we have been considering: "A man is justified by faith *[alone]*, apart from observing the law" (Romans 3:28). There is a variation of this false teaching, however, that is a bit more difficult to discern: the error of broadening the definition of faith to include works.

In his book, *Evangelism Explosion,* author D. James Kennedy, who has many commendable things to say elsewhere, falls into this error. Also, as will be made clear in the excerpt that follows, Kennedy is an advocate of "decision theology." This is from the final part of a section entitled, "Extended Presentation of the Gospel":

> Rene, you have just heard the greatest story ever told—the Good News, the Gospel of Jesus Christ about the greatest offer ever made. Now, Rene, the question God is asking you is simply this: **Do you want to receive the gift of eternal life?** This gift that the Son of God left his throne and went to hell on the cross to procure for you, would you like to receive it?
>
> Oh, yes, I would.
>
> **. . . You receive eternal life by receiving the person of Jesus Christ. . . .** He says, "Behold, I stand at the door and knock; (the door of your life) if any one hear my voice, and open the door, I will come in to him, and will sup with him, and he with me". . . . He will come into your life and make you **his child** and an **heir** of an eternal fortune **if you receive him.** Rene, would you like to ask Jesus Christ to come into your life as your Savior today?
>
> Oh, yes.

---

[20]*Ibid.*, Sess. 6, chapter 16, p. 41.

> Let me say one other thing. I'll say it very plainly. When Christ comes into a life as **Savior** he comes to do something for you: **to forgive you and give you eternal life.** But, also he comes as **Lord.** He comes as **Master and King.** He comes to demand something of you. He says there is a throne room in your heart and that throne is rightly his. He made you. He redeemed you. He bought you. He says that he wants to take his rightful place on the throne of your life. **Are you willing to yield your life, to surrender your life, to him, out of gratitude for the gift of eternal life?**
>
> Yes, I would like to.
>
> **Would you like to repent of your sins and follow him?** That means that you will turn from what you have been doing that is not pleasing to him and follow him as he reveals his will to you in his Word. Is this what you would like to do?
>
> I would like to try.
>
> All right, Rene. **The Lord is here right now.** We can go to him now in **prayer** and we can tell him that **you want to cease trusting in your own strivings and you want to put your trust in Christ the Lord for your salvation and receive him as your personal Savior.** Is this truly what you want?
>
> Yes.
>
> All right. May I point out to you, Rene, that the Lord is **looking at your heart more than he is listening to your lips.** He says, "Ye shall seek me and find me when ye seek for me with all of your heart." If this is really what you mean, then the Lord will hear your prayer and grant you eternal life.

This, then, is the prayer he suggests:

> Lord Jesus, I want you to come into my life right now. (She repeats each phrase). I am a sinner. I have been trusting myself and my own good works. But now I put my trust in thee. I accept you as my own personal Savior. I believe you died for me. I receive you as Lord and Master over my life. Help me to turn from my sins and to follow you. I accept your gift of eternal life. I am not worthy of it but I thank you for it. Amen.

> Rene, . . . by a simple act of faith you have put your trust in Jesus Christ for your salvation. Did you mean that?
>
> Yes, I did.[21]
>
> The commitment section then ends with the assurance that since Rene is now trusting Christ alone for salvation, she has the assurance of eternal life.

"He comes as **Lord.** He comes as **Master and King.** He comes to demand something of you. He says there is a throne room in your heart and that throne is rightly his. . . . **Are you willing to yield your life, to surrender your life, to him, out of gratitude for the gift of eternal life?"** To express thoughts such as these when talking about faith is to broaden the definition of faith to include the works that follow. It is a mingling of justification with the Christian's subsequent life of sanctification.

What happens when "Rene" discovers that the sinful flesh hasn't given up its efforts to control her? What happens when she yields to a temptation of Satan, when she surrenders to a sinful desire of the flesh, when she in a moment of weakness permits someone or something else to occupy the throneroom of her heart? If the essence of faith in Jesus is not simply trust in his finished work but includes the new life that follows, "Rene" will begin to doubt whether she really has faith.

It is true that faith is never alone but always produces works. Justification is always followed by sanctification. But it is equally true and of first importance that justification is by faith alone and never includes the works that follow. That truth the evangelist needs to communicate clearly.

Practical questions

It would do well for us to pause here for a moment and ask a few practical questions:

Should one speak about faith in an evangelism presentation?

C. F. W. Walther writes in Thesis XIII of his *Law and Gospel:*

> The Word of God is not rightly divided when one makes an appeal to believe in a manner as if a person could make himself be-

---

[21]D. James Kennedy, *Evangelism Explosion* (Wheaton, IL: Tyndale House, 1970), pp. 51-55 (emphasis in the original).

> lieve or at least help toward that end, instead of preaching faith into a person's heart by laying the Gospel promises before him.[22]

Walther maintains:

> You may spend a lot of time telling men that they must believe if they wish to be saved, and your hearers may get the impression that something is required of them which they must do. They will begin to worry whether they will be able to do it, and when they have tried to do it, whether it is exactly the thing that is required of them. Thus you may have preached a great deal about faith without delivering a real sermon on faith.[23]

And again:

> A preacher must be able to preach a sermon on faith without ever using the term *faith.* It is not important that he din the word *faith* into the ears of his audience, but it is necessary for him to frame his address so as to arouse in every poor sinner the desire to lay the burden of his sins at the feet of the Lord Jesus Christ and say to him: "Thou art mine, and I am Thine."[24]

Walther's point is not that the word "faith" should never be mentioned (He himself writes, "I do not mean to say that you must not preach about faith"[25]), but that the preacher should above all be concerned about proclaiming the message through which the Holy Spirit *produces* faith.

The same is true when a person "preaches" one-on-one as an evangelist. It is not inappropriate to talk about faith. The apostle Paul certainly did not hesitate to do so. In the most complete Pauline evangelistic message recorded in the Scriptures, we hear Paul telling the people in Antioch of Pisidia, "Through Jesus the forgiveness of sins is proclaimed to you. Through him *everyone who believes* [emphasis added] is justified from everything you could not be justified from by the law of Moses" (Acts 13:38,39). His answer to the question of the jailer at Philippi, "What must I do to be saved?", was, "Believe in the Lord Jesus, and you will be saved" (Acts 16:30,31).

---

[22]C. F. W. Walther, *Law and Gospel,* translated by W. H. T. Dau from the German edition of 1897 (St. Louis: Concordia, 1928), p. 260.

[23]*Ibid.*, p. 261.

[24]*Ibid.*, p. 260.

[25]*Ibid.*, p. 261.

Confessional Lutherans, in fear of "decision theology," tend to back away from doing as Paul did at Philippi. They should be made aware that when they say to a person, as Paul did to the jailer, "Believe in the Lord Jesus, and you will be saved," that is not a law command a person must fulfill but a gospel promise God himself carries out. It is able to effect what it offers, for the gospel is the means by which the Holy Spirit calls people to faith (cf. 2 Thessalonians 2:14). Evangelists, therefore, should not hesitate to conclude an evangelism presentation with the gospel promise, "Believe, and you will be saved."

Another reason for speaking about faith in an evangelism presentation is to counteract false views of faith, perhaps picked up from some previous exposure to Christianity, that may be confusing the person.

The individual may be thinking of faith as a work of the law he or she must do to be certain of forgiveness. Or the person might have heard that true faith must be accompanied by an emotional experience of some sort. Or there may be the misconception that faith is more than simply accepting the finished work of Christ.

A third reason for speaking about faith in an evangelism presentation is to give people an opportunity to confess with their mouths the faith the Holy Spirit may have worked in their hearts. The evangelist can then rejoice with them over what the Holy Spirit has done for them.

Accordingly, following a presentation of God's word of wrath, the law, and his word of promise, the gospel, the evangelist might say something to this effect:

> Jesus Christ has done it all—for you. He has lived the perfect life God demanded of you. And God has credited his perfect life to your account. He has taken your sins, the sins which merit only death and hell, upon himself. And God has credited his death as your death. You are free. What God demands of you—holiness and no sin—God gives to you through Jesus. There is nothing you have to do. There is nothing you can do. The work is finished.
>
> God is certainly a gracious God to have done all of this for you, isn't he?
>
> Now, the Bible says, "God so loved the world [that includes you, doesn't it?] that he gave his one and only Son, that *whoever believes in him* shall not perish but have eternal life" (John 3:16).

God promises, "Believe in the Lord Jesus, and you will be saved."

What about you? Do you see what God demands of you? Yes, he requires absolute holiness and perfection.

How well have you lived up to God's demands? Yes, you—and I also—have sinned and fall short of the perfection God demands.

What have you earned by your sin? Yes, the wages of sin is death. There is no way you can achieve what God demands of you through your own efforts, is there? No matter how hard you try you will come up short.

Do you see what God has done for you? He sent Jesus, his Son, into the world, didn't he? What kind of life did Jesus live in your place? Yes, an absolutely perfect life. Where did God put your sins? That's right, on the cross of Jesus. What has God done with Jesus' holy life? Yes, he credited it to your account.

Do you believe that Jesus did all of this *for you?*

If the person answers in the affirmative, the evangelist might respond:

I'm happy to hear that. That is what it means to believe in Jesus Christ: to recognize him as the one who did in your place what you could not do for yourself, and that what he did counts for you in the sight of God.

What is God's promise to those who believe in Jesus? Yes, they will not perish, but have eternal life. Of what can you be sure right now—because of Jesus? That's right, eternal life is yours. It is God's gift to you—through Jesus.

The assumption is that the above would be in dialogue form, with the person being given opportunity to respond each step along the way.

As the evangelist reviews the essentials of the message of salvation, he may meet with responses that indicate the person has not yet come to see himself as sinner and Jesus as Savior. The evangelist, therefore, may have to back up and do some further work in one area or another.

On the other hand, through the evangelist's message the person may have come to recognize himself as a sinner deserving God's condemnation. And he may have come to trust in Jesus Christ as the one who has rescued him from condemnation. The evangelist can at that point assure him that he is a believer in Jesus, that forgiveness of sins and a right standing with God are now his personal possession.

Approaching the subject of faith in this way in an evangelism presentation keeps the spotlight on faith's object, Jesus Christ. And it also helps keep it clear that faith is not something produced by the individual, but is rather a Spirit-wrought "yes" to the message of sin and grace.

A second practical question suggests itself:

Should one discuss the new life of sanctification when presenting the evangelism message?

In general, it would be wise to follow the advice of Luther as quoted in the Formula of Concord:

> We certainly grant that we must teach about love and good works too. But it must be done at the time and place where it is necessary, namely, when we deal with good works apart from this matter of justification. At this point the main question with which we have to do is not whether a person should also do good works and love, but how a person may be justified before God and be saved. And then we answer with St. Paul that we are justified alone through faith in Christ, and not through the works of the law or through love—not in such a way as if we thereby utterly rejected works and love (as the adversaries falsely slander and accuse us) but so that we may not be diverted (as Satan would very much like) from the main issue with which we here have to do into another extraneous matter which does not belong in this article at all.[26]

To make it as clear as possible that one's standing in the eyes of God is not at all dependent on works that follow, it is better in general to conclude an evangelism presentation with God's promise. Tell the person the good news of forgiveness and acquittal because of Jesus' perfect life and sacrificial death, which is assured by the resurrection and received by faith. Let the floodlights shine brightly on God's saving grace. Close the visit in that light. Let the discussion of good works go until another time.

The person may, however, ask about the place of good works. Then a brief reply is in order that clarifies the relationship between justifi-

---

[26]Solid Declaration, Article III, 29.

cation and sanctification. The evangelist will want to make it clear that one doesn't do good works to merit God's favor. One doesn't love in order to be loved. Rather, as the Scriptures state, "We love because he first loved us" (1 John 4:19).

The evangelist may bring this out by means of a simple illustration. He or she might say something to this effect:

> Suppose you are out swimming and all of a sudden suffer severe cramps in both legs. You are struggling to keep afloat and are tiring rapidly. You are in grave danger of drowning. But then someone sees your predicament, swims out to you, and brings you safely to shore.
>
> What kind of feeling would you have toward that person? Yes, obviously you would be thankful. You would likely do whatever you could to show your thankfulness. Probably you would never be able to do for the person exactly what he had done for you, but you would want to do something to show your gratitude.
>
> The Lord has done a lot more than rescue you from drowning, hasn't he? He has saved you from eternal death. How do you feel toward him? You are thankful, aren't you? How can you show your thankfulness? You can't do for God what he has done for you, but you can demonstrate your gratitude by trying to live in a way that pleases him.
>
> That is where good works come in. They are the believer's way of saying thank you to God for the gift of forgiveness of sins and eternal life through Jesus. They are not a way to earn credit in God's eyes, but a way to thank him for crediting to you Jesus' perfect life and sacrificial death, which is all you need for eternal life.

With Luther, however, I am of the opinion that unless there is a compelling reason to do otherwise, such a conversation should take place at a different time from the presentation of the basic message of evangelism, lest sanctification become mingled with justification in the mind of the hearer. Christians do need to hear, as St. Paul puts it, that "we are God's workmanship, created in Christ Jesus to do good works" (Ephesians 2:10); but that is not the foundation of the Christian faith. First lay the foundation. Teach justification by God's grace through the redemption that came by Christ Jesus, received by faith. Then build on that foundation.

2—The Means of Grace

God in his overflowing grace has declared the whole world to be not guilty because of Jesus' substitutionary life and death. By Spirit-given faith and by faith alone, the individual sinner receives the full benefit of Jesus' finished work: forgiveness of sins, a right standing with God, assurance of life eternal. One more element in God's plan of salvation remains to be discussed: the delivery system. How does the Holy Spirit create faith in the heart of a person to accept Christ's completed work? That brings us to a consideration of the means of grace.

The means of grace rightfully occupy a key place in Lutheran theology. With the Scriptures, the Lutheran church confesses the means of grace to be the way by which the Holy Spirit of God both offers and confers to the individual all the blessings procured by Christ through his life and death. Through the means of grace, God the Holy Spirit conveys to people the gift of forgiveness of sins won by Christ and works faith in the heart to accept this forgiveness. The means of grace are the link between Christ's cross and a person's heart.

What the means of grace are

Strictly speaking, there is only one means of grace: the gospel. The gospel, says St. Paul, "is the power of God for the salvation of everyone who believes" (Romans 1:16). "Our Savior, Christ Jesus . . . has destroyed death and has brought life and immortality to light," writes Paul. How do freedom from death as well as life and immortality become one's personal possession? "Through the gospel," he says (2 Timothy 1:10).

Paul reminds the Corinthians of the gospel he had preached to them—the message of Christ crucified, buried, and risen. "By this gospel you are saved," he tells them (1 Corinthians 15:2).

Writing to the Thessalonians, Paul closely connects the Holy Spirit's work with the gospel:

> From the beginning God chose you to be saved *through the sanctifying work of the Spirit* and through belief in the truth. He called you to this *through our gospel,* that you might share in the glory of our Lord Jesus Christ. (2 Thessalonians 2:13,14)

> *Our gospel* came to you not simply with words, but also with power, with *the Holy Spirit.* (1 Thessalonians 1:5)

In keeping with passages such as these, the Lutheran Confessions attach the saving work of the Holy Spirit to the gospel: "The Holy

Spirit . . . is not given and received through the law but through the preaching of the Gospel."[27]

This does not mean that the law has no place in evangelism, of course. "Through the law we become conscious of sin" (Romans 3:20). Rather than being a means of *grace,* however, the law is a means of *diagnosis* through which God brings the sinner to the point where he or she recognizes the need for help. The law's place is to accuse, to expose, to condemn, to lead the sinner to cry out, "Help! There's no way out. What can I do?" Such was the effect of the law upon Luther. In his highly autobiographical hymn, "Dear Christians, One and All, Rejoice," he writes:

> My own good works availed me naught,
> No merit they attaining;
> My will against God's judgment fought,
> No hope for me remaining.
> My fears increased till sheer despair
> Left naught but death to be my share
> And hell to be my sentence.[28]

That is the work of the law. The law always accuses, always condemns. As such it serves an important preparatory role in the church's work of evangelism. The only time it should not be used by the evangelist, in fact, is when its message of condemnation has already struck terror into the heart of the sinner.

In determining whether or not to use the law, the evangelist needs to carefully distinguish between symptoms and disease. Most people recognize that all is not right with their lives. The evangelist will work with people who are weighed down with such negatives as unhappiness, anxiety, boredom, emptiness, restlessness, dissatisfaction, feelings of worthlessness, frustration, to mention just a few of the burdens people carry around with them.

All of these, however, are only symptomatic of the real problem. It is not a proper use of the gospel to apply it directly to such symptoms. Treating symptoms doesn't cure the disease. Rather, the law needs to be used to reveal the source of all these problems in a person's life. The person needs to see that his deepest problem is a spiritual one: his estrangement from God. To make that clear is the law's intended purpose.

---

[27]Formula of Concord, Solid Declaration, Article VI, 11.

[28]Hymn 377, stanza 3, in *Christian Worship* (Milwaukee: Northwestern Publishing House, 1993).

In our conversations with the unchurched, we might seek to turn their attention away from the symptoms to the disease—and ultimately to its cure—by saying something to this effect:

> I really feel for you in what you are going through [elaborate according to the circumstance]. But (I don't know if you have ever thought about this) there is an even deeper problem involved here. What you are experiencing is just a symptom of the fact that things are not what they were intended to be in this world.
>
> God created a perfect world in which there was no sadness, sickness, or death, no feelings of emptiness or dissatisfaction, no frustrations and anxiety. All of God's creation—and that includes his highest creation, human beings—was in a perfect relationship, or fellowship, as the Bible calls it, with its Creator. With that perfect harmony between Creator and creature came perfection in everything else.
>
> But then humanity rebelled against its Creator. This rebellion severed that perfect relationship with God. When things aren't right between a person and his or her Creator, every aspect of life is affected. A broken vertical relationship between people and God results in a broken horizontal relationship between people and people.
>
> The key to it all, then, is the need for one's relationship with God to be restored. Then everything else will fall into its proper place.
>
> What about you? Do you think that you are in a right relationship with God?

At this point the evangelist might want to use the helpful diagnostic questions: "If you were to die tonight, are you sure you would have eternal life?" And, "If you were to die tonight, and God were to ask you, 'Why should I let you into my heaven?', what would you tell him?" Or, he or she could simply ask, "Would you like me to share with you what the Bible says about what it takes to get into a right relationship with God?" The evangelist can then present the message of sin and grace.

At the close of the presentation, the evangelist will want to return to the symptom(s) which led into a discussion of the spiritual disease of mankind and its cure. He or she might say something along these lines:

I am not going to promise you that God will instantly remove all your problems. The Bible says that because we are living in a fallen world, Christians, too, will endure tribulations.

But this I can say because God promises it: God will make everything that happens in your life work out for good (cf. Romans 8:28). He will either remove your burdens or give you the strength to endure them. He may also help you understand why he is permitting them to occur (cf. 2 Corinthians 12:7-9). And he gives you the assurance that one day you will be able to lay down all your burdens when he welcomes you into his perfect heaven.

In my experience of bringing God's message of salvation to people over a number of years, I would have to disagree with Ralph Quere, who contends, "We can presuppose the law; we probably won't have to preach it."[29] Rather, since people tend to blame their problems on everything but a faulty relationship with God, the evangelist probably will have to preach the law.

Quere correctly states, however, that "our message should focus not on the law that terrifies but on the gospel that justifies."[30] The law always remains God's "alien" work. The gospel is the means of grace. Evangelists, too, would do well to give attention to Walther's 25th thesis in his *Law and Gospel:*

> The Word of God is not rightly divided when the person teaching it does not allow the Gospel to have a general predominance in his teaching.[31]

Elaborating on this thesis, Walther quotes 1 Corinthians 15:3: "What I received I passed on to you as of first importance: that Christ died for our sins according to the Scriptures." He then applies that verse to seminary students who would soon be pastors:

> The apostle . . . regarded all other matters as subordinate to his primary subject for preaching, namely, the Gospel concerning Christ.

---

[29]Ralph W. Quere, *Evangelical Witness—The Message, Medium, Mission, and Method of Evangelism* (Minneapolis: Augsburg, 1975), p. 15.

[30]*Ibid.*, p. 15.

[31]C. F. W. Walther, *Law and Gospel,* trans. by W. H. T. Dau (St. Louis: Concordia, n.d.), p. 403.

> Now, do not merely listen to this statement of the apostle, but think of the time when you will be the pastor of a congregation and make a vow to God that you will adopt the apostle's method, that you will not stand in your pulpits sad-faced, as if you were bidding men to come to a funeral, but like men that go wooing a bride or announcing a wedding. If you do not mingle Law with the Gospel you will always mount your pulpit with joy. People will notice that you are filled with joy because you are bringing the blessed message of joy to your congregation. . . . Your hearers will be spiritually starved to death if you do not allow the Gospel to predominate in your preaching. They will be spiritually underfed because the bread of life is not the Law, but the Gospel.[32]

What Walther had to say about the pastor standing in the pulpit and preaching to a congregation applies with equal validity to a Christian sitting in a living room and evangelizing an individual. He comes as a servant of the *gospel.* With Walther, the evangelist knows that the "ultimate aim in . . . preaching of the Law must be to preach the Gospel." He understands that "the Law is merely an auxiliary doctrine; it is not the real doctrine of Christ."[33]

The law is the means of diagnosis. As such it serves a necessary function. The gospel, however, is the means of grace.

Where do we find the gospel? The answer of the Scriptures: The gospel is to be found in the Word, which also contains the law; and it is to be found in baptism and in the Lord's Supper (the sacraments), which are gospel only. The gospel in the Word and the sacraments—these are the means by which the Holy Spirit of God conveys and confers forgiveness, new life, and salvation. That is also the way the Lutheran Confessions speak of the means of grace. In the article immediately following the article on justification by faith, the Augsburg Confession states:

> Through the Word and Sacraments, as through instruments, the Holy Spirit is given, and the Holy Spirit produces faith, where and when it pleases God, in those who hear the Gospel.[34]

The Confessions add a fourth and a fifth way by which the gospel is communicated: through "the power of the keys" and through "the

---

[32]*Ibid.*, p. 406.

[33]*Ibid.*, pp. 404,405.

[34]Article V, 2.

mutual conversation and consolation of brethren."[35] It is just as correct, however, to see these not as additional means, but as two specific ways by which the gospel in the Word is conveyed. "The power of the keys" has to do with the announcement of forgiveness of sins to the penitent sinner. "The mutual conversation and consolation of brethren" is a reminder that the gospel is proclaimed not just formally from a pulpit, but wherever and whenever Christians speak the word of absolution to another person. To speak of the means of grace, then, as the gospel in the Word and the sacraments, adequately and clearly describes how God offers the forgiveness won by Christ and creates the faith to accept that forgiveness.

God confers identical blessings to people through the gospel in the Word or through the sacraments. Only the form is different. The Lutheran Confessions put it this way:

> The Word and the rite [sacrament] have the same effect, as Augustine said so well when he called the sacrament "the visible Word," for the rite is received by the eyes and is a sort of picture of the Word, signifying the same thing as the Word. Therefore both have the same effect.[36]

The Confessions are simply echoing the way the Scriptures speak. The Scriptures say of the gospel in the Word: *"Faith* comes from hearing . . . the word of Christ" (Romans 10:17). St. Paul tells Timothy that "the holy Scriptures . . . are able to make you wise for *salvation* through faith in Christ Jesus" (2 Timothy 3:15). Peter reminds the recipients of his first letter, "You have been *born again* . . . through the living and enduring word of God" (1 Peter 1:23).

The Scriptures ascribe the same saving power to baptism. Peter tells the multitude on the first Pentecost Day, "Be baptized, every one of you, in the name of Jesus Christ *for the forgiveness of your sins.* And you will receive the gift of the Holy Spirit" (Acts 2:38). Baptism, writes Paul, is a *"washing of rebirth* and renewal by the Holy Spirit" (Titus 3:5). Peter says, "Baptism . . . *saves* you . . . by the resurrection of Jesus Christ" (1 Peter 3:21).

The Lord's Supper is no less a means of grace. Jesus says, "This is my body. . . . This is my blood . . . poured out for many *for the forgiveness of sins"* (Matthew 26:26,28).

As we reach out to unbelievers with the means of grace, a certain logical order suggests itself. We will generally begin with the gospel

---

[35]Smalcald Articles, Part III, Article IV.

[36]Apology of the Augsburg Confession, Article XIII, 5.

in the Word, proceed to baptism, and then, following further instruction, offer the gospel in yet another way: through the Lord's Supper. In all three ways, however—the gospel in the Word, baptism, and the Lord's Supper—we are working with the same living and powerful instrument, through which the Holy Spirit himself comes with every spiritual blessing won by Christ.

When evangelists bring the gospel to people, they can be confident that the Spirit's own power is in operation, raising up the spiritually dead, giving sight to the spiritually blind, turning enemies of God into his friends. Only the means of grace can and, according to God's promise, will accomplish such miracles.

The Lutheran Confessions again and again emphasize the value and absolute necessity of the means of grace. To give just a few examples:

> One cannot deal with God or grasp him except through the Word.[37]

> Through the preaching of and meditation upon the holy Gospel of the gracious forgiveness of sins in Christ there is kindled . . . a spark of faith which accepts the forgiveness of sins for Christ's sake and comforts itself with the promise of the Gospel. And in this way the Holy Spirit, who works all of this, is introduced into the heart.[38]

> We must firmly hold to the conviction that God gives no one his Spirit or grace except through or with the external Word which comes before. Thus we shall be protected from the enthusiasts—that is, from the spiritualists who boast that they possess the Spirit without and before the Word. . . . We should and must constantly maintain that God will not deal with us except through his external Word and sacrament. Whatever is attributed to the Spirit apart from such Word and sacrament is of the devil.[39]

"There is no need of climbing up into heaven to obtain remission of sins," says Luther. "God has put the forgiveness of sins into holy Baptism, into the Lord's Supper, and into the Word. Yes, he has put it into the mouth of every Christian when he comforts you and assures

[37]*Ibid.*, Article IV, 67.

[38]Formula of Concord, Solid Declaration, Article II, 54.

[39]Smalcald Articles, Part III, Article VIII, 3 and 10.

you of the grace of God through the merit of Jesus Christ, so that you should accept and believe it just as if Christ himself had with his own mouth assured you of it."[40]

Faulty concepts of the means of grace

It is not at all difficult to understand why the Confessions and Luther spoke so frequently and so strongly about the means of grace. For one thing, as seen above, the Scriptures themselves place great emphasis on the means of grace as the way God has chosen to both offer and confer forgiveness, new life, and salvation. To emphasize them, then, is simply to be faithful to the Scriptures.

In addition, there were many erroneous views of the means of grace that needed to be refuted. They came from several quarters, from Roman Catholic theology and from the followers of Calvin and Zwingli. They arose even from some who had once stood firmly at the side of Luther, e.g., Carlstadt and Melanchthon.

The issue, putting it very simply, is this: How does one know where he or she stands with God? Does assurance come from something *internal and subjective,* e.g., from one's feelings or from confidence in an action one has performed? Or does assurance spring from something *external and objective,* from God's Word of promise? Which is the real means of grace, a divine promise or a human feeling or action?

Roman Catholicism

Roman Catholic theology sees the means of grace as doing no more than offering some help to the individual who is still largely responsible for working out his own salvation. The Lutheran Confessions speak of "the papists and scholastics . . . who taught that by his natural powers man can start out toward that which is good and toward his own conversion, and that thereupon, since man is too weak to complete it, the Holy Spirit comes to the aid of the good work which man began by his natural powers."[41]

According to Roman Catholic theology, the Holy Spirit assists a person by an infusion of God's enabling grace through the sacraments. That enabling grace, in turn, helps the person work toward furthering his justification. Justification is seen as a *process* of be-

---

[40]*St. Louis Edition,* XIII, 2439ff., as quoted in Francis Pieper, *Christian Dogmatics,* Vol. 3 (St. Louis: Concordia, 1953), p. 208.

[41]Formula of Concord, Solid Declaration, Article II, 76.

coming just in God's eyes and the means of grace, particularly the sacraments, as a way of assisting in that process. One of the canons of the Council of Trent put it this way:

> If anyone says that men are justified either by the sole imputation of the justice of Christ or by the sole remission of sins, to the exclusion of the grace and the charity [love] which is poured forth in their hearts by the Holy Ghost, and remains in them, or also that the grace by which we are justified is only the good will of God, let him be anathema.[42]

As this canon from the Council of Trent brings out, Roman Catholicism's faulty teaching on the means of grace springs directly from its faulty doctrine of justification. If God has not declared the world to be not guilty solely through Christ's work, then obviously the means of grace cannot be the way by which God conveys that message to the world. Since more needs to be done, the means of grace in Roman Catholicism becomes the way by which God, with sacrament-infused grace, enables the individual to finish the work.

The effect of such a doctrine of the means of grace is a perpetual uncertainty. This is consistent with Roman Catholic theology: "No one can know with the certainty of faith . . . that he has obtained the grace of God,"[43] i.e., that he has received enough grace and acted on it properly to make him certain of salvation.

Contrast that with the way the Scriptures speak: Justification is not a process but a verdict that God in Christ has declared the sinful world not guilty; and the means of grace are the way by which God conveys that verdict and creates the faith to accept it. The result for the individual? Certainty, based on the external Word and promise of God.

Calvinism

Calvinistic, or Reformed, theology separates regeneration from the means of grace. It speaks of an immediate, i.e., without means, rather than a mediate operation of the Holy Spirit.

The Lutheran Confessions strongly insist that "we must condemn with all seriousness and zeal, and in no wise tolerate in the church of God, the enthusiasts who imagine that without means, without

---

[42]H. J. Schroeder, trans., *Canons and Decrees of the Council of Trent,* Sess. 6, can. 11 (St. Louis: B. Herder Book Co, 1941), p. 43.

[43]*Ibid.*, Chapter IX, p. 35.

the hearing of the divine Word and without the use of the holy sacraments, God draws man to himself, illuminates, justifies, and saves him."[44]

Luther writes in his treatise, *Against the Heavenly Prophets:*

> When God sends forth his holy gospel he deals with us in a two fold manner, first outwardly, then inwardly. Outwardly he deals with us through the oral word of the gospel and through material signs, that is, baptism and the sacrament of the altar. Inwardly he deals with us through the Holy Spirit, faith, and other gifts. But whatever their measure or order the outward factors should and must precede. *The inward experience follows and is effected by the outward.* God has determined to give the inward to no one except through the outward [emphasis added].[45]

Calvinistic, Reformed, theology turns the two around. It begins with inward, immediate experience, and follows with the external Word. Let a modern day Calvinist, Herman Hoeksema, speak:

> Regeneration is an immediate work of the Holy Spirit, independent of the preaching of the Word.[46]

> It takes place in the very depth of man's existence. It is a new birth, a being born from the very start. . . . It *precedes* all mediate work of God in us. . . . It consists of *an infusing, implanting, of new life* [emphasis added].[47]

He goes on to say: "Regeneration is not even as such a matter of [a person's] own experience, seeing that it does not take place within, but below the threshold of his consciousness. It is therefore independent of age and can take place in the smallest infants. We may even take for granted that . . . God usually regenerates his elect children from infancy."[48] With that, Hoeksema in effect dismisses the need for baptism as a means of regeneration.

What is the purpose of the preaching of the gospel if the Holy Spirit regenerates apart from any means? The gospel causes "the

---

[44]Formula of Concord, Solid Declaration, Article II, 80.

[45]*American Edition,* Vol. 40 (Philadelphia: Fortress Press, 1958), p. 146.

[46]Herman Hoeksema, *Reformed Dogmatics* (Grand Rapids: Reformed Free Publishing Association, 1966), p. 642.

[47]*Ibid.*, p. 462.

[48]*Ibid.*

sprouting out of the seed of the new life,"[49] that is, it helps the already regenerated person to grow in his or her Christian life. In other words, the gospel in Reformed thinking has more to do with sanctification than justification.

As different as Roman Catholic and Reformed theology are in many points, they converge in the way they handle the means of grace. Both speak of an infused grace, as Pieper brings out:

> Rome conceives of saving grace as a current which flows into man by way of the many Papistic means of grace if man "does not place an obstacle in its way," while Calvinism thinks of saving grace as a current which, like lightning, strikes immediately and hence irresistibly. Both take saving grace to mean, not the mercy or favor of God in Christ, but a good quality implanted in the heart of man.[50]

Calvinism, consistently held to, cannot produce assurance in the heart any more than can Roman Catholicism. Both rely on an invisible, internal working of the Spirit rather than on the external, objective promises of God in the means of grace.

Arminianism

There is a third way by which the means of grace are robbed of their full power. That is the way of Arminianism, which assigns the responsibility of conversion, at least to a degree, to man, who cooperates with God (called synergism) to become a Christian. The Confessions reject

> the teaching of the synergists, who maintain that in spiritual things man is not wholly dead toward that which is good, but only grievously wounded and half-dead. As a result, his free will is too weak to make a beginning and by its own powers to convert itself to God and to obey the law of God from the heart. Nevertheless, after the Holy Spirit has made the beginning and has called us by the Gospel and offers his grace, the forgiveness of sins, and eternal life, then the free will by its own natural powers can meet God and to some degree—though only to a small extent and in a weak way—help and cooperate and prepare itself for the grace of God, embrace and accept it, [and] believe the Gospel.[51]

---

[49]*Ibid.*, p. 463.

[50]Francis Pieper, *Christian Dogmatics,* Vol. 3 (St. Louis: Concordia, 1953), p. 121.

[51]Formula of Concord, Solid Declaration, Article II, 77.

The synergist thus adds a third cause of conversion. It is effected, not just by the Holy Spirit working through the means of grace, but also through the will of man, which cooperates with the Holy Spirit. The gospel is thereby reduced to an offer, which the person must decide either to accept or to reject. The real power thus resides in the person who makes the decision rather than in the gospel. In effect, man's will rather than the gospel becomes the means of grace.

The weakness of such a view, which transfers the power for conversion from the means of grace to the will of man, can be illustrated by the story told by Herman Gockel about the little boy who, on a wintry day, was walking with his father on an icy sidewalk. The little boy slipped and fell. Raising himself from the sidewalk, he said, "Daddy, I think I had better hold on to your hand." They came to another slippery spot. The little boy's feet went out from under him. He lost his grip on his father's hand and fell again. Getting up once more, this time he said, "Daddy, I think *you* had better hold *my* hand." Now if they came to an icy stretch, his father could hold tightly to him and he would be safe.[52]

One who thinks that all is well between him and his God because he decided to accept Christ is like that little boy who thought he was safe because he was holding onto his father's hand. Such a person is safe and secure only so long as *he* keeps holding on.

On the other hand, one who knows that all is well between him and his God because God himself, through the gospel, has taken hold of him is like the little boy whose hand is being tightly held by his father. Such a person can be sure that nothing, even death, can cause his Father's hand to let go of him (cf. Romans 8:38,39). Using the picture of a shepherd and his sheep, Jesus, the Good Shepherd, promises those whom he has brought into his flock, "They shall never perish; no one can snatch them out of my hand" (John 10:28).

We have purposely taken the time to review at considerable length what the Scriptures and the Lutheran Confessions say about the means of grace, as well as to examine the erroneous views the Confessions reject. Two reasons come to mind. For one thing, it serves as a reminder that we need to exercise careful discernment when reading material on evangelism that is not drawn from the well of scriptural, confessional Lutheran theology. The terminology may be the same; the meaning, however, is not always identical. It is flavored by the theological system from which the literature springs.

---

[52]Herman W. Gockel, *My Hand in His* (St. Louis: Concordia, 1966), pp. 136,137.

Secondly, our intention has been to impress on our minds what a blessing for evangelism Lutherans have in their scriptural understanding and use of the means of grace. Paul Eickmann brings this out nicely in the closing words of an essay, "The Seminary's Unchanging Foundation in a Changing World: *Sola Fide*," delivered on the occasion of the 125th anniversary of Wisconsin Lutheran Seminary:

> What makes Lutherans distinctive in their evangelism efforts? All Christians more or less plainly confess Christ. But only Lutherans who have remained anchored in the Scriptures confess the means of grace as God's promise of forgiveness, as an invitation to receive his mercy, spoken by the Lord himself to us lost sinners in our dying world. While many conservative Protestants demand, "Believe what the Bible says," Lutherans have good news, "Christ Jesus came into the world to save sinners. He has forgiveness, life, and salvation for everyone in his word."
>
> As they are able, Lutheran Christians can certainly tell "what Jesus means to me." That is a confession of faith. But they will also make their confession to the means of grace as God's own objective promises of peace and life. They will point to the sacraments as God's work not ours. They will urge adults to be baptized and to bring their children to baptism. They will invite the lost to find comfort in the liturgy, with its words of absolution, and in sermons which proclaim Christ crucified and risen.[53]

The means of grace are the great treasure the Lord has entrusted to his church. Justification and faith to accept justification—that is entirely in God's hands. But the means of grace—that the Lord has placed into our hands, to use them and to use them faithfully.

When we recognize that the gospel in Word and sacrament is the *powerful* means by which the Lord conveys the message of justification and works faith to accept that message, we will use these means with boldness and confidence.

When we recognize that the gospel in Word and sacrament is the *only* means by which the Holy Spirit accomplishes this work, we will feel compelled to use them whenever and wherever we can. Though the Lord could bring people to faith and salvation apart from the means of grace, he has chosen not to. "Faith comes from hearing" (Romans 10:17).

---

[53]*Wisconsin Lutheran Quarterly,* 86:3, Summer 1989, p. 191.

Let the Confessions remind us once more that if we have the means of grace, the gospel in Word and sacrament, we have all we need to be evangelists:

> It is God's will to call men to eternal salvation, to draw them to himself, convert them, beget them anew, and sanctify them through this means and in no other way—namely, through his holy Word (when one hears it preached or reads it) and the sacraments (when they are used according to his Word). . . .
>
> All who would be saved must hear this preaching.[54]

That is where evangelism comes in. Hearing implies that someone is talking.

Practical Questions

From this review of the doctrine of the means of grace a number of related questions pertaining to evangelism come to mind. First,

What is the place of prayer in evangelism?

Confessional Lutheran evangelists hardly have to be told that it is not proper to invite an unbeliever to pray to become a believer. Contrary to Reformed theology, which maintains that "the means of grace . . . are the Word, Sacraments, and prayer,"[55] Lutherans correctly hold that prayer is not a means of grace. Prayer is a fruit of faith, not a means to attain faith. Only the gospel in Word and sacrament can transform an unbeliever into a believer.

On the other hand, the evangelist, who himself or herself is a Christian and therefore can pray, will certainly not want to neglect the considerable benefits that come from prayer. The evangelist will want to pray for such things as:

- good government that permits the spread of the gospel (cf. 1 Timothy 2:1-4)
- open doors for the gospel (cf. Colossians 4:2,3)
- the ability to clearly present the gospel (cf. Colossians 4:4)
- the rapid spread of the gospel (cf. 2 Thessalonians 3:1)

---

[54]Formula of Concord, Solid Declaration, Article II, 50,52.

[55]Charles Hodge, *Systematic Theology,* Vol. 3 (New York: Charles Scribner's Sons, 1893), p. 466.

- boldness to proclaim the gospel (cf. Acts 4:29; Ephesians 6:19)
- the conversion of people to whom they bring the gospel (cf. Romans 10:1)
- God's blessing on others who are proclaiming the gospel (cf. many of the above passages)
- more workers to be sent into the Lord's harvest field (cf. Luke 10:2)

Is it fitting to include prayer in connection with an evangelism visit? *Before the visit* it is only natural for the evangelist to go to the Lord in prayer asking for his blessing upon the Word he hopes to share. *After the visit* he will want to keep in his prayers the people to whom he has witnessed.

During the visit, oral prayer on the part of the evangelist, though not an integral part of evangelism, is fitting under certain circumstances. For example, the person may be going through a difficult time in life and might ask the evangelist to pray for him or her. The Scriptures urge that "intercessions . . . be made for everyone" (1 Timothy 2:1). What better time is there to respond to such a prayer request than at the time it is made!

Or, upon hearing the gospel, the person may confess faith in Jesus as Savior. It is hardly out of place at such a time for the evangelist not only to *say,* "I thank the Lord that you have been led to that confession," but to *pray,* "Lord, I thank you that you have brought __________ into your family." Rather than proceeding directly with such a prayer, however, the evangelist would be well-advised to ask the person's permission: "Would you like me to have a prayer, thanking the Lord for what he has done for you today?"

Consider one other scenario: You have had the opportunity to bring the message of law and gospel to an individual. The person is struggling with one or more of the scriptural truths you have shared with him. He may be having trouble with the idea that the person who has tried hard to live a good life is no closer to salvation than one who is living a flagrantly ungodly life. He might be finding it difficult to accept the fact that he cannot do at least something to get right with God. Or his problem may be that he cannot imagine that God would want someone like him in his family, with all the bad things he has done in his life.

The evangelist will seek to deal with these difficulties as they come to light by reviewing and amplifying some of the law-gospel truths he has already shared. Having done that, he might well ask the individual, "Would you like me to pray for you that, as you think about what we've discussed tonight, the Lord help you overcome these hurdles and lead you to trust in Jesus as your Savior?" If the response is positive, such a prayer would be very much in place right then and there.

In summary, though prayer is not a means of grace, the evangelist will gladly heed the encouragement of St. Paul to "pray continually" (1 Thessalonians 5:17) in connection with the work of evangelism—before, during, and after his contacts with people.

A second practical question:

Should the gospel ever be withheld in an evangelism presentation?

We will want to remember what the gospel is, a proclamation of objective justification, that God has declared the whole world to be not guilty through Christ. It is a message that has in it the power to lead a person to believe what it proclaims. Pieper reminds us:

> Among all nations and in all climes not a single person can be found whom we would be deceiving if we not only assured him, but affirmed it with an oath in the name of God: "Through Christ God is reconciled to you, does not impute your sins to you, but forgives them."[56]

Knowing that, we should be very hesitant to withhold the gospel from a person.

An individual might be having trouble accepting the fact that he is a sinner meriting nothing but damnation. The law has still not accomplished its work of leading him to despair of any hope of saving himself. Should the evangelist proceed with the gospel? The validity of the gospel does not depend on whether or not the person is contrite and looking to Christ only for salvation. If that were the case, one could bring the gospel only to those who are already believers.

This does not mean, of course, that a person will receive the blessings the gospel promises apart from contrition and faith. It does mean, however, that the evangelist can confidently tell what Christ has done for the person's justification. Whether or not the person receives that message in faith, the message is still valid. And, of great importance to the evangelist, it is the powerful means by which God's Holy Spirit can turn the person's heart from unbelief to trust in Jesus.

---

[56]Francis Pieper, *Christian Dogmatics,* Vol. 3 (St. Louis: Concordia, 1953), p. 195.

There are times, however, when it is not possible or not proper to proceed with the gospel. In his instructions to the Twelve when he sent them out on a first, brief mission trip, Jesus said, "If anyone will not welcome you or listen to your words, shake the dust off your feet when you leave that home or town" (Matthew 10:14). We should not force ourselves on people. If they refuse to listen to what we have to say, the responsibility for their rejection rests upon them. "It will be more bearable for Sodom and Gomorrah on the day of judgment" (Matthew 10:15) than it will be for those who refuse to listen to the gospel.

We should take care, though, how we approach people. We should be, as Jesus told the Twelve, "as innocent as doves" (Matthew 10:16). The word translated "innocent" (Greek, *akeraios*) literally means "unmixed." It was used of metals and of wine with the idea of purity, not mixed with any other elements. In its figurative sense it has the meaning of not being mixed with evil, guile, deceit, and the like. We will want to approach people with the proper motivation of love for their souls.

We will also want to be "as shrewd as snakes," as Jesus said in the same passage. The word translated "shrewd" (Greek, *phronimoi*) could also be translated "wise," "intelligent." St. Paul writes, "Be wise in the way you act toward outsiders; make the most of every opportunity. Let your conversation be always full of grace, seasoned with salt [i.e., pure and wholesome], so that you may know how to answer everyone" (Colossians 4:5,6). St. Peter speaks of the need for a kind and gentle approach: "Always be prepared to give an answer to everyone who asks you to give the reason for the hope that you have. But do this with gentleness and respect" (1 Peter 3:15).

We will not want to speak or act in a manner that gets in the way of our message. We don't want people to reject us because of our offensive approach with the result that we don't gain a hearing for our message.

Nevertheless, as Jesus indicates, there are times when people, in spite of all we do to approach them in a loving, genuine manner, will refuse to listen. From such we can only turn away and go elsewhere. The gospel is withheld because people refuse to listen to it.

Jesus also tells us, "Do not give dogs what is sacred; do not throw your pearls to pigs. If you do, they may trample them under their feet, and then turn and tear you to pieces" (Matthew 7:6,7). With these words Jesus indicates that there may be times when we should withhold the beautiful pearl of the gospel from people even if they would permit us to speak.

In the context of evangelism, the "pigs" and the "dogs" are not unbelievers in general, since we are told to bring the gospel to unbelievers. Undoubtedly the picture is that of scoffers who are openly mocking everything that the evangelist is saying. If the person, to use Jesus' picture, is trampling the Word under feet, if he is blatantly profaning everything that is sacred, the time has come to stop talking.

Those who refuse to hear and those who scoff at what is said should not be forgotten by the evangelist, however. They should become the objects of his prayers. And, to make sure that it truly is the Word and not him they are rejecting, the evangelist would do well to return at another time to bring the same message, but perhaps with a different approach. Or, someone else might be sent to see if the individual might be more willing to listen to another person.

Should the gospel ever be withheld in an evangelism presentation? Only under circumstances that make it impossible to share the message because people refuse to listen or openly ridicule what is said. Generally speaking, though, one would not withhold the gospel in an evangelism call.

Another question suggests itself in connection with the doctrine of the means of grace:

What is the role of apologetics in evangelism?

Apologetics, according to the dictionary, is "the branch of theology dealing with the defense and proof of Christianity."

In one sense, apologetics has no place at all in evangelism. It may be possible to come up with rational, logical arguments that demonstrate the folly of unbelief, since the truth is neither irrational nor illogical. Such arguments, however, no matter how skillfully presented, will not have the effect of turning a person from unbelief to faith.

Conversion is a supernatural work, brought about by the Holy Spirit. The only effective means of transforming an unbeliever into a believer, therefore, is to use the means by which the Holy Spirit works. That is why Christ's commission to his disciples was to preach repentance and forgiveness of sins (cf. Luke 24:47).

Our call as Christians is not to *prove* the gospel but to *proclaim* it. The gospel by its very nature is self-authenticating. Apologetics cannot replace the preaching of law and gospel. It is not a substitute for the means of grace.

On the other hand, apologetics can properly serve a helping role in evangelism. It can assist in clearing away misconceptions that may have resulted in a person being unwilling to listen seriously to what the Scriptures say.

Pieper nicely illustrates the proper role of apologetics in his discussion of belief in the divine origin of the Scriptures:

> Besides the Christian certainty . . . of the divinity of Scriptures, which is produced by the self-attestation of Scripture, there is also a purely human conviction . . . of the divine authority of Scripture, which is based on arguments of reason. . . . All divine works bear the divine stamp, by which reason can see that they are not the product of man. One will hardly mistake an artificial flower for a natural one. Now, Scripture is as much a work of God, "God's Book," as is the created universe. And as a natural, rational observation of the creation reveals God as its Creator (Romans 1:18ff.), so, too, a natural, rational study of Holy Scripture points to God as its author. When we compare the Holy Scriptures according to content and style with other "Bibles" in the world, e.g., with the Koran, the other Sacred Books of the East, etc., when we think of the victorious march of Christianity through the world, though its teaching is an offense to Jews and foolishness to the Greeks, when we recall the astounding effects of the religion taught in the Scriptures on individuals and whole nations, then a reasonable reason cannot do otherwise than conclude that the Scriptures must be divine and confess that it is more reasonable to grant the divinity of Scripture than to deny it. This is the domain of apologetics.[57]

Pieper then wisely counsels that one should not put too much stock in apologetics, but also that one should not think too lightly of its value:

> It would be *overestimation* [emphasis added] if we imagined that any one could be converted by such rational arguments. A man becomes a Christian, in every single case and until the Last Day, only in one way: by way of *contritio* [contrition] and *fides* [faith]; that is, he must experience the divine judgment of condemnation, which the Law, speaking through Scripture, produces . . . and believe in the remission of his sins through the Gospel, proclaimed in Scripture.
>
> The arguments which call forth only a human faith . . . would be *underestimated* [emphasis added] if we declared them to be ut-

[57]*Ibid.*, Vol. 1, pp. 309,310.

> terly worthless. . . . Such rational arguments serve to show how frivolous are the judgments of unbelief against the divinity of Scripture. . . . Arguments of reason, historical arguments, etc., can . . . be of service in the conversion of a person by inducing those outside the Church to read or hear the Word of God itself and so come to faith in the Word by the operation of the Holy Ghost through the Word.—But we must not imagine that the presentation of such arguments of reason is a necessary prerequisite for the proclamation of the Word of God.[58]

In my years of calling on the unchurched, I have often used arguments similar to the ones Pieper offers here. In my experience, the best place for such apologetics is in response to objections that arise in the course of witnessing. In other words, one doesn't set out to prove the divine origin of the Scriptures, or a six-day creation, or a worldwide flood.

One simply tells what the Word says. In so doing the evangelist may meet with objections, which often stem from faulty information the person has received from one source or another. Somewhere along the way, for example, someone has told him that the Bible has been copied so many times that no one can know for sure what it really says. For the evangelist to take a few minutes to show how the manuscripts of the Bible have been preserved over the years—that is the role of apologetics. It won't make a Christian of a person, but it may well result in his willingness to keep listening. If apologetics has accomplished that, it has done its job.

One further question comes to mind:

Where does "friendship evangelism" fit into the picture?

Strictly speaking, there is no such thing as friendship evangelism. There is friendship, and there is evangelism. They are two different entities.

If we combine the two, we end up with the kind of thinking demonstrated in the following statement:

> People today who respond to the Christian faith . . . are those who respond to the love and caring of Christ's people, not to a set of ideas or theological statements. People are not talked into the kingdom. They are loved in. Reflecting God's unconditional

[58] *Ibid.*, pp. 310,311.

love is the essence of the Christian gospel. And love is experienced, not verbalized.[59]

The truth is, people *are* "talked into the kingdom." The Holy Spirit does the work. He carries it out, however, through the words Christians speak, not through the acts of love they display.

At the same time, it is not difficult to discern a connection between friendship and evangelism. Friendship can be a way in, a door through which one walks with the gospel.

In many ways friendship is a setting more conducive to evangelism than trying to share the gospel with a total stranger. For one thing, it is quite natural to desire to share good news with a friend. What better news can a Christian offer to another than the message of salvation through Jesus! After Matthew was called by Jesus to serve as one of the Twelve, he invited his friends to a meal so they, too, could meet Jesus (Matthew 9:9-13). Philip, likewise, brought his friend Nathanael to Jesus (John 1:45,46).

Second, there is a relationship of mutual trust and respect in a friendship. You would not expect a friend to exploit you or take advantage of you. You would therefore be more likely to listen to a friend when he talks about spiritual matters than to a stranger. The fact that a friend is sharing the gospel does not make the gospel any more powerful, of course, but it may well incline the person to give a fair hearing to it.

Third, a setting of friendship allows for an unhurried and repeated sharing of the gospel. You don't have to say it all at once, if the circumstances don't seem to warrant it. You don't have to force the situation. The Lord willing, you will have more than one opportunity to point your friend to the cross. Later in the book we will be talking about the value of sequencing calls on the unchurched, each time building on what has been said previously. What has to be carefully planned and structured in a congregational setting can happen naturally friend to friend.

Fourth, friendship gives one a window on another person's life, which can uncover opportune moments for talking about spiritual matters. The Scriptures make it clear that all unbelievers are at all times equally unreceptive to the gospel. Certain circumstances may arise, however, which result in a person's being willing to listen to the message of sin and grace. Something happens that knocks the

---

[59]W. Charles Arn, in *Church Growth: State of the Art,* C. Peter Wagner, ed., (Wheaton: Tyndale House, 1986), pp. 66,67.

props of security out from under a person. He loses his job. Problems with children or marital difficulties are overwhelming him. He is suffering from an illness or has been touched by the death of a loved one. By permitting these kinds of things to happen, God may well be telling a person that he is not as self-sufficient as he thinks he is. It's a wakeup call. As John P. Meyer put it, "In a loose sense, anything that causes a sinner to stop and think may be termed a call."[60]

Who is in a better position to take advantage of such an opening than a friend? You know what is going on in his or her life. Much better than most, therefore, you can be there to "strike while the iron is hot." As you help your friend in his time of need, you can point him to his greatest need, that of a right standing with God. And you can direct his gaze to the cross, God's marvelous method of meeting that need.

Fifth, friendship permits a person to observe a Christian in action at close hand over a period of time—for months, even years. As you let the light of your faith shine (Matthew 5:16), in time your friend may be led to ask questions about the source of your joy, or strength, or hope, or patience, or courage, or whatever he may have observed in you. Then you will want to "be prepared to give an answer to [the one] who asks you to give the reason for the hope that you have" (1 Peter 3:15). You can point your friend to the source and power of your life—forgiveness of sins and new life through Jesus Christ.

Since friendship can offer excellent opportunities for evangelism, we might ask: Is it proper to cultivate friendship or at least some kind of relationship with an unbeliever with the specific intent of evangelizing him or her?

There are two sides to this issue. On the one hand, Christians with the heart of the Good Shepherd will look upon the lost in the way he did. They will see them as "harassed and helpless, like sheep without a shepherd." And, with Jesus, they will have "compassion on them" (Matthew 9:36).

A new neighbor moves in. It soon becomes evident that the family is unchurched. A coworker in the office reveals that he or she has no religious affiliation. The Christian neighbor or coworker knows there is nothing these people need more than to be introduced to the salvation Christ won for them. So, rather than avoiding contact with them,

---

[60]John P. Meyer, *Dogmatics Notes,* Vol. 2 (Mequon: Seminary Mimeographing Co., 1956), p. 62.

the Christian will seek to cultivate some kind of relationship, which in time might permit the sharing of the message of salvation.

On the other hand, Christians will not pretend love and friendship in an attempt to win a hearing for the gospel. The apostle Paul tells the Corinthians:

> We have renounced secret and shameful ways; we do not use deception, nor do we distort the word of God. On the contrary, by setting forth the truth plainly we commend ourselves to every man's conscience in the sight of God. (2 Corinthians 4:2)

Paul refused to resort to "secret and shameful ways," ways that were not open and above board, to win people. He didn't use "deception" (Greek, *panourgia*), which literally means "a readiness to do anything," an "end justifies the means" philosophy. The noble end of sharing the gospel does not justify ignoble means to achieve that end.

Such a manipulative approach, besides being contrary to God's will, is probably not going to escape the unbeliever's notice, as was brought out in a letter to the editor in a secular news magazine. The writer was responding to an article about the evangelism practices of a particular congregation:

> The recruiting practices (called "evangelism" in the article) are successful primarily because deception is used: a potential recruit is not told he or she is being recruited but that a friendship is being built. The "friendship," however, is contingent upon the recruit's joining the group. If the person does not join, the relationship is at least cooled and, at most, stopped altogether. The friendship technique is successful with people at points of emotional vulnerability: college students, those new in town, people in transitions of one sort or another and the lonely. Genuine Christianity does not need deception to work and grow.[61]

Christians should not hide from non-Christians. They'll never get the message out that way. It is quite proper to cultivate a relationship with a non-Christian. But always be open and above board. Never pretend you are what you are not. And when the Lord provides opportunities to speak, then be ready to do so.

Before concluding this section on friendship evangelism, we should also note that much of what we have said about friendship on a per-

---

[61]*Time Magazine,* June 8, 1992, p. 18.

sonal level, especially helping people in time of need, is also applicable on a congregational or church body level. The Scriptures say, "As we have opportunity, let us do good to *all* people [emphasis added]" (Galatians 6:10). That is one way by which Christians, not just individually but also corporately, can let the light of their faith shine in a dark world (Matthew 5:16).

We can rightfully speak of a social aspect of a congregation's or church body's ministry. Confessional Lutherans tend to become nervous, and rightfully so, when the word "social" is attached to "gospel." The idea of the social gospel is that the church's mission is to alleviate societal problems with the purpose of making this world a better place in which to live. Some, stretching this idea to its limit, advocate so-called liberation theology, which encourages the "oppressed" to rise up in arms, if necessary, to free themselves from economic, political, or social oppression.

It should go without saying that when we speak of a social aspect of a congregation's or church body's ministry, we are not talking about the social gospel. Advocates of the social gospel define the church's mission in materialistic terms. The Scriptures define the church's mission in spiritual terms. The church is to preach repentance and forgiveness of sins, law and gospel. Its primary concern will always be for people's souls.

On the other hand, Christians will not want to turn a blind eye or deaf ear to people's physical needs. When Jesus sent out the Twelve, he not only gave them authority to drive out evil spirits with the powerful Word but also "to heal every disease and sickness" (Matthew 10:1). Jesus demonstrated thereby the same concern for soul and body he himself had exhibited in his own ministry.

The connection with evangelism? Helping people in a time of need is a way by which Christians, both individually and corporately, can establish a point of contact with a non-Christian. That in turn may provide an opportunity to share the means of grace.

Acts 3 provides an instructive example of this. Peter and John went up to the temple at the time of prayer. There they healed a lame beggar, an act of love toward a person in need. The sight of the formerly lame beggar "walking and jumping, and praising God" drew a large crowd, which was "filled with wonder and amazement at what had happened to him" (Acts 3:8,10). That was an opening for Peter. It was a point of contact that gave him an opportunity to preach a message of sin and grace (Acts 3:12-26).

As I have been working on this chapter, I have been reading a delightful book, a history of a century of world mission work in the Wisconsin Evangelical Lutheran Synod (WELS).[62] The book gives some good examples of how our missionaries, as they responded to the needs of people, established points of contact that made it possible to do the work of evangelism.

Back in the winter of 1918–19, a severe flu epidemic was taking the lives of many of the Apaches in Arizona's Fort Apache Reservation. Missionary Edgar Guenther visited Apache Chief Alchesay, who had contracted the flu, and in the absence of the doctor administered some of the medicine he had brought along. This mission of mercy made a deep impression on the chief. In fact, he and Edgar Guenther became very close friends. Three years after Guenther's first visit Chief Alchesay, together with 100 members of his tribe, was baptized into the Christian faith.[63]

A second example is more contemporary: the medical mission work carried on since 1961 by WELS in Central Africa, first in Zambia and then also in Malawi. Over the years thousands of people have been helped through this ministry of mercy. The writer asks, "How well has the medical program served its stated purpose as an arm of the mission?" He answers:

> The program stands in its own right as a ministry of mercy and compassion. An older African one day told one of our nurses, "If you were not here, we would be dying like flies." As an arm of the mission the medical program has shown the love of Christ to the people and in this way has helped break down some barriers to the gospel.[64]

These two examples, Guenther in Apacheland and the medical mission in Central Africa, illustrate two related, but not completely identical, ways of how responding to people's needs can serve the purpose of evangelism. Both are examples of Christian love in action. Neither employed "secret and shameful ways" to win souls for Christ. Neither resorted to "deception" (2 Corinthians 4:2).

Yet there is a difference. The former was more of a spontaneous, the latter more of a planned, intentional approach. Missionary Guenther helped a person in need. That point of contact, in turn, provided the opportunity for Guenther to bring the gospel to the chief.

---

[62]Theodore A. Sauer, project director, Harold R. Johne and Ernst H. Wendland, ed., *To Every Nation, Tribe, Language, and People* (Milwaukee: Northwestern, 1992).

[63]*Ibid.*, pp. 42,43.

[64]*Ibid.*, p. 198.

In the case of the African medical mission, there was a twofold plan right from the beginning. The intent was to show mercy to people in their physical need and to serve as a point of contact through which healing for the soul could be administered:

> Not to be forgotten is the direct gospel ministry carried on at the clinics through the daily devotions in God's word . . . , the spiritual counsel for the ailing and their families, as well as the emergency baptisms of many babies at the clinics. . . . The angels of heaven have been given good reason to rejoice at the healing of souls as well as of bodies that has occurred through the years in the medical mission program.[65]

My long-time coworker in San Jose, California, Mark Sprengeler, has been serving for a number of years as a missionary in Hong Kong. His point of contact with people generally is the need they feel to learn the English language. He may be teaching English in small groups to as many as 50 people at any given time.

Similar to the medical mission in Africa, he has two purposes in teaching English to the Chinese people in Hong Kong. For one thing, it is a way for him to display the love of Christ. He is giving these people something that will likely be of benefit to them in their lives.

But he also prays that these classes will provide some open doors through which he can enter with the means of grace. He makes that intention clear to people right at the outset. He tells them he is a Christian, that he is happy to be teaching them English, but that he especially wants to share with them the message of Christianity. Somewhere along the course of instruction, as the Lord provides the opportunities, he does just that. No manipulation. No deceit. Yet it is a planned evangelism approach on the basis of what he has found to be an effective way to make contact with people.

Making contact with people at their point of need is also applicable to the work of evangelism on the home front. The Scriptures make it clear that no one will come to faith apart from the gospel. For that to happen, Christians, who have the gospel, need to come into contact with non-Christians, who do not have the gospel. The Scriptures do not prescribe how this contact should be made. That is left up to the believer's sanctified Christian judgment.

---

[65]*Ibid.*

Sometimes non-Christians will walk into a church and there hear the gospel. More often, though, the gospel will have to be brought to them. A kindly deed, done spontaneously to help a person in his or her time of need, may be just the point of contact the Lord uses to enable the Christian to touch even deeper needs—as Missionary Guenther discovered.

Or a person or congregation may, like the African medical mission, plan an approach to meeting certain needs of a person or a group of people with the intent of using that point of contact to bring people the means of grace.

A congregation may, for example, establish a food pantry, both to help people in their physical needs and to share the means of grace. On the church body level, WELS has done something similar through the parachurch organization, WELS Lutherans for Life. Counselors seek to help pregnant women see the value of the life that has taken form within them. Also, as the opportunity arises, they use the situation to talk about their Savior.

Again, Paul's counsel in 2 Corinthians 4 needs to be followed: Don't manipulate. Don't deceive by practicing a spiritual "bait and switch" technique, advertising one thing and then surprising people with something else. Be open, transparent, up front with people.

The means of grace are absolutely indispensable to salvation. Christians, therefore, will strive to make contact with non-Christians so they, too, can hear the joyous news, "Son, be of good cheer, your sins are forgiven."

3—The Church

The Holy Spirit is the Lord, the Giver of life. He gives life by generating faith in the heart through the means of grace. By so doing he unites believers with their God and also with other believers in "the holy Christian church, the communion of saints."

A proper understanding of the mission and the ministry of the church is crucial to the work of evangelism. What is the church? What is the mission Christ has given to his church? Who are the ministers of the church? These are some of the questions we will be looking at in this and the following section. We will also be exploring the implications for evangelism in the answers we give to these questions.

Definition

The Lutheran Confessions define the church in simple fashion:

> The church in the proper sense is the assembly of saints who truly believe the Gospel of Christ and who have the Holy Spirit.[66]

> The church . . . is God's true people, reborn by the Holy Spirit.[67]

The church is people, but not just any people. The church is the people of God, believers and believers only. The church is comprised of those and only those "whose names are written in heaven" (Hebrews 12:23). It consists of those "who have been sanctified in Christ Jesus, saints by calling" (1 Corinthians 1:2, NASB). All who belong to it are "without stain or wrinkle or any other blemish." Justified by faith, they are "holy and blameless" in God's eyes (Ephesians 5:27). The church is the communion of saints.

The church is one. It is the body, of which Christ is "the head" (Ephesians 5:23). Luther writes in the Large Catechism:

> I believe that there is on earth a little holy flock or community of pure saints under one head, Christ. It is called together by the Holy Spirit in one faith, mind, and understanding. It possesses a variety of gifts, yet is united in love without sect or schism.[68]

The church is universal. It consists of "all those everywhere who call on the name of our Lord Jesus" (1 Corinthians 1:2), that is, who truly worship God in faith. The Confessions describe the church as "made up of true believers and righteous men scattered throughout the world."[69]

The church is necessary for salvation—in this sense: The church is the sum total of believers in Jesus Christ, yesterday, today, and tomorrow. Only believers in Christ have the promise of eternal salvation. To say that there is no salvation outside of the church is simply another way of saying that there is no salvation outside of faith in Christ Jesus. Coming to faith in Jesus and becoming a member of the church are not two different things. When the Holy Spirit converts a person through the means of grace, he also incorporates the person into the body of Christ, the church. Both are equally the work of the Holy Spirit, and both occur at the same time. There are no believers outside the holy Christian church.

---

[66]Apology of the Augsburg Confession, Articles VII and VIII, 28.

[67]*Ibid.*, 14.

[68]The Creed, Third Article, 51.

[69]Apology of the Augsburg Confession, Articles VII and VIII, 20.

The church is invisible in that its exact makeup is not discernible to the human eye. Since faith is a matter of the heart, only "the Lord knows those who are his" (2 Timothy 2:19). Invisible does not mean non-existent, however, as the Confessions bring out:

> We are speaking not of an imaginary Church, which is to be found nowhere; but we say and know certainly that this Church, wherein saints live, is and abides truly upon earth; namely, that some of God's children are here and there in all the world, in various kingdoms, islands, lands, and cities, from the rising of the sun to its setting, who have truly learned to know Christ and his Gospel.[70]

This statement from the Confessions echoes the way the Scriptures frequently connect the church with a specific geographical setting. The Scriptures speak of the church in Jerusalem, for example, in Antioch, in Corinth, in Rome, in the house of Aquila and Priscilla and in the house of Philemon. This does not mean that there are many churches, however, but that the one church is to be found in many places.

Marks of the church

There is a real church. It is found wherever God's children, believers in Jesus Christ, may be. But faith in Jesus Christ is invisible. The Holy Spirit, who brings people to faith, likewise cannot be discerned with the human eye. How, then, can one discern where the church is present? One has to look for that which is visible, the means of grace, by which the Holy Spirit brings people to faith and keeps them in the faith. The Confessions call the means of grace the "marks of the church." The church is

> an association of faith and of the Holy Spirit in men's hearts. To make it recognizable, this association has outward marks, the pure teaching of the Gospel and the administration of the sacraments in harmony with the Gospel of Christ. . . . Where God's Word is pure, and the Sacraments are administered in conformity with the same, there certainly is the Church, and there are Christians.[71]

---

[70]*Ibid.* (This quotation is from the German version and taken from the *Concordia Triglotta* [Minneapolis: The Mott Press, 1955]).

[71]*Ibid.*, 5 (The final sentence is from the German version. It is taken from the translation of the *Concordia Triglotta*).

The Augsburg Confession simply says, "The church is the assembly of saints in which the Gospel is taught purely and the sacraments are administered rightly."[72]

Wherever the gospel is purely taught and the sacraments rightly administered, there is the church. This is true because we have the promise of God, "My word that goes out from my mouth . . . will not return to me empty, but will accomplish what I desire and achieve the purpose for which I sent it" (Isaiah 55:11). God's purpose in sending out his Word is to create and sustain faith. Where there is faith, there are Christians. Where there are Christians, there is the church.

The difference between any visible gathering of people around the Word and sacraments and the holy Christian church is that a visible gathering, such as a congregation, may contain unbelievers who are pretending to be believers. Jesus brought that out in his parable of the dragnet, which contained both good and bad fish (Matthew 13:47-50). God, who alone can read the heart, is the only one who can distinguish between the true believer and the hypocrite in any gathering of people around the means of grace.

It is because of the believers who are present that any visible gathering around the Word and sacraments, whether it be a congregation or an association of congregations such as a synod, can rightfully be called "church." Because unbelievers may also be present, however, the holy Christian church cannot be equated with any one visible gathering of people, as Roman Catholicism maintains; nor can it be equated with the sum total of all congregations and church bodies. The holy Christian church consists of believers and believers only.

This does not in any way diminish the importance of gathering in visible groupings around the means of grace, however. The writer of the letter to the Hebrews says:

> Let us consider how we may spur one another on toward love and good deeds. Let us not give up meeting together, as some are in the habit of doing, but let us encourage one another—and all the more as you see the Day approaching. (Hebrews 10:24,25)

Assembling with other Christians, generally within a local congregation, to be strengthened and encouraged and to be strengtheners and encouragers of others, is not optional for Christians. It is God's will. It is not necessary for salvation, however. Circumstances could

[72]Article VII, 1.

make it impossible for a believer to assemble with others around the means of grace. For example, he may be in an area where all of the existing churches have departed from the "pure doctrine of the gospel." But inability to be a member of a church does not deprive a person of *a* place in *the* church. Only unbelief does that.

Growth of the church

In their evangelism work, Christians need to keep clear the distinction between Church (the holy Christian church) and church in the sense of a congregation or church body. Evangelism has to do directly with Church building and only indirectly with church building.

It is not incorrect to say that God wants his Church to grow, when we understand Church as the "communion of saints." The Lord is described by Peter as "not wanting anyone to perish, but everyone to come to repentance" (2 Peter 3:9). Paul writes, "God our Savior . . . wants all men to be saved and to come to a knowledge of the truth" (1 Timothy 2:3,4). The Church grows when the Holy Spirit, through the means of grace, brings people to repentance and a saving knowledge of the truth. The role of the evangelist is to be a channel through which the Lord funnels the means of grace to people.

Nor is it wrong to say that God desires to see orthodox congregations and church bodies grow. He is pleased to see the Holy Spirit gather Christians in growing numbers around the gospel rightly preached and the sacraments properly administered. Within such congregations they can be nourished with the truth, which sets people free and keeps them free (cf. John 8:31,32). John Fritz puts it very strongly in his *Pastoral Theology,* written especially for pastors of confessional Lutheran churches:

> As long as there are any unchurched people living in the territory of a Christian congregation, that congregation should seek to win them for Christ (Luke 14:21-23). For this purpose a Christian congregation should seek to grow in membership (Acts 2:41; 4:4). If a congregation which is located in a territory of many unchurched people does not grow in membership, this does not speak well for it nor for its pastor; much less so, of course, if it even loses in membership.[73]

---

[73]John H. C. Fritz, *Pastoral Theology* (St. Louis: Concordia, 1932), p. 286. Fritz makes it clear that he is not simply playing a "numbers game" by continuing: "Before being admitted to membership, strangers (non-Lutherans and non-Christians) must of course be thoroughly indoctrinated and make a confession of the Christian religion as believed and confessed by the Lutheran Church on the basis of the Word of God" (p. 286).

Confusion sets in, however, when Church growth and church growth are placed on an equal plane. Church Growth Movement leader C. Peter Wagner, for example, defines evangelism as "persuading people to become followers of Jesus Christ [Church growth] *and* responsible members of local churches [church growth].[74] Donald McGavran, the acknowledged "father" of the Church Growth Movement, writes:

> The Church Growth perspective takes a high view of the church. . . . We hold the church to be a necessary part of God's plan for the salvation and discipling of men and nations. They must not only believe in Jesus Christ but must become responsible members of his church. . . . Believers must become a part of the church; otherwise the reality of their belief is in question.[75]

As it turns out in practice, the major emphasis of the Church Growth Movement has been on adding numbers to visible churches. Wagner writes: "We need to measure the outcome of our activities in some way, and responsible church membership is a reasonable measurement."[76]

If growth in church membership is the way congregations measure the success of their evangelistic endeavors, then the primary question is no longer: What is needed to bring people out of darkness to light, out of death to life? Instead the question becomes: What can we do to make our church—its buildings and grounds, its people, its worship, its programs—as attractive as possible so as to bring more people in? That this has become the primary concern of "church growth" practitioners quickly becomes clear when one studies their literature.

This is not to say that congregations should be unconcerned about their buildings and grounds, or about being friendly to visitors, or about making their worship vibrant and uplifting. It is to say, though, if what people need most is to become a part of the holy Christian church, the communion of saints, then the primary work of evangelists must be to use the means the Spirit employs to bring people to a conviction of their sins and to trust in Jesus as Savior. The

---

[74]C. Peter Wagner, *Your Church Can Grow* (Glendale, CA: Regal Books, 1976), p. 141.

[75]Donald A. McGavran and Win Arn, *Ten Steps for Church Growth* (San Francisco: Harper and Row, 1977), pp. 30,31.

[76]C. Peter Wagner, *Strategies for Church Growth* (Ventura, CA: Regal Books, 1987), p. 54.

church growth that primarily interests God is that of the holy Christian church.

Mission of the church

The closing verses of the four Gospels give us a clear picture of the mission Christ has entrusted to his church. Each of the Gospels ends with a similar commission.

Matthew 28:18-20—Make disciples

At the end of Matthew, Jesus gives what has come to be known as the Great Commission:

> All authority in heaven and on earth has been given to me. Therefore go and make disciples of all nations, baptizing them in the name of the Father and of the Son and of the Holy Spirit, and teaching them to obey everything I have commanded you. And surely I am with you always, to the very end of the age (Matthew 28:18-20).

Jesus begins by assuring his disciples, assembled on a mountain in Galilee, that he is the Lord of the church, the one with "all authority in heaven and on earth." He, the risen Lord, has conquered Satan and his hellish host and is about to return to his Father. There, at the right hand of the Father, he now reigns "far above all rule and authority, power and dominion, and every title that can be given, not only in the present age but also in the one to come" (Ephesians 1:21).

Having assured them that their victorious Savior stands behind them, Jesus then says, "Therefore go." The word translated "go" is a participle (*poreuthentes*), literally, "having gone." It is not the main verb of the sentence. Jesus' assumption, however, is that what he tells them to do ordinarily will not happen unless the disciples go to people.

What is it that Jesus commissions the disciples to do? He tells them to "make disciples of all nations." The word translated "make disciples" (*matheteusate*) is an imperative. It is the main verb of the sentence: "Having gone, make disciples. . . ."

What is a disciple? The Greek word from which it is derived means "to learn." A disciple, then, literally is a learner. In the way the four evangelists—Matthew, Mark, Luke, and John—and the book of Acts use it, however, it is generally synonymous with a follower of Jesus Christ, a believer.

Is "make disciples" the best translation of the word *matheteusate?* In its intransitive use (without a direct object) the word means "to be a disciple." Here it is used transitively. Its object is "all nations," the heathen, unbelievers who do not yet know Christ as Savior. "'Disciple' all nations," says Jesus. What does this mean? Most, if not all, contemporary versions, e.g., the NET, NASB, New King James, take it in the way the New International Version translates it: "Make disciples of all nations." The King James Version, however, rendered it "teach all nations." This is a possible meaning of the word (cf. Matthew 13:52, where the same Greek word is used and is properly translated "instructed").

In the verse before us, however, "make disciples" is clearly the meaning. That is evident by the two words that qualify and describe the activity: "baptizing" and "teaching." These two participles explain how Christ's commission will be carried out. First, by baptizing. The Scriptures make it clear that through baptism, a means of grace, God washes away sin (Acts 2:38). Baptism is called a "washing of rebirth" (Titus 3:5), a way by which the Holy Spirit converts people from spiritual death to spiritual life. In short, through baptism, God the Holy Spirit turns an unbeliever into a believer, or, what is the same thing, a disciple of Christ. Accordingly, when Christ says "'Disciple' (*matheteusate*) all nations by baptizing them," *matheteusate* can mean nothing other than to make disciples, to turn unbelievers into believers; for that is the Spirit-produced effect of baptism.

Second, Jesus said, "Make disciples of all nations, . . . teaching them to obey everything I have commanded you." This is the important follow-up to baptism. Note that Jesus is not only saying, "Teach them everything I have commanded you," but "Teach them *to obey* everything I have commanded you." The word translated "to obey" (Greek: *terein*) also means to guard, to hold firmly to. One Greek-English lexicon points out that the word is "suggestive of present possession." You cannot obey, guard, or hold firmly to that which you do not already have. In saying "teaching them to obey everything I have commanded you," Jesus is telling his church that its mission of making disciples does not end with baptism. He is picturing people who have already heard the Word and been baptized, who have become disciples, and who now need to be taught to continue to adhere to everything they have learned. Commenting on these words, R. C. H. Lenski put it this way:

> A living reception in the heart is meant, an assimilation in faith, one that will henceforth control and mold the entire char-

> acter and life. Hence also this teaching will be so dear to the heart that no man will be allowed by false teaching to take it away or in any way to alter it.[77]

In short, "teaching them to obey everything I have commanded you" includes the believer's life of sanctification that follows upon his or her becoming a believer through baptism. This, too, was a part of Christ's mission mandate.

"Make disciples of all nations, baptizing them and teaching them to obey everything I have commanded you," says Jesus. They were to make people Jesus' disciples by employing the means of grace (baptism in particular), through which the Holy Spirit creates faith. And then they were to help people grow as disciples as, through the Word, they taught them to obey, to guard, and to hold fast to everything Jesus had commanded, i.e., all of his Word.

Jesus concludes his Great Commission with the promise: "And surely I am with you always, to the very end of the age" (Matthew 28:20). Paul reminds the Ephesians, "He who descended [to this earth to rescue us from Satan's clutches] is the very one who ascended higher than all the heavens, in order to fill the whole universe" (Ephesians 4:10). When Christ's church goes out with baptism and the Word, it never goes alone. Where as few as two or three gather around the gospel and then go with the gospel to make disciples, Christ will always be present.

The group Christ commissioned on the mountain in Galilee was small in number and not particularly strong in faith. Matthew, in fact, says that "some doubted" (verse 17). Yet they could go out in confidence. They had Christ's authority behind them, Christ's presence with them, and Christ's powerful gospel working for them.

Mark 16:15-18—Preach the gospel

The Gospel of Mark records another end-of-ministry commission of Christ:

> Go into all the world and preach the good news to all creation. Whoever believes and is baptized will be saved, but whoever does not believe will be condemned. And these signs will accompany those who believe: In my name they will drive out demons; they will speak in new tongues; they will pick up snakes with

---

[77]R. C. H. Lenski, *Interpretation of St. Matthew's Gospel* (Columbus, Ohio: Lutheran Book Concern, 1932), p. 1159.

> their hands; and when they drink deadly poison, it will not hurt them at all; they will place their hands on sick people, and they will get well. (Mark 16:15-18)

Though this commission took place in Jerusalem rather than Galilee, in one sense the setting is similar. Once again Jesus is speaking to people who, humanly speaking, were not very promising candidates to fulfill his commission. In the verse directly before this commission, we are told that when Jesus appeared to the Eleven, "He rebuked them for their lack of faith and their stubborn refusal to believe those who had seen him after he had risen" (Mark 16:14).

They, however, were to be conveyers of a message that far transcended their weakness. They were to "preach [Greek *keruxate,* literally, "be heralds of"] the gospel." As in the Matthew commissioning account, the "go" with which the commission begins is a participle, "having gone." The mandate is: Be heralds of the gospel. The assumption is that to do this the disciples will be going to those who have not yet heard and believed it.

Again, as in Matthew, the scope is as broad as the world for which Christ lived and died. Jesus tells us elsewhere, "This gospel of the kingdom will be preached in the whole world as a testimony to all nations, and then the end will come" (Matthew 24:14).

Mark's commissioning account includes a few things not found in Matthew's. For one thing, on this occasion Jesus added, "Whoever believes and is baptized will be saved, but whoever does not believe will be condemned" (Mark 16:16). The heralding of the gospel will meet with one of two responses: faith or unbelief. When the seed is sown, some falls on the beaten path and never takes root; and some falls on good ground, springs up, and produces an abundant crop (cf. Matthew 13:3-23). The same seed produces two different results. Paul says that the one who brings the gospel, and thus the gospel itself, is to those who reject its message "the smell of death"; but to those who accept what it offers the gospel is the "fragrance of life" (2 Corinthians 2:16).

The gospel is powerful. It never leaves its hearers where they were before they heard it. Either they will, by the Holy Spirit, believe and be saved, or they will reject its message and be damned.

Mark adds a second item not found in Jesus' commission in Matthew. The Lord promised to accompany the preaching of the gospel with external signs: "These signs will accompany those who believe: In my name they will drive out demons; they will speak in new tongues; they will pick up snakes with their hands; and when they drink deadly poison, it will not hurt them at all; they will place their hands on sick people, and they will get well" (Mark 16:17,18).

Some in our day, lacking confidence in the power of the means of grace, are looking to such powerful external signs to create faith. They assert that there is a close relationship between signs and wonders and the growth of the New Testament church. John Wimber uses Paul's ministry at Corinth to illustrate this point:

> Perhaps the activity best suited to the use of [extraordinary] spiritual gifts is the area of evangelism. This was Paul's testimony to the Corinthians concerning his initial efforts in their lives: "My message and my preaching were not in persuasive words of wisdom, but in demonstration of the Spirit and of power" (1 Cor. 2:4, NASB). In Athens, he had used persuasive words with meager results. At his next apostolic stop, Corinth, many believed. It appears that in Corinth Paul combined proclamation with demonstration, as Christ had done throughout his ministry. . . . I call this type of ministry that Paul had in Corinth power evangelism. . . . The explanation of the gospel comes with a demonstration of God's power through signs and wonders. . . . In order to see God's church multiply as it is doing in the rest of the world, the Western church must become involved in power evangelism.[78]

Our purpose here is not to enter into a discussion of the whole charismatic movement. That, obviously, is a subject in itself. Suffice it to say at this point that a careful study of Paul's ministry makes it clear that it was carried out in conformity with what he himself wrote:

> "Everyone who calls on the name of the Lord will be saved." How, then can they call on the one they have not believed in? And how can they believe in the one of whom they have not heard? And how can they hear without someone preaching to them? . . . Consequently, faith comes from hearing the message, and the message is heard through the word of Christ. (Romans 10:13,14,17)

The failure of Wimber and others to recognize how the gospel creates and sustains faith stems from their failure to recognize and appreciate the power that the gospel has in and of itself. Note how

---

[78]C. Peter Wagner, ed., *Church Growth: State of the Art* (Wheaton: Tyndale House, 1986), pp. 223,224.

Wimber separates God's power from the gospel when he says that "the explanation of the gospel comes with a demonstration of God's power through signs and wonders." The *gospel,* according to Wimber, apparently is something that is simply *explained,* something that human logic can chew on and make a rational decision about, while *signs and wonders demonstrate God's power* and thus move one to make a favorable decision about the gospel.

Christ did promise that signs and wonders would accompany the preaching of the gospel. Paul's words in 2 Corinthians indicate, however, that this was a promise given specifically to the apostles. He writes, *"The things that mark an apostle*—signs, wonders and miracles—were done among you with great perseverance" (2 Corinthians 12:12). Likewise, the writer of the letter to the Hebrews states that when "those who heard him [Christ]" (a clear reference to the apostles) went out with the gospel, "God also testified to it by signs, wonders and various miracles" (Hebrews 2:3,4). The Scriptures do not lead us to expect that God will accompany the preaching of the gospel with such external signs and wonders today.

The real power, today as in the days of the apostles, resides in the gospel. "Preach the gospel." That is the commission. "Preach the gospel *to all creation."* That is the scope of the commission. "Whoever believes and is baptized will be saved, but whoever does not believe will be condemned" (Mark 16:16). That is the result of carrying out the commission.

Luke 24:46-49—Preach repentance and forgiveness of sins

> [Jesus] told them, "This is what is written: The Christ will suffer and rise from the dead on the third day, and repentance and forgiveness of sins will be preached in his name to all nations, beginning at Jerusalem. You are witnesses of these things. I am going to send you what my Father has promised; but stay in the city until you have been clothed with power from on high." (Luke 24:46-49)

At the end of Luke's Gospel we find yet another of our Lord's commissions to his church. It was most likely given on the first Easter evening. The risen Lord had suddenly appeared to his disciples who were huddled in fear behind locked doors. After offering evidence that it was really he and not a ghost, he reminded them that it had been God's plan, prophesied in the Scriptures, for him to suffer, die, and rise. "This," he said to them, "is what is written: The Christ will suffer and rise from the dead on the third day" (Luke 24:46).

The message of the Christ who suffered, died, and rose, foretold by the prophets, fulfilled by Jesus—that was what the church would take out into the world. Jesus summarizes that message with these words: "Repentance and forgiveness of sins will be preached in his name to all nations" (Luke 24:47).

The word translated "preached" is the same word used in the Mark 16 commissioning account. Jesus' disciples would be heralds of "repentance and forgiveness of sins." This is simply another way of saying they would be law and gospel proclaimers. The law convicts sinners of their sinfulness; the gospel promises and delivers forgiveness to the convicted sinner. That is what repentance is: sorrow over sin and turning in faith to Jesus for forgiveness. As his disciples brought the law and the gospel to people, the result would be repentance, and with that would come the assurance of forgiveness of sins.

Jesus also identifies the scope of his commission: "Repentance and forgiveness of sins will be preached in his name *to all nations.*" The church would be going to all people everywhere who had not yet come to repentance and received the forgiveness of sins. This they would do, "beginning at Jerusalem."

On the day of his ascension Jesus expanded somewhat on this commission when he promised his followers: "You will be my witnesses in Jerusalem, and in all Judea and Samaria, and to the ends of the earth" (Acts 1:8). The gospel would flow out from Jerusalem in ever-widening circles until finally the whole globe would be encompassed with the message of forgiveness of sins and new life in Christ.

That is the way the gospel spreads yet today. It is only natural to begin where one is and then to spread out in ever widening circles. A local congregation's program of outreach will concern itself largely with those within its reach, its own "Jerusalem." Through its fellowship in a larger body, such as a synod, the congregation also preaches repentance and forgiveness of sins beyond its "Jerusalem" to the ends of the earth.

In the Great Commission of Matthew 28, Jesus promised his own personal presence as his church went out into the world to make disciples. Here in the Luke passage Jesus assures his church of the presence and power of the Holy Spirit: "I am going to send you what my Father has promised; but stay in the city until you have been clothed with power from on high" (Luke 24:49). Disciples of Christ can "preach repentance and forgiveness of sins" with all confidence. Backing them up is the very Spirit of God, the Lord, the Giver of life.

John 20:21-23—I am sending you to forgive and retain sins

> Jesus said, "Peace be with you! As the Father has sent me, I am sending you." And with that he breathed on them and said, "Receive the Holy Spirit. If you forgive anyone his sins, they are forgiven; if you do not forgive them, they are not forgiven." (John 20:21-23)

The setting for these verses is quite certainly the same as that of the commission recorded in Luke 24. It was the night of the first Easter. Jesus appeared to the apostles. He calmed their fears with the greeting, "Peace be with you!" These words assured them that all was right between them and their God. By his substitutionary work on their behalf, peace had been established between God and the world.

Now they were to go and bring this message of peace to others. Sent by Christ himself, filled with the Holy Spirit, they are given the awesome responsibility of handling the keys to the kingdom of heaven. They are to tell people the good news that in Christ their sins have been forgiven. Those who receive their message in faith can be assured that heaven's doors are open wide to them. Those who reject it must be told that the doors of heaven are closed as long as they refuse to repent and believe the gospel.

Summary

We might synthesize these four commissioning passages as follows:

The Author of the Commission:

- the one who assures us of peace with God through his suffering, death, and resurrection
- the Lord of the church and the universe, who has been given all authority in heaven and on earth

The Commissioned:

- Christ's disciples, that is, the holy Christian church

The Commission:

- preach the good news of repentance and forgiveness of sins
- make disciples of all nations, baptizing them and teaching them to obey everything Christ commanded

The Scope of the Commission:

- all nations, all creation, beginning at home and spreading out to the world

The Method:

- the church, sent by Christ, will go with the good news to those who are not yet disciples

The Result:

- some will believe, receive forgiveness, and be saved
- others will reject, forfeit forgiveness, and be condemned

The Promise:

- Christ will be with his church always, to the very end of the age
- the Spirit, promised by Christ, will likewise be present and active as the church carries out its mission

Such is the mission that Christ, in his last days before returning to his Father, set before his church.

Practical questions

A discussion of the church and its mission gives rise to a number of practical questions:

Is the mission of the church to preach the gospel or to make disciples?

The two—preaching the gospel and making disciples—are closely connected. Making disciples is the goal, or end result, our Lord had in mind. He does not want any to perish, but all to come to repentance and faith. He wants all to be saved, to come to a heart knowledge of the truth. Preaching the gospel (employing the means of grace) is the means by which the Lord will achieve his goal of making disciples and so of gathering in his elect before he returns.

Therefore, it is not a question of either/or. Christ has commissioned his church to make disciples by preaching the gospel in Word and sacrament. That is the church's mission. Joh. Ylvisaker brings this out in his harmony of the Gospels. Summarizing the commissions at the end of the Gospels, he says:

> [Jesus] gives the disciples the task to go and preach the Gospel to every creature, to make all nations his disciples by baptizing

and teaching them, and thus to incorporate them into his kingdom.[79]

It is true that only God the Holy Spirit can effect the end result of making a disciple out of an unbeliever; all we can do is sow the seed. But it is also true that our Lord, by speaking specifically of making disciples in his commission to his church, is encouraging it to keep that intended goal in mind when it does its seed sowing.

This goal has implications for evangelism. For one thing, if the mission of the church is to make disciples by preaching the gospel, we will not be content with a quick, one-time sowing of the seed. If possible, we will continue to water and cultivate the seed we have sown. We will keep working with people, using the means of grace the Lord has given us, until such a time as the Holy Spirit accomplishes the miracle of making disciples out of them.

It may well happen, of course, that somewhere along the way people refuse to listen any further. The seed does at times fall on the beaten path. Though the Lord does not want any to perish, some will. Though the Lord wants all to be saved, not all will taste the salvation won by Christ. If evangelists have faithfully sown the seed, they should not look upon themselves as failures when some stubbornly cling to unbelief.

There is another benefit in remembering that making disciples by preaching the gospel is the mission Christ gave to his church. It serves as a reminder to believers that the Lord of the church has enlisted them as his valued partners in the building of his church. The Holy Spirit alone can bring people out of spiritual death into spiritual life. The Spirit alone can ultimately accomplish the miracle of making disciples. But the Spirit does not operate apart from the means of grace. And it is through our use of the means of grace that the Spirit works. When Christians speak the gospel, the Spirit works repentance and conveys forgiveness of sins.

Jesus said to Simon Peter, "*I* will build my church" (Matthew 16:18). But he sends believers, as he sent the apostle Paul, "to open [people's] eyes and turn them from darkness to light, and from the power of Satan to God" (Acts 26:18).

In a discussion of the mission of the church another question suggests itself:

---

[79]Joh. Ylvisaker, *The Gospels* (Minneapolis: Augsburg, 1932), p. 781.

What is the relationship between outreach and nurture?

As brought out above in our brief exposition of Matthew 28:18-20, Jesus himself has answered that question. From the Great Commission, the church receives its charter to make disciples of all the nations of the earth by baptizing them and also by nurturing those who have been made disciples ("teaching them to obey everything I have commanded you"). Those who have *become* disciples through the means of grace are also to be given opportunity to *grow* as disciples.

In the most important sense every disciple is a finished product. When the Holy Spirit makes people disciples through the means of grace, he applies to them personally the full benefits of Christ's perfect life and substitutionary death. Christ's holiness is credited to their account and their sins are no longer counted against them. Disciples are saints—holy in God's eyes, a full part of his family, 100% ready for eternity.

In another sense, though, disciples are far from finished. They remain, as the word "disciple" implies, learners. One's learning does not, or at least should not, end with baptism and after being taught the bare essentials of the Word of God.

Jesus spent three years teaching the Twelve, covering every area of the Christian life. "Come, follow me," he invited them, "and I will *make* you fishers of men" (Matthew 4:19). "He appointed twelve," Mark tells us, "designating them apostles—that they might be with him and that he might send them out to preach" (Mark 3:14). The order is significant. First they were to be with Jesus, learning from him. Then they were to go out to preach the gospel to others.

The apostle Paul likewise emphasized nurture in his work. On his first missionary journey, he made many disciples in the cities of Antioch, Iconium, Lystra, and Derbe. At the close of this journey Paul retraced his steps, "strengthening the disciples and encouraging them to remain true to the faith" (Acts 14:22); and he also "appointed elders for them in each church" (Acts 14:23) who would continue with the nurturing of these new disciples.

That wasn't all. On his second missionary journey, Paul visited these same congregations for the third time. As a result we are told that "the churches were strengthened in the faith" (Acts 16:5).

On his third journey, Paul remained in Ephesus for three years. He spent most of that time teaching. Luke tells us, "He took the disciples with him and had discussions daily in the lecture hall of Tyrannus" (Acts 19:9). As a result of these years of teaching, Paul could later tell the elders of the congregation at Ephesus, "I have not hesitated to proclaim to you the whole will of God" (Acts 20:27). Paul nurtured people by teaching them "everything" Jesus had commanded.

Paul states his purpose in Colossians, "We proclaim him [Christ], admonishing and teaching everyone with all wisdom, so that we may present everyone perfect [literally, "complete," "having reached the goal"] in Christ" (Colossians 1:28). The church is faithful to Christ's commission to make disciples of all nations, both when it reaches out to unbelievers with the means of grace, and when it nurtures believers with the same means.

All of this has a direct bearing on evangelism. As disciples grow in their faith by solid nurture in God's gracious Word, they grow both in their zeal and in their ability to bring that same Word to others. As someone has well put it, "One might as well exhort a woman with a barren womb to have children as to exhort a sterile church to evangelize or respond to missions."

Nurture *fuels* evangelism. As God's people "grow in the grace and knowledge of [their] Lord and Savior Jesus Christ" (2 Peter 3:18), as they "mature," growing up toward "the whole measure of the fullness of Christ" (Ephesians 4:13), they recognize ever more fully what a blessing it is to be disciples of Jesus Christ. That, in turn, leads them to want others to have what they have.

Nurture also *equips* for evangelism. When God's people are taught the truths of his Word, they are able then to pass on to others those same truths.

In a congregation or church body that takes God's Word seriously there will always be a tension between outreach and nurture. Such a tension is not unhealthy, for it indicates that the congregation or church body is committed to both. The only way to completely eliminate that tension is to ignore one or the other.

Both nurture (which includes the training of workers for the church) and outreach require time as well as human and material resources, all of which are limited. Among Christians there will be ongoing debate as to the proper allocation of these scarce resources. There may not always be agreement. That, however, is to be expected. God's Word does not specify what percentage of a congregation's or church body's resources should be devoted to outreach and what percentage to nurture. When God's people recognize that the church's mission includes both outreach and nurture, they will seek under God to give both their due. In so doing, they can be sure that God's will is being done and that his kingdom will continue to come both externally and internally.

A third question:

What do planning, goal setting, making use of statistical studies, etc., have to do with the mission of the church?

None of the above has anything directly to do with the church's mission. The mission of the church is to make disciples by employing the means of grace. Properly used, however, such activities can assist congregations and church bodies as they seek to carry out this mission.

A congregation may find it helpful, for example, to put together a community profile to help it understand the people among whom it is working. Such a community profile would provide information about the congregation's "parish area" on such things as the percentage of unchurched people; the numbers, locations, and kinds of churches in the area around the church; projected growth (or decline) of population; areas of projected population growth; economic characteristics; ethnic and social makeup (blue collar? white collar? predominantly singles? young families with children? middle aged? retired?). Such information can help a congregation as it plans an outreach strategy. It can do the same for a church body as it plans where and when to establish new mission congregations.

Gathering such data and then using it to assist in outreach planning is in accord with sound stewardship principles. Stewardship in the broad sense includes careful, faithful use of everything the Lord has entrusted to us. On the top of the list is certainly the gospel, by which the Holy Spirit makes disciples. Many, if not most, congregations are faced with the fact that there are more unchurched people in their area than congregational resources (primarily people and time) with which to reach them. Congregations will want to plan how best to employ these limited resources to reach a maximum number of people with the gospel.

The apostle Paul was faced with the same challenge in his ministry. When the Holy Spirit directed the church at Antioch of Syria to send Paul and Barnabas out with the gospel, it does not appear that the Spirit set their itinerary. From all indications they had to make their own plans.

The world was his field. Where should he go? A careful study of the three missionary journeys reveal certain features of Paul's mission strategy. He carried out his work largely in the most strategic cities of an area. The gospel could radiate from these cities to surrounding areas. He utilized the synagogue as a "bridge" to the community. He was determined to concentrate his efforts in areas where the gospel had not yet been preached (cf. Romans 15:20).

The book of Acts gives us several examples of specific plans Paul made. On his second journey, Paul apparently made plans to preach the gospel in the province of Asia. Toward the close of his second journey, he told the Ephesians that his plan was to return and spend more time with them, which is precisely what he did. At the end of his third journey, he asked the Ephesian elders to come out to the coast to meet him. His plan was to get to Jerusalem for Pentecost (cf. Acts 20:16). He, therefore, did not have the time to travel all the way into Ephesus. And always in the back of Paul's mind was his long-range goal to bring the gospel to Spain (cf. Romans 15:28).

There was order and direction, careful planning, in Paul's travels. But at the same time there was flexibility. He was always open to the Lord's leading. When the Lord directed Paul's path to Europe through the "Macedonian call," he willingly adapted his plans to the Lord's direction (cf. Acts 16:6-10). He fully realized that it is the Lord who opens doors, not man, and that God's plans, therefore, had priority over his.

The strategy Paul followed is instructive to us today, teaching us to strike a wholesome balance between planning and goal-setting on the one hand, and a flexibility that is open to the Lord's leading on the other. James, the Lord's brother, warns us not to be overconfident about our own plans: "Now listen, you who say, 'Today or tomorrow we will go to this or that city, spend a year there, carry on business and make money.' Why, you do not even know what will happen tomorrow" (James 4:13,14).

We can become so caught up in one-year, five-year, and ten-year plans that we fail to catch the gentle nudging of the Lord to move in directions different from what we have plotted. "Macedonian calls" can still occur today. Not every call is the call of God, but the Lord can still lead his church in this way. The newly-converted Paul's humble petition, "What should I do, Lord?" (Acts 22:10 NET), is a good prayer for congregational and church body leaders yet today as they make plans to reach out with the gospel to their communities and to the world.

We should add here a word of caution, sounded well by Robert Koester. He reminds us that planning and goal setting are improper when they intrude into areas God has reserved for himself. Koester writes:

> In our sphere of responsibility, the means are the end. The ultimate end for which we hope—the conversion of souls—is God's responsibility. . . . The nature of the gospel forces us to focus on

> *preaching* the gospel. It is within these parameters that we must devise goals, visions and methods. . . . The issue does not revolve around whether a person has zeal to win the lost. The issue revolves around whether that zeal is confined to the area of our responsibility or whether we move outside of it. The result is that in the former case, the integrity of the Gospel is maintained, while in the latter it is compromised. . . . My concern is to remain within the circle of my responsibility.[80]

Koester's well-taken point is that we can, and perhaps should, be setting *ministry* goals, e.g., number of evangelism calls we intend to make or number of new missions we plan to open, but that we should not be setting goals in the area that is God's doing, i.e., producing results. We can only plant and water the seed; God makes it grow (cf. 1 Corinthians 3:6). The Augsburg Confession puts it this way:

> Through the Word and the sacraments, as through instruments, *the Holy Spirit is given, and the Holy Spirit produces faith, where and when it pleases God,* in those who hear the Gospel [emphasis added].[81]

Planning, goal setting, and utilizing statistical studies can serve a helpful purpose as long as we do not employ them to try to take over what is God's rightful sphere of activity. No amount of planning, goal setting, or visionary thinking will make the church grow. That is God's work. Such activity can help the church, though, in its work of determining when, where, and how to plant the seed.

A final practical question on the church and its mission:

Does the scope of the church's mission include members of other churches?

The pastoral theology textbook, *The Shepherd Under Christ,* states:

> Evangelism must be carried on in such a way that it does not seek to make converts of those who are active members in a Christian church. The pastor himself will avoid *proselytizing* and warn his members against it. Those people who are members of a church that confesses the one true God (the triune

---

[80]Robert J. Koester, *Law and Gospel: The Foundation of Lutheran Ministry with Reference to the Church Growth Movement* (Milwaukee: Northwestern Publishing House, 1993), pp. 133,136,145,146.

[81]Article V, 2.

God, including recognition of Jesus as God) and acknowledge redemption through Christ cannot be considered "unchurched." Treating them as prospects is to interfere in another church's ministry (Acts 20:28; 1 Peter 4:15).[82]

The word "proselyte" occurs only four times in the Greek New Testament (Acts 2:10; 6:5; 13:43; Matthew 23:15). In each case it has to do with a Gentile who has become a convert to Judaism. The word does not bear a negative connotation in the Scriptures.

When the noun "proselyte" or the verb "to proselytize" is used in confessional Lutheran circles, however, it has the narrower meaning of visiting members of another Christian congregation or denomination with the intention of persuading them to leave that congregation or denomination (sometimes called "sheep-stealing"). Such action would violate two biblical doctrines, that of the church and that of the divine call. Carl Lawrenz writes:

> Clinging to the scriptural teaching that the presence of believers, the presence of the church, must be concluded and apprehended by us on the basis of the presence of the marks of the church [the means of grace], Lutherans from Luther down have not been ready to question altogether even in the case of the Roman Catholic Church . . . its character as a church. They have remembered that even this church, in spite of its horrendous doctrinal errors, still adheres to the three ecumenical creeds, uses them in its services, still acknowledges the triune God and Christ as the divine Redeemer, still reads the Gospels and Epistles in its services as God's Word, above all still has and performs holy baptism as instituted by the Lord.[83]

Luther, for example, in his comments on Galatians 1:2, writes:

> So today we still call the Church of Rome holy and all its sees holy, even though they have been undermined and their ministers are ungodly. . . . Nevertheless there remain in it baptism, the Sacrament, the voice and text of the Gospel, the Sacred Scriptures, the name of Christ, and the name of God.[84]

---

[82]Armin W. Schuetze and Irwin J. Habeck, *The Shepherd Under Christ* (Milwaukee: Northwestern Publishing House, 1981), p. 240.

[83]Carl Lawrenz, "A Definitive Study of Proselytizing," *Wisconsin Lutheran Quarterly,* 73:1, Jan. 1976, p. 32.

[84]*American Edition,*Vol. 26 (St. Louis: Concordia, 1963), p. 24.

"On the basis of these considerations," Lawrenz writes, "we cannot approach an active member even of the Roman Catholic Church as though he were an unchurched heathen and as though he had no relation to a Christian ministry, no matter how great our fears may be about his faith and his salvation because of the horrendous errors by which he is being tyrannized in his heterodox church and by its ministry."[85] To do so would give the false impression that our church body and denomination is the only saving church on earth and is virtually identical with the holy Christian church.

The doctrine of the call is also involved in this issue. When a Christian congregation, even a heterodox one, extends a divine call, a certain bond is established between pastor and people. He is the called shepherd of the flock. Proselytizing seeks to sever the bond between shepherd and sheep. Lawrenz writes:

> An orthodox Christian or an orthodox pastor cannot simply brush that relationship aside and presume to take over the role of spiritual shepherd and overseer with respect to the members of such a [i.e., heterodox] congregation. . . . It is not a light thing to ignore or to violate the spiritual rights of even the weakest of God's royal priests, those tyrannized by false teachers, or to make light of the sacredness of a divine call in itself, even though the person who has that call misuses it and does not carry it out faithfully.[86]

Obviously, if the marks of the church are entirely lacking, the church and its ministry are not present. Those who belong to such organizations are valid mission prospects. *The Shepherd Under Christ* puts it this way:

> Any religious group that denies the divinity of Christ does not know the true God. . . . Members of such groups (e.g., Jehovah's Witnesses, Mormons, Christian Scientists) are properly considered unchurched.[87]

Two things remain to be said, both of which are referred to in *The Shepherd Under Christ*. For one thing, "the confessional deterioration in many so-called Christian churches causes increasing difficulty

---

[85]Lawrenz, *op. cit.*, p. 33.

[86]*Ibid.*, p. 32.

[87]*Op. cit.*, p. 240.

in determining their Christian status."[88] The remarks of Lawrenz on this point are worth hearing:

> We cannot, of course, discount or minimize the difficulty with which one is often confronted in the present era of rapid confessional deterioration in the matter of determining which congregations and which ministries still can and must be respected as Christian in spite of the grave errors with which they are infested. This is particularly true concerning those extremely liberal and doctrinally indifferent Christian denominations which have a strong congregational polity, so that each congregation functions and acts almost like an independent unit. The decision becomes difficult in these instances also because these congregations do not subscribe to a common confessional statement and frequently also have no fixed order of service which all their congregations follow and which could assure the presence of a basic Christian message.
>
> It is somewhat different in the case of those liberal churches on the other hand in which every congregation has committed itself formally to common confessional statements which still present the basic Christian truths and who still follow a fixed order of service which includes the ecumenical creeds, prescribed Scripture lections from the Gospels and the Epistles that are regularly read, fixed prayers with rich Christian content, and who sing traditional Christian hymns, hymns from an authorized hymnal of the past full of rich evangelical messages. It often happens with reference to such churches that the simple worshippers absorb better things and more that is in harmony with Christian truth and the gospel than their called ministers intend to offer.[89]

Lawrenz concludes: "No matter how great the difficulty of decision may be regarding the evaluation of certain churches and their ministry, it must always be made on the basis of the presence or non-presence of the marks of the church, and thereby the presence of its ministry."[90]

His advice is sound. One should not be too quick to conclude that the marks of the church are entirely lacking in a congregation or

---

[88]*Ibid.*

[89]*Op. cit.*, pp. 34,35.

[90]*Ibid.*, p. 34.

church body, and therefore members of a particular heterodox church are fair territory for the church's work of evangelism.

Second, as *The Shepherd Under Christ* puts it:

> When . . . members of erring Christian churches seek information in their search for the truth, a forthright answer must follow without fear that this could raise the charge of proselytizing (1 Peter 3:15).[91]

This speaks to the important question, "What, then, is the responsibility of orthodox Christians and Christian congregations over against members of heterodox churches?" A distinction needs to be made between testifying to the truth and proselytizing. The former is the ongoing call of every Christian. John Fritz correctly states:

> A pastor or any other Christian has no right to break into the flock of another pastor. This, however, should not keep any pastor or any Christian from bearing testimony to the truth when called upon to do so or whenever opportunity presents itself to do so, e.g., when I am making a house-to-house canvass for the purpose of finding the unchurched, or when I meet a person in a public vehicle . . . or at some other public place or in my own home and am asked in reference to my faith, or the difference between the creed of my church and the creed of another church or in reference to any religious question, or if the drift of a conversation presents such an opportunity, I should not hesitate to confess the truth and give a good account of my faith; that is not only not forbidden, but directly commanded.[92]

To think of yet another example, if someone visits a church service, it is entirely proper to pay a visit to that person. If it is discovered that the individual is a regular member of another Christian church, even a heterodox one, we should not try to get him or her to leave that church and join ours. It is not proselytizing, however, for the evangelism caller to present the gospel in every home he is invited to enter. Proclaiming the gospel is not proselytizing.

A congregation can also proclaim the gospel even to the heterodox through the mass media. Radio and television services, placing devotional material in hospitals, nursing homes, and doctors' and dentists' waiting rooms, disseminating sound, confessional Lutheran

---

[91]*Op. cit.*, p. 240.

[92]John H. C. Fritz, *Pastoral Theology* (St. Louis: Concordia, 1932), p. 58.

publications through a church body's publishing house—these are a few of the ways by which orthodox Christian congregations can get their message out to their community. Such public testimony is not proselytizing; for, as Fritz puts it,

> we are not singling out anyone in particular with the intention of estranging him from his own church, but are in this world bearing witness to the truth as God has commanded us, saying, "Go ye into all the world, and preach the gospel to every creature" (Mark 16:15; 1 Peter 2:9; Matthew 5:13-16).[93]

4—The Ministry

Definition

It stands to reason that if the *mission* of the church is to make and nurture disciples, then the church's ministry will center around the *means* by which the Holy Spirit accomplishes this mission. That is the way the Scriptures and likewise the Lutheran Confessions speak.

When Christ commissioned his church, he thereby also established its ministry: preach the gospel and administer the sacraments (cf. Matthew 28:19ff; Mark 16:15ff; Luke 24:47ff; John 20:21ff). The Augsburg Confession defines the ministry of the church in this way:

> In order that we may obtain this faith [i.e., saving faith in Christ], the ministry of teaching the Gospel and administering the Sacraments was instituted.[94]

The Formula of Concord puts it even more simply. It speaks of "the ministry of the church, the Word proclaimed and heard."[95]

In line with the way the Scriptures and Confessions speak, the Wisconsin Evangelism Lutheran Synod states in a doctrinal statement entitled Theses on the Church and Ministry: "Christ instituted one office in his Church, the ministry of the Gospel."[96] The ministry of the church, its sole ministry, is the ministry of the gospel. It is to preach and teach the Word and to administer the sacraments.

---

[93]*Ibid.*

[94]Article V, 1.

[95]*Ibid.*, Solid Declaration, Article XII, 30.

[96]This statement, prepared by the Doctrinal Commission of the WELS, was adopted in 1969 by the 40th Convention of the Wisconsin Evangelical Lutheran Synod.

The priesthood of all believers

That ministry Christ has given to his whole church. The Confessions state:

> The keys [i.e., the gospel ministry] were given to the church and not merely to certain individuals: "Where two or three are gathered in my name, there am I in the midst of them" (Matt. 18:20). Finally, this is confirmed by the declaration of Peter: "You are a royal priesthood" (1 Pet. 2:9).[97]

This statement, with its quote from 1 Peter 2:9, touches on a subject dear to the heart of Martin Luther: the priesthood of all believers. In this verse Peter gives all believers four significant titles: "You are a chosen people, a royal priesthood, a holy nation, a people belonging to God."

These titles have a number of things in common. For one thing, each of them was used by God in the Old Testament to describe his people, Israel. Second, each of these titles is a statement of fact. Christians do not have to strive to *become* "a chosen people, a royal priesthood, a holy nation, a people belonging to God." That is what Christians *are*. A third point of similarity is that each title is portraying the same truth as every other title; for each is a description of the holy Christian church, the communion of saints. The church is a "chosen people." The church is a "royal priesthood." The church is a "holy nation." The church is a "people belonging to God."

"You are a chosen people." "My people, my chosen," God called the people of Israel (Isaiah 43:20). Both words are significant. The word translated as "people" (Greek, *genos*) has in it the idea of being in the family. "Chosen" is a reminder that the formation of this particular family was God's doing entirely. We think, for example, of how God chose Abraham out of all the peoples on earth, chose him and his descendants to be his people through whose promised Descendant all the nations of the earth would be blessed.

God has now given this title to Christians. All believers in Jesus are God's "chosen people," chosen "according to the foreknowledge of God the Father, through the sanctifying work of the Spirit" (1 Peter 1:2).

"You are a . . . royal priesthood." This and the next two titles are drawn from Exodus 19:5,6, where the Lord instructed Moses what to

---

[97]Smalcald Articles, On the Power and Primacy of the Pope, 68,69.

tell the Israelites who were assembled at the foot of Mt. Sinai. Moses was to remind Israel of what the Lord had done to Egypt on their behalf and how he had carried them "on eagles' wings" to this place of freedom. "Now," says the Lord, "if you obey me fully and keep my covenant, then out of all nations you will be my treasured possession. Although the whole earth is mine, you will be for me a kingdom of priests and a holy nation."

One cannot help but notice the conditional character of this covenant. *If* Israel would obey God and in that way keep its part of the covenant, *then* God would look upon this people as his treasured possession, a kingdom of priests, and a holy nation.

Israel, we know, failed miserably to live up to its side of the covenant. What Israel by disobedience gave up, however, God by the new covenant of Jesus' blood has graciously given—to his church. The apostle John exclaims, "To him who loves us and has freed us from our sins by his blood, and has made us to be a kingdom and priests to serve his God and Father—to him be glory and power for ever and ever!" (Revelation 1:5,6).

"Royal priests" is the title Christians possess. They are priests who belong to and are in the service of the king. Through Jesus they stand in a royal position, with no one over them except God himself.

"You are a . . . holy nation." The word translated as "holy" (Greek, *hagios*) has in it the idea of being set apart *from* something as well as for something. As with Israel of old, God has called Christians to himself. He has set them apart *from* the ungodly, unbelieving world and *for* a brand new life of dedicated, consecrated service.

"You are a . . . people belonging to God." Christians are God's own special possession, "bought at a price" (1 Corinthians 6:20), "not with perishable things such as silver or gold, . . . but with the precious blood of Christ, a lamb without blemish or defect" (1 Peter 1:18,19). "Our great God and Savior, Jesus Christ . . . gave himself for us," writes Paul to Titus, "to redeem us from all wickedness and to purify for himself a people that are his very own, eager to do what is good" (Titus 2:13,14). "Once you were not a people," says Peter, "but now you are the people of God" (1 Peter 2:10).

Christians do not have to suffer from an identity crisis. They know who they are. Christians are "a chosen people, a royal priesthood, a holy nation, a people belonging to God."

Nor must Christians be uncertain regarding their purpose. These four titles, "chosen people," "royal priesthood," "holy nation," "a people belonging to God," R. C. H. Lenski reminds us, are not "static but dynamic."[98] Christians have become something for a purpose. Peter clearly states that purpose: "that you may declare the praises of him who called you out of darkness into his wonderful light" (1 Peter 2:9).

That is what God looked for from Israel, "the people I formed for myself," he says, "that they may proclaim my praise" (Isaiah 43:21). Now he looks for praise from his new people.

The purpose of every Christian is to "declare" (Greek, *exangello*) God's praises. This is an action word, a word that has in it the idea of telling out, making widely known. It carries in it a picture of conveying to those on the outside a message that is known to those on the inside.

Christians' purpose is to tell out God's "praises," his excellencies (Greek, *aretas*), his shining, eminent qualities, his wonderful deeds, to tell the world how great God is, a greatness that is to be seen especially in his saving acts. As he rescued Israel from slavery, so he has rescued the world from the worst slavery of all. As he destroyed Israel's enemies by the Red Sea, so he has destroyed even greater enemies by the cross and empty tomb of Jesus. The best "spiritual sacrifice" (1 Peter 2:5) Christians can offer up to God as priests of God is to declare the praises of the one who, by the gospel, has effectively called them out of the darkness of sin, unbelief, and death into the light of forgiveness, faith, and life.

The titles Peter here puts forward are the common possession of all Christians. All Christians, as priests of God, share in the purpose of declaring to others the wonderful works of God. Luther writes:

> Peter [in 1 Pet 2:9,10] names the people and the congregation very clearly, and he calls them all together a royal priesthood and commands them to preach the deeds of God who has called them. . . . Thereby the Holy Spirit teaches us that ointments, consecrations, tonsures, chasubles, albs, chalices, masses, sermons, etc., do not make priests or give power. Rather, priesthood and power have to be there first, brought from baptism and common to all Christians through the faith which builds them upon Christ the true high priest, as St. Peter says here.[99]

---

[98]R. C. H. Lenski, *The Interpretation of the Epistles of St. Peter, St. John and St. Jude* (Columbus: Wartburg Press, 1945), p. 102.

[99]*American Edition,* Vol. 39 (Philadelphia: Fortress Press, 1970), pp. 236,237.

The church father Jerome said something similar back in the fourth century. "Baptism," he said, "is the ordination of the laity."

Luther was also insistent in maintaining that, in view of passages such as 1 Peter 2:9, all Christians possess the means of grace and have the right—the duty, in fact—to use them. He writes, "No one can deny that every Christian possesses the Word of God and is taught and anointed by God to be priest. . . . But if it is true that they have God's Word and are anointed by him, then it is their duty to confess, to teach, and to spread [his Word]."[100] George Sweazey puts it this way: "The effect of the Reformation was not to destroy the priesthood and leave a church of laymen, but to destroy the laity and leave a church of priests."[101]

In line with the way Luther speaks, Wilbert Gawrisch writes,

> The priesthood of the New Testament is universal. It belongs to all believers. All of them are royal priests. All of them, therefore, also possess the ministry of the Spirit, the authority and right to preach the Gospel and administer the sacraments. Jesus gave the Great Commission not only to the apostles, but all his disciples. . . . Every Christian possesses the Ministry of the Keys.[102]

John Schaller, president of Wisconsin Lutheran Seminary from 1908-1920, wrote in an article entitled, "The Origin and Development of the New Testament Ministry":

> The Holy Scriptures incontrovertibly show that the ministry, that is, the commission to preach the gospel, is given to every Christian; that at conversion not only the ability but also the impetus for this preaching is implanted in him; and that the gospel by its very nature as a *message* presupposes this preaching activity and at the same time by the effect it has guarantees it will occur.[103]

The shepherds, for example, whose hearts had been touched *by* the angel's message (Luke 2:10-12) could not help but do something *with* that message: "They spread the word concerning what had been told

---

[100]*Ibid.*, p. 309.

[101]George E. Sweazey, *Effective Evangelism* (New York: Harper and Row, 1953), p. 90.

[102]Wilbert R. Gawrisch, "A Royal Priesthood Proclaiming God's Praise," *Wisconsin Lutheran Quarterly,* 75:4, Oct. 1978, p. 287.

[103]Translated in the *Wisconsin Lutheran Quarterly,* 78:1, Jan. 1981, p. 38.

them about this child" (Luke 2:17). The woman at Jacob's well did the same as she told her fellow townspeople about Jesus (John 4:29).

All of God's people are called to serve as priests in their private lives. This is their *personal ministry.* They can do this in two ways. First, by the testimony of a godly life they function as the salt of the earth and the light of the world (cf. Matthew 5:13-16). This may well be the primary way by which Christians will be able to touch bases with an increasingly secularized society, which is not necessarily hostile to religion but simply doesn't find it particularly relevant or meaningful. The testimony of a Christian's life may well lead a person to ask about "the reason for the hope we have" (1 Peter 3:15). That may be the opening the Lord provides for the Christian to share the life-giving, life-changing gospel.

Christians carry on their personal ministry as priests of God also by the testimony of their lips. Jesus told the demoniac of Gerasa out of whom he had driven a legion of demons, "Go home to your family and tell them how much the Lord has done for you, and how he has had mercy on you" (Mark 5:19). Schaller gives a few examples of such private functioning by God's priests:

> When Christians at a social gathering privately discuss with one another the great deeds God has done to accomplish the salvation of sinners, even if this is in a most informal way, the gospel is then under discussion, and the one who gives expression to it is carrying on the ministry. When a member of the family or a Christian neighbor who is not a pastor, yes, when a mother, sister, or Christian neighbor lady offers a sick person the comfort of the forgiveness of sins or in some other way strengthens his patience by pointing to the goodness of God our Savior, spiritual priests and priestesses are functioning in the New Testament ministry.[104]

Public ministry of the gospel

God's priests can put their priestly function into action in a second arena, that of the *public ministry,* that is, ministry of the gospel, which one is called to do in the name of and on behalf of one's fellow Christians.

Essentially there is no difference between the ministry Christ has given to every Christian and the public ministry. The Scriptures do not assign any duties to public ministers that have not also been as-

---

[104] *Ibid.*, p. 39.

signed to every believer. There are certain functions of the ministry of the gospel, however, that can hardly be carried out by all at the same time without disorder and confusion, e.g., preaching in the worship service and administering the sacraments when the congregation is gathered together. There are also functions of the ministry for which all Christians are not equally trained or gifted. It is for this purpose that Jesus instituted the public ministry of the gospel. Luther writes,

> You should put the Christian into two places. First, if he is in a place where there are no Christians he needs no other call than to be a Christian, called and anointed by God from within. Here it is his duty to preach and to teach the gospel to erring heathen or non-Christians, because of the duty of brotherly love, even though no man calls him to do so. . . . Second, if he is at a place where there are Christians who have the same power and right as he, he should not draw attention to himself. Instead he should let himself be called and chosen to preach and to teach in the place of and by command of the others.[105]

The Lutheran Confessions put it this way: "Nobody should preach publicly in the church or administer the sacraments unless he is regularly called."[106]

The form of the public ministry of the gospel most familiar to us in our day is the pastoral office. It is the broadest and most comprehensive in scope, since the pastor is called to oversee the entire ministry of the gospel within the congregation. The pastoral office, however, is not the only possible form of public ministry. The New Testament gives several other examples, e.g., apostles, prophets, elder/overseers, deacons, evangelists, pastor/teachers, and teachers.

Luther recognized that the public ministry should not be equated with and restricted to the pastoral office. August Pieper, in an article examining Luther's doctrine of the church and ministry, points out that Luther "does not declare this particular species, the local pastorate, to be divinely instituted in contrast to other species of the public preaching ministry or the preaching of the Word, but that rather he declares this species to be divine together with the other species."[107] Besides the office of pastor Luther includes under the public preaching

---

[105]*American Edition,* Vol. 39 (Philadelphia: Fortress Press, 1970), p. 310.

[106]Augsburg Confession, Article XIV.

[107]August Pieper, "Luther's Doctrine of Church and Ministry," translated in the *Wisconsin Lutheran Quarterly,* 60:4, Jan. 1963, p. 258.

office and ministry of the Word and sacraments "teachers, preachers, lectors, priests (whom men call chaplains), sacristans, schoolmasters, and whatever other work belongs to these offices and persons."[108]

Schaller, likewise, says,

> As soon as a group of Christians gather together as such in any manner and at any place and the existing congregation can in that way be recognized, the responsibility for preaching which every individual Christian has as a believer remains unchanged. Through the fact that a number of Christians are together, however, the need for mutual confession and mutual edification quite naturally arises. From this an obligation arises for the whole group which the individual Christian does not have: because of its own need it must make provisions to let the Word of Christ ring out in its gathering. *That* [emphasis added] this takes place is essential; how it takes place is incidental and depends on the circumstances of the congregation and on the opportunity. Among us it usually delegates to a single individual the responsibility to do the formal, solemn preaching on a regular basis, to conduct the public worship services, and in addition to serve the individual members of the congregation with the Word according to their needs. These things could also be arranged in an entirely different way since the pastorate in the form which is customary among us was very likely totally unknown in apostolic times. . . . As soon as the congregation has established any such ministry and has called the men for it, God gives it his approval and calls the men whom he bestows on this church gifts and assures them that they have been appointed by the Holy Ghost.[109]

More recently Carl Lawrenz wrote, "There is . . . no direct word of institution for any particular form of the public ministry. . . . The one public ministry of the gospel may assume various forms as circumstances demand. These forms need not embrace all the functions of the public ministry. . . . Through the Word the Holy Spirit guides the believers in their common faith to establish the adequate and wholesome forms which fit every circumstance, situation and need."[110]

---

[108]*Ibid.*, p. 258.

[109]John Schaller, "The Origin and Development of the New Testament Ministry," *Wisconsin Lutheran Quarterly,* 78:1, Jan. 1981, pp. 50,51.

[110]Carl J. Lawrenz, "The Scriptural Truths of the Church and Its Ministry," *Wisconsin Lutheran Quarterly,* 82:3, Summer 1985, p. 183.

Christians, then, can function as priests in two arenas. They all serve at all times as priests in their private lives (*personal ministry*). And, should the congregation of believers call them to do so, they can also serve in some portion of the *public ministry* of the church.

We can apply this directly to the church's work of evangelism. When properly qualified lay people are asked to assist with the outreach program of the congregation in the name of and on behalf of the congregation, they then are serving in the church's public ministry, no less than the pastor—though the scope of their work will be narrower.

We should perhaps add a note here that the Scriptures do not limit service in the public ministry to men. Women, too, may serve in the public ministry of the church. To say that women teachers in the elementary schools of the church are serving in the public ministry, for example, is in keeping with the way the Scriptures speak. They are serving in the name of and by call of the congregation.

Likewise, there is nothing in the Scriptures to prevent a woman from serving in the name of the congregation as a part of its evangelism committee or as one of those the congregation asks to visit the unchurched on its behalf. The Bible does speak, however, of a role relationship between men and women that needs to be maintained. A woman should therefore not be asked to serve in a form of ministry that inherently includes authority over a man (cf. 1 Timothy 2:11-14), e.g., serving as a pastor, an elder, or the head of a decision-making committee whose makeup includes both men and women.

The Scriptures encourage women as well as men, however, to share their faith with others. That can be done as a part of their personal ministry as priests of God; it can also be carried out by some—men and women—as a part of the public ministry of the congregation.

The role of the pastor

In an extended editorial in the *Wisconsin Lutheran Quarterly* Armin Schuetze asks, Is the pastor a shepherd or is he a coach?[111] In the editorial he brought out well that it is not a matter of either/or. The Scriptures assign both roles to the pastor. Both are valid and necessary, and both have implications for the congregation's work of evangelism. The pastor is a shepherd, a nurturer of the flock entrusted to his care. A pastor is also a coach. The Scriptures don't use the

---

[111]Armin W. Schuetze, "A Shepherd or a Coach?", *Wisconsin Lutheran Quarterly,* 74:1, Jan. 1977, pp. 3-11.

word coach, of course, but they do teach what this term denotes. The Scriptures say that Christ gives called spiritual leaders to his church to equip the saints for serving their Lord (Ephesians 4:12).

Nurturer of the saints

The very title "pastor" means shepherd. That title is thus a beautiful description of a major part of his call. He is to "pastor," to shepherd, the flock. At the end of his third missionary journey, the apostle Paul used that title when he addressed the assembled elders of the church at Ephesus:

> I have not hesitated to proclaim to you the whole will of God. Keep watch over yourselves and all the flock of which the Holy Spirit has made you overseers. *Be shepherds of the church of God,* which he bought with his own blood. I know that after I leave, savage wolves will come in among you and will not spare the flock. Even from your own number men will arise and distort the truth in order to draw away disciples after them. So be on your guard! Remember that for three years I never stopped warning each of you night and day with tears. Now I commit you to God and to the word of his grace, which can build you up and give you an inheritance among all those who are sanctified. (Acts 20:27-32)

The apostle Peter uses the same term in his words to the elders of the churches, to whom he wrote,

> To the elders among you, I appeal as a fellow elder, a witness of Christ's sufferings and one who also will share in the glory to be revealed: *Be shepherds of God's flock* that is under your care, serving as overseers—not because you must, but because you are willing, as God wants you to be; not greedy for money, but eager to serve; not lording it over those entrusted to you, but being examples to the flock. And when the Chief Shepherd appears, you will receive the crown of glory that will never fade away. (1 Peter 5:1-4)

These two passages point to some of the functions of a shepherd. A shepherd *feeds* his flock. The food the spiritual shepherd dispenses is, as Paul puts it, "the word of his [God's] grace," the green pastures of the gospel in Word and sacrament.

A shepherd *guards* the flock. Today, as then, "savage wolves," false teachers with their destructive heresies, threaten to destroy the flock. The shepherd guards the flock both by preaching and teaching the truth and by warning against error.

A shepherd *guides* the flock. In humility, "not lording it over" those entrusted to him, the shepherd guides the flock by leading it along the paths that are pleasing to God. With the apostle Paul, he will be intent on proclaiming "the whole will of God" to the members of his flock.

As a nurturer, then, the pastor feeds, guards, and guides the flock. He does this through his regular preaching and teaching of the Word and administration of the sacraments.

A ministry of nurturing the saints is bound to have an impact on the congregation's work of evangelism. The more thoroughly God's people are nurtured by Word and sacrament, the more they become conformed to the image of Christ. And the more they are conformed to Christ's image, the more effectively they will be able to function as salt and light in the world.

To be such nurturers of others, pastors themselves must be nurtured. The pastor must resist the temptation to be constantly on the go. He needs to take time out regularly for his own personal, devotional study of the Word. One cannot give to others what he himself has not received. A young pastor once asked a well-known preacher of his day, Charles Spurgeon, the secret of his success. "Knee work, young man! Knee work!" he replied. A daily quiet time, soul-feeding time, nurtures the nurturer. The apostles in the early church recognized the need for regular time alone with their Lord (cf. Acts 6:1-6); God's called shepherds today also need to "grow in the grace and knowledge of [their] Lord and Savior Jesus Christ" (2 Peter 3:18).

A pastor, as nurturer of the flock, also needs to devote a sufficient amount of time to preparing the spiritual food, his sermons and Bible studies, which he will set before the flock. Again, the implications for evangelism are not difficult to ascertain. A properly nurtured flock will be a strong and healthy flock. A strong and healthy flock will represent well the name of Christ in home, neighborhood, school, factory, shop, and office.

It is also in place to remind ourselves that the shepherd leads by example. His attitude toward and activity in the work of evangelism will have an effect on the congregation's attitude and activity. The pastor is, humanly-speaking, in a key position to help or hinder the evangelistic efforts of a congregation, just as his attitude toward a Lutheran elementary school or the Sunday school goes a long way in influencing his congregation's attitude toward the same.

The pastor will soon learn that he cannot push his people into evangelism. He needs to lead them, as Peter writes, "Not lording it over those entrusted to you, but being examples to the flock" (1 Peter 5:3).

The ministries of both Jesus and the apostle Paul illustrate the importance of a leader's example. Jesus said to his disciples, *"Follow me,* and I will make you fishers of men" (Matthew 4:19). From being with Jesus, following him day by day, his disciples learned first-hand the importance of seeking out the lost. They heard him call Zacchaeus down from the sycamore tree and observed how he spent the day with him (Luke 19:1ff.). They noted how he gave of his valuable time to the woman at Jacob's well (John 4:1ff.). They listened to his parables of the Lost Sheep, the Lost Coin, and the Lost Son (Luke 15:1ff.). They observed how he wept over the city of Jerusalem (Matthew 23:37-39). Time spent with him gave them opportunity to catch his evangelistic fervor.

The apostle Paul also led by example, an example he urged others to emulate. He tells the Philippians, "Whatever you have learned or received or heard from me, or seen in me—put it into practice" (Philippians 4:9). He exhorts the Corinthians, "Follow my example, as I follow the example of Christ" (1 Corinthians 11:1). A part of that example was his zeal for the conversion of the heathen. Those who had observed him in action knew exactly what he meant when he wrote, "Woe to me if I do not preach the gospel" (1 Corinthians 9:16).

A pastor likewise is an example—first of all in his personal ministry as a priest of God, a calling that he retains in common with all believers even while serving in the public ministry. The pastor, who not only is encouraging his members to share the gospel with a friend or to bring a neighbor to church or to a Bible information class, but is seeking to do the same himself, serves as a fine role model for the congregation. He is practicing what he preaches.

The pastor can also serve as an example in his public ministry. He can make it clear that outreach is a vital part of his call by setting aside time on a regular basis for calling on the unchurched. There are certain factors that militate against pastors being examples to the flock in the work of evangelism. There is, for one thing, the time factor. Other duties such as hospital and shut-in calls, counseling, board and committee meetings, funerals, marriages, in addition to preparation for preaching and teaching, can easily consume every moment of a pastor's time, especially in the larger congregation.

The pastor has to contend constantly with the "squeaky wheel gets the grease" syndrome. He will not feel the same pressure from the unchurched in the community to visit them as he will from his own members. That means he will have to *make time* for outreach work. He may find it helpful to set aside a particular evening each week for calling on the unchurched. He may be able to delegate some of the work he is doing, as the apostles in the early church did (cf. Acts 6:1-6), to free up more time for evangelism. He may find it advisable to "bunch" meetings into a single night rather than spread them out over several evenings. Or, the congregation perhaps should be thinking about enlarging the full-time pastoral staff.

Then there is the competency factor. Some pastors may feel more competent and comfortable preaching the gospel from a pulpit than they do sharing it one-on-one with an unbeliever. Some, it is true, will have a greater ability to communicate the gospel to an unbeliever than others. God gives different gifts to different people. Yet even those whose strong gifts do not lie in the area of evangelism can overcome a good share of their fears and inhibitions simply in the doing. One, to a great extent, learns to preach by preaching, to teach by teaching, to counsel by counseling. So it is also with the work of evangelism.

In addition to doing the work of an evangelist himself, there are other ways by which the spiritual shepherd can provide evangelism leadership in the congregation. A pastor with a heart for evangelism will, among other things,

- include evangelism applications ("Go and tell") where appropriate in his preaching
- talk about evangelism in Bible classes and write about it in newsletters, pastoral letters, etc.
- stress in his youth and adult instruction classes that evangelism is a normal, vital part of a Christian's life
- give the work of evangelism its due in the official meetings of the congregation, with regular reports on work being done and work being planned
- seek to have the ministry of outreach represented on the congregation's church council
- remember the unchurched when planning and conducting the church's worship
- urge that a fair share of the congregation's budget be designated for outreach

- remember the unchurched when developing the annual program of the congregation

The need for the pastor to be a shepherd, a feeder and leader of the flock that has called him to be their shepherd, can hardly be emphasized too strongly. There is, in fact, a close correlation between shepherding and equipping. It begins with shepherding. Shepherds feed the flock with the spiritual food of Word and sacrament. Spiritual food produces spiritual growth. As members of the flock grow in their faith, they are being equipped to be Christ's ambassadors wherever he has placed them. In that respect, as Schuetze puts it, we can properly say that "to feed is also to equip."[112]

Equipper of the saints

Yet at the same time, the Scriptures do assign to the pastor the specific role of equipping the saints, of seeing to it that they are trained to serve their Lord according to their gifts:

> [Christ] gave some to be apostles, some to be prophets, some to be evangelists, and some to be pastors and teachers, to prepare God's people for works of service, so that the body of Christ may be built up. (Ephesians 4:11,12)

Paul mentions four groups of spiritual leaders in this passage: apostles, prophets, evangelists, and pastor/teachers. Of these four groups, apostles and prophets are no longer present in the church today. The apostles were eyewitnesses of Jesus' ministry and his specially chosen Spirit-inspired spokesmen, through whom he gave to the church the New Testament of the Scriptures. Prophets functioned in the days before the completion of the New Testament. They would, from time to time, receive messages from the Holy Spirit they were to transmit to the church (Agabus, for example, in Acts 11:28).

Evangelists, it appears, were those, like Philip, who brought the gospel to people for the first time. Eusebius writes, "In foreign lands they [evangelists] simply laid the foundations of the faith. That done they appointed others as shepherds, entrusting them with the care of the new growth, while they themselves proceeded . . . to other countries and other places."[113] Evangelists still exist as gifts of the ascended Christ to his church today, while the office of pastor/teacher apparently corresponds most closely to that of our pastor today.

---

[112]*Ibid.*, p. 8.

[113]Eusebius, *Ecclesiastical History,* 3.37.2.

St. Paul mentions both an immediate and an ultimate purpose of these gifts of Christ to his church: "to prepare God's people for works of service, so that the body of Christ may be built up." The word translated "prepare" (Greek, *katartizo*) has in it the idea of making fit or suitable, restoring to a former condition, putting in order, equipping. It is used to speak of restoring walls that have been broken down (Ezra 4:12), of mending torn fishing nets (Matthew 4:21), of restoring people who have sinned (Galatians 6:1). All such uses have in them the thought of making things or people what they ought to be. That is Paul's point in this passage. Spiritual leaders are not called to do all of the work of the ministry by themselves. A major part of their work is to get God's people ready for serving God, both in the world and in the church.

The immediate purpose of Christ's gift of spiritual leaders to his church is that the saints might become prepared and equipped for "works of service." The ultimate purpose is "so that the body of Christ may be built up." Building up, internal and external growth, occurs when the spiritual leader prepares and equips the saints for service instead of trying to carry out the whole ministry himself. All of God's people are gifted, and the use of these gifts in the gospel ministry of the church contributes to the growth of the kingdom. Armin Schuetze stated it well: "*Everyone a Minister* is not only the title of a book[114] but true of every Christian."[115]

John R. W. Stott writes,

> The New Testament concept of the pastor is not of a person who jealously guards all ministry in his own hands, and successfully squashes all lay initiatives, but of one who helps and encourages all God's people to discover, develop and exercise their gifts. His teaching and training are directed to this end, to enable the people of God to be a servant people, ministering actively but humbly according to their gifts. . . . Thus, instead of monopolizing all ministry himself, he actually multiplies ministries.[116]

Multiplication is the principle that guided Jesus in his training of the Twelve. He preached the gospel of the kingdom to the multitudes

---

[114]Oscar E. Feucht, *Everyone a Minister* (St. Louis: Concordia, 1974).

[115]Armin W. Schuetze, "A Shepherd or a Coach?", *Wisconsin Lutheran Quarterly,* 74:1, Jan. 1977, p. 7.

[116]John R. W. Stott, *God's New Society: The Message of Ephesians* (Downers Grove: Inter-Varsity Press, 1979), p. 167.

and healed their diseases; but he spent special time with the Twelve, equipping them for their ministries. In fact, the closer Jesus came to his last days on earth, the less time he spent with the multitudes and the more time he gave to the Twelve; for it was through these men that his message would be carried on. They not only needed to be taught but needed to become capable of teaching. In this way the message of the kingdom would be multiplied in ages to come.

The apostle Paul followed the same principle of multiplication. As did Jesus, Paul preached to the multitudes, but he spent special time training certain coworkers such as Timothy and Titus. He tells Timothy, "The things you have heard me say in the presence of many witnesses entrust to reliable men who will also be qualified to teach others" (2 Timothy 2:2). Four generations are mentioned here. Paul not only teaches Timothy but teaches him how to teach others. Timothy will pass on the message to reliable men and will prepare them for their ministries, so that they in turn will be qualified to teach others.

"He gave . . . some to be pastors and teachers, to prepare God's people for works of service." These words make it clear that equipping the saints is not merely a sideline but an integral part of the public ministry. One reason Christ instituted the public ministry was so that all the saints might become equipped for their ministry, their service to God using the gifts they have received from him.

Applying this principle specifically to the work of evangelism, the pastor would do well to think in terms of equipping, or training, two groups in the congregation for outreach with the gospel. The first group is the congregation as a whole. The pastor will want to train all the members of the congregation to become more adept at sharing the basic message of salvation in an informal way (as a part of their personal ministry) within their own personal mission field—their circle of unchurched family members, friends, and neighbors. He can accomplish this through periodic "how to" Bible classes on evangelism. He can also include some basic instruction on Christian witnessing as a part of his youth and adult instruction classes.

The pastor will also want to spend time with a smaller number of people, giving them more intensive training, as Jesus did with the Twelve. Just as a congregation generally offers a teacher training course to prepare some to teach Sunday school, so it is fitting that it offer an evangelism training course to prepare some to participate in the congregation's public ministry of outreach with the gospel.

In summary, the pastor serves the church's work of evangelism both in his role as shepherd and as coach. As a shepherd, through his regular preaching and teaching, as well as through his personal example, he nourishes, guides, and guards the flock and thus equips it to live as God's people, as salt and light, in the world. As a coach, he equips *all* the members of his flock for their *personal ministries* by training them in the fundamentals of witnessing; and he equips *some* of the members of the flock for assisting in the *public ministry* of the congregation by offering them more intensive training in reaching out with law and gospel to the lost and dying.[117]

5—Preservation

We will look very briefly at yet one more aspect of the work of the Holy Spirit, the Lord, the Giver of life. Not only does the Spirit bring people to faith, he also enables them to grow in faith, and he keeps them in the faith to the end.

It is God's will that Christians grow in their faith (cf. 2 Peter 3:18). He wants them to mature in their understanding and appreciation of the fact that he has blessed his children "with every spiritual blessing in Christ" (Ephesians 1:3). Freedom from guilt, certainty of everlasting life, the luscious "fruit of the Spirit" (love, joy, peace, etc.), guidance from the Word for daily living, strength from above for godly living, assurance of heard and answered prayers, the encouraging fellowship of other believers—this is just a partial listing of what is meant by the "every spiritual blessing" God has given to each of his children without fail. In Christ, the child of God lacks nothing. As God's children grow in their faith, they are able to appropriate these many blessings more fully and thus to personally experience them more deeply. That, too, is a part of God's gracious will for his children.

God also wants his children to experience the joy of serving him, according to their gifts, as productive members of the body of Christ (cf. Romans 12:1-8; 1 Corinthians 12). His will is that they live the life of good works he has "prepared in advance for [them] to do" (Ephesians 2:10).

Finally, God wants his children to "stand firm" in faith "to the end" (Matthew 24:13). "Be faithful, even to the point of death," says the risen and exalted Christ, "and I will give you the crown of life" (Revelation 2:10).

---

[117]Some portions of the above section on the ministry have been adapted from an essay of the author, "Equipping the Believers As Disciples," presented to the 49th Biennial Convention of the Wisconsin Evangelical Lutheran Synod in 1987.

It is not true, as Calvinistic theology contends, that "once you believe, you can never be lost, you can never go to hell."[118] A believer can fall away. The fact that the Scriptures warn against apostasy testifies to that fact (cf. 1 Corinthians 10:12; Hebrews 6:4-6; 10:26-31). One only has to think of Judas as a concrete example of the fact that once saved does not necessarily mean always saved. The Lutheran Confessions are echoing the Scriptures when they condemn those "who deny that those who have once been justified can lose the Holy Spirit."[119]

Those involved in the work of evangelism, therefore, will not consider their work finished as soon as people confess faith in Jesus as their Savior. They will want to do what they can to help new converts grow as disciples and remain disciples until the day their lives on earth come to an end.

The Holy Spirit uses the same means of grace to produce growth and preservation of faith that he uses to bring about the miracle of conversion. Evangelists, therefore, will seek to get those they have evangelized involved in the life and work of the congregation, because through their fellowship with a Christian congregation, new converts will be in regular contact with the means of grace in Word and sacrament. As they are regularly nourished by the gospel, they will produce the fruits and works that faith engenders. And, by the same gospel, they will be kept in the faith until the Lord calls them home.

This conviction, that spiritual life is built up and maintained by spiritual food, is the rationale behind giving attention to new member assimilation in the congregation. Suggestions relating to how a congregation can go about the work of assimilation will be the subject of a subsequent chapter.

+ + + + + + +

In looking back to what we have covered in this chapter, two indispensables stand out: the Holy Spirit and the means of grace. Through the means of grace the Holy Spirit brings people to faith. Through the means of grace the Holy Spirit gathers those he has converted into the body of Christ, the church. The ministry of the church, both personal and public, is to administer the means of grace. The building up and preservation of believers in the faith is again the work of the Spirit through the means of grace.

---

[118]Edwin H. Palmer, *The Five Points of Calvinism* (Grand Rapids: Baker, 1980), p. 68.

[119]Augsburg Confession, Article XII, 7.

The implication for evangelism is clear: The church's work of evangelism needs to center around dispensing the means of grace. In that way the Holy Spirit, the Lord, the Giver of life, is given the opportunity to carry out his work of calling and gathering God's elect, of enlightening and sanctifying them, and of keeping them with Jesus Christ in the one true faith.

+ + + + + + +

In the first three chapters of this book, under the theme, "We Believe," we have sought to summarize from the Scriptures and Lutheran Confessions what Lutherans believe and how what Lutherans believe relates to evangelism. In the second part, "Therefore We Speak," our intention is to demonstrate how these scriptural insights can be put to work in a practical way in a congregation's program of evangelism.

Part Two

Therefore We Speak—

The Practice of Evangelism in the Congregation

Chapter Four: Creating a Congregational Mission Mindset

A very close connection exists between the theology of evangelism and the practice of evangelism. As we mentioned in the introduction to this text, theology propels evangelism. What we *believe* inspires and informs what we *speak*. We believe—therefore we speak. In what follows, our intention is to present in broad strokes how a congregation might put into practice the biblical principles that formed the subject matter of the first half of the book.

It should be mentioned that what we will bring out in the remaining chapters of this book is not meant to be prescriptive. That is, it is not our intent to tell any congregation exactly how to carry out the work of evangelism in its midst. What we believe—our theology—*is* prescriptive. True theology is based on the unchanging truths of Scripture. "Thus says the Lord" is non-negotiable. How we organize and structure ourselves on a congregational level for putting our theology into practice is *not* prescriptive. This is not to say that a congregation is free to do whatever it pleases. A congregation's practice of evangelism is a reflection of its theology. The fact that altar calls are not a part of Lutheran worship, for example, is based on the Scripture's doctrine of conversion. Nevertheless, there is much room for diversity of practice within the framework of the Bible-based theology to which we hold. Congregational circumstances and the gifts of pastors and members—to mention just two of a number of variables—will dictate how a particular congregation in a particular time and place will structure and organize itself for evangelism.

We should add, however, that it is wise for a congregation to take some conscious, deliberate steps to incorporate outreach to the community as a part of its overall program. No one will have to urge a congregation to set up some way to care for the church's property, or to oversee the congregation's program of education, or to manage the church's finances. Everyone recognizes that this work needs to be done, and everyone knows that some organization and structure is necessary for it to be done effectively.

It is easier for the congregation's work of evangelism to be relegated to the background. If the property of the church is not being cared for, many will notice it. If the church is not involved in outreach, that will not be nearly so noticeable (The unchurched in the community will not be complaining vocally that no one is calling on them!). Consequently, it is important for a congregation, knowing that a part of its mission is to preach the gospel also to those who do not yet know Christ as Savior, to take some definite steps to include evangelism in its overall program. Nurture and outreach go together.

The subject discussed in the chapter before us is "Creating a Congregational Mission Mindset." We will look at three more topics in the chapters that follow:

Planning and Organizing for Outreach

Establishing an Evangelism Calling Program

Assimilating the New Member

We noted in a previous chapter that the pastor would do well to think in terms of equipping, or training, two groups in the congregation for outreach with the gospel. The first group is the congregation as a whole. The pastor will want to see to it that all the members of the congregation are sensitive to the fact that God has put them into their own personal mission field, that is, their circle of family members, friends, coworkers, and neighbors. He will then want to help his members become more adept at sharing the basic message of sin and grace with those in their personal mission fields.

Robert Kolb is right when he says that because many members feel "incapable of defending their God, they shrink from embarrassing him."[1] As a result, they are often silent at times when they would like to be speaking up. Congregational members often need more than just *encouragement* to "do the work of an evangelist" (2 Timothy 4:5). They also need some basic *how to* training. That is one of the topics of this chapter on creating a congregational mission mindset: impressing on the individual member that he or she has a vital role to play in carrying out God's gracious will that all be saved and come to a knowledge of the truth (cf. 1 Timothy 2:4).

In the second part of this chapter, we will look at the congregation as a whole and talk about developing a *corporate* mission mindset, which will be reflected in the congregation's worship, its educational agencies, and its fellowship activities.

---

[1]Robert Kolb, *Preaching the Gospel Today* (St. Louis: Concordia, 1984), p. 13.

1—Building an Every Member Mission Mindset

Three basic assumptions underlie the importance of seeking to create a mission mindset on the part of every member. The first assumption is that Jesus Christ is the only way to life with God, now and forever. We believe Jesus when he says, "I am the way and the truth and the life. No one comes to the Father except through me" (John 14:6). We take seriously the assertion of the apostle Peter that "salvation is found in no one else, for there is no other name under heaven given to men by which we must be saved" (Acts 4:12).

The second assumption is that the only way people will come to believe in Jesus and be saved is through hearing the gospel (cf. Romans 10:17). The gospel is "the power of God for the salvation of everyone who believes" (Romans 1:16).

The third basic assumption is that if we want people to be able to hear the gospel, believers, who have the gospel, need to come into contact with unbelievers, who do not have the gospel. This communication can occur in two basic ways. Unbelievers can come to us. They can, for example, visit church on a Sunday morning and there hear the message of sin and grace. Members, therefore, need to be encouraged to invite their friends and relatives to *come* with them to a worship service, a Bible class, or other church event where they have the opportunity to hear the gospel. Some, seeking rest for a troubled conscience or answers to personal problems, may visit church upon the invitation of a Christian family member or friend. Others, though they may feel no special need to do so, may come simply out of respect for the friend who invites them.

Given the nature of the unbeliever, however, simply inviting him or her to come to church may not be the most effective way to connect the person with the message of salvation. By nature, non-Christians are like the people of Gerasa who pleaded with Jesus to "leave their region" (Mark 5:17). Jesus had driven a legion of demons out of one of their countrymen. The demons had then entered a herd of 2,000 pigs and caused them to rush down a steep cliff into the Sea of Galilee, where they drowned. The pigs apparently had been the livelihood of the Gerasenes. Upon seeing what had happened to their pigs, the Gerasenes wanted to put as much space as they could between themselves and the one who had interfered so drastically with their lifestyle. They didn't want to be close to Jesus.

It is no different today. Christians, along with the healed demoniac of Gerasa (cf. Mark 5:18), have a great desire to be with Jesus. That's what makes Sunday worship a high point of their week. For believers, to be with Jesus, to hear him speak to them in his Word, to receive his body and blood in the Holy Supper, to join with fellow Christians in singing his praises—that is a foretaste of heaven itself. Unbelievers, however, who may know *about* Jesus but don't *know* him as their Savior, do not share such sentiments. If they think at all about Jesus, about Christianity, it is more likely that they will look upon Jesus as one who interferes with their lives, one who makes them feel guilty about things they know they shouldn't be doing. It is not natural for an unbeliever to want to come to Jesus, since all the natural man can see in him is law and judgment.

We can learn from Jesus' instructions to the Gerasene demoniac. Though this man wanted to return with Jesus to Galilee, Jesus said to him, "Go home to your family and tell them how much the Lord has done for you, and how he has had mercy on you" (Mark 5:19). Christ has commissioned his whole church to go also, to "go into all the *world* and preach the gospel to all creation" (Mark 16:15), not to wait for the world to come to us.

When the demoniac went back to his fellow Gerasenes, he had an obvious point of entry. The people of Gerasa knew what his situation had been before Jesus had come and driven out the demons. He could simply point them to the one who, in mercy, had done this great thing for him.

More often than not, however, it is the cumulative effect of a Christian's words and actions that provides a hearing for the gospel. Leighton Ford tells the story of a highly gifted Asian student who received a scholarship to attend a Christian college in the United States. When she arrived in the States, she was a non-Christian; by the time she left, she had become a Christian. The person through whom she was brought to faith in Christ was a rather quiet, reserved young woman. When asked how this student had been used to bring her to faith in Jesus, the Asian student replied, "She built a bridge from her heart to mine, and Christ walked over it."[2]

One can discern three distinct steps in such "bridge-building" evangelism. The first step is to *establish a relationship* with a person. The second step, once a relationship of mutual trust and respect has been established, is to *be alert to opportune moments* for imparting the truths of the gospel. The third step is to actually *communicate the gospel.* In some situations, an opportunity to do so might present it-

---

[2]Leighton Ford, *Good News Is for Sharing* (David C. Cook: Elgin, 1977, abridged ed.), p. 61.

self quite quickly. In other cases, it might require more time. Christians, who know that no unbeliever will come to repentance and faith apart from hearing the message of sin and grace, will want to look for opportune moments to communicate to those in their personal mission fields the great news of what Jesus Christ has done for them and how he has had mercy on them. A key part of a congregation's program of outreach will be to impress continually on all members that wherever they live is their personal mission field. Then offer guidance to them in establishing relationships with people, in watching for opportune moments, and in communicating the gospel.

We touched lightly on this subject in part two of chapter 3 when we discussed the concept of "friendship evangelism."[3] Now we want to explore how to put "friendship," "bridge-building" evangelism into practice.

Establish relationships

Building a bridge from one person to another with the ultimate goal of being able to communicate the gospel begins with establishing relationships with people.

Identify your personal mission field

A helpful first step in establishing relationships is to identify one's personal mission field. Studies have shown that a typical church member has on the average six to eight unchurched friends or acquaintances, a figure that may vary greatly, of course, from place to place and situation to situation. This is the Christian's personal mission field. This number of unchurched friends or acquaintances has been described by some as the Christian's FRAN network (his **F**riends, **R**elatives, **A**ssociates, and **N**eighbors). Even a relatively small congregation of 100 members may have as many as 600-800 unchurched people whose lives are in some degree or other intertwined with members of the congregation—quite a mission field!

Church historian Kenneth Scott Latourette observed regarding the Christians in the early church: "The primary change agents in the spread of the faith . . . were the men and women who earned their livelihood in some purely secular manner, and spoke of their faith to those whom they met in this natural fashion."[4] That is true today

---

[3]The reader may want to refer to pages 113-120 to review what friendship evangelism is and what it is not.

[4]Kenneth Scott Latourette, *A History of the Expansion of Christianity,* Vol. 1 (New York: Harper, 1937), p. 116.

also. Friendship or kinship ties often provide excellent openings for bringing the life-giving gospel to people who do not yet know Christ. Christians, who with their God want none to perish but all to come to repentance (cf. 2 Peter 3:9), would do well to give serious thought to identifying those whom God has placed into their personal mission fields. Who is there among my friends, relatives, coworkers, classmates, neighbors who does not yet know Jesus as Savior?

In addition to recognizing the mission field into which God has placed us, we can also seek to expand our mission field. Jesus intentionally stopped at the tree in which Zacchaeus was sitting and said, "I must stay at your house today" (Luke 19:5). He had to do this because Zacchaeus was in need of the salvation he had come to bring. Jesus "had to go through Samaria" (John 4:4) because there was a woman there who needed to hear about the living water which would satisfy her thirst forever.

Christians today, too, can be on the lookout for those who may be lacking the one thing needed. Some, living in an urban setting, have intentionally become "van watchers" in their neighborhoods. They stop in shortly after new families have moved in to welcome them to the neighborhood. In a gesture of friendship, they might bring their new neighbors a plate of baked goods and offer to help them become acquainted with their new community. From such small beginnings friendships are sometimes forged, which can give rise to an opportunity to pass on to their new friends the one message that saves.

Take time with people

Establishing relationships obviously involves more than simply identifying those in one's circle of friends and neighbors who are not Christians. It also means taking time with such people. Jesus did that, though he was a busy person. It wasn't as though he had nothing else to do when he spent the day at the house of Zacchaeus. Jesus was a man on a mission, on the last leg of his final journey to Jerusalem. He knew he had come to earth "to give his life as a ransom for many" (Mark 10:45). He knew his death would take place in Jerusalem. What he would accomplish in Jerusalem would affect every man, woman, and child who ever had lived or ever would live. Ahead of Jesus in Jerusalem was important business indeed, and yet he took time for just one person, an outcast at that. "The Son of Man came to seek and to save what was lost," he said (Luke 19:10). Zacchaeus was one of the lost; Jesus, therefore, did not hesitate to spend some valuable moments with him.

Time is a precious commodity. When husbands and wives both work out of the home, as is the case with the majority of families today, they treasure the few hours they have together as a family. Sociologists of our day speak of the phenomenon of "cocooning," of people shutting themselves up in their homes after work and on the weekends as a refuge from the fast pace of life all around them. The result? Though one lives in a neighborhood, he may never get to know his neighbors. Christians need to remember that non-Christians will not be able to be brought to a saving knowledge of Jesus unless they hear about him. That implies the importance, the necessity, in fact, of Christians making contact with non-Christians.

There is another form of cocooning on the part of Christians that can have an equally adverse effect on gospel outreach: Many Christians tend to spend time only with fellow Christians. This is especially prevalent in congregations with Lutheran elementary schools. The tendency is for families to forge their social contacts within the church and school. This is understandable. It is natural for Christians to desire and enjoy fellowship with Christians. They have many things in common that non-Christians do not share with them. But again, few will be converted to Christianity if Christians remain isolated from non-Christians. "You are the salt of the earth," Jesus told his disciples (Matthew 5:13). It has been well said that in order to be the salt of the earth, Christians have to get out of the salt shaker. To use another picture, Christians need to venture out from the fortress, the safety of the four walls of the church, into the world—specifically, into their own personal mission fields—where people are living and dying without Christ.

Let your light shine

In that mission field, in our association with unchurched friends and neighbors, what shall we do? Where shall we begin? In his Sermon on the Mount, Jesus suggests that the starting point may well be the non-verbal, but not invisible, testimony of the Christian life: "You are the light of the world," Jesus tells his followers. "A city on a hill cannot be hidden. Neither do people light a lamp and put it under a bowl. Instead they put it on its stand, and it gives light to everyone in the house. In the same way, let your light shine before men, that they may see your good deeds and praise your Father in heaven" (Matthew 5:14-16). In a practical application to this declaration of Jesus, the apostle Peter urges believing wives married to unbelieving husbands, "Be submissive to your husbands so that, if any of them do not believe the word, they may be won over without words by the behavior of their wives, when they see the purity and reverence of your lives" (1 Peter 3:1,2).

Both Jesus and Peter are talking about what we might call "pre-evangelism." Letting the light of my faith shine is not going to bring anyone to faith; but it may make a person curious about the source of my faith-life. Then I can, with the demoniac of Gerasa, tell what great things God has done for me and how he has had mercy on me.

"Light shining," displaying my faith by a life of love, is an excellent form of pre-evangelism, for, as Arthur McPhee observes, "Most men and women are not looking for religion, nor do they often have the time or inclination to ask themselves questions about the meaning of life, nor do they perceive themselves as miserable sinners in need of forgiveness. But most men and women are looking for love. . . . If you demonstrate by the way you live and relate to others that the love of God has become a reality in your experience, then you have something that is hard for people to walk away from."[5]

Joseph Aldrich writes in the same vein:

> God's evangelistic strategy is beauty. Evangelism starts with the beauty of God, and it also involves a beautiful bride, the church. God desires that through our lives the world will see his beauty. . . . There is God's evangelistic strategy in a nutshell: He desires to build into you and me the beauty of his own character, and then put us on display. . . . We can compare this beauty to music. . . . After a neighbor has seen that you are a person of integrity, and that you care about him, a time will come when, having heard the music, . . . some will want to hear the words to that music.[6]

While I was serving in the parish ministry in San Jose, California, one of the families of our congregation solicited my advice on how to bring the gospel to a new family on the block. The family was Hindu, recently arrived from India. I admitted that I wasn't quite sure of how to go about doing this. I suggested that perhaps the best thing would be simply to be good neighbors and wait for the opportunity to present itself to speak about spiritual matters.

---

[5]Arthur McPhee, *Friendship Evangelism* (Grand Rapids: Zondervan, 1978), pp. 56,75.

[6]Joseph C. Aldrich, "Lifestyle Evangelism—Winning through Winsomeness," *Christianity Today,* Vol. 27, No. 1, January 7, 1983, p. 13.

The families had children about the same age. They began to play with each other. In time the Hindu family approached our members and said, "We enjoy having our children play with your children. There's something different about them, something we really like." That was the beginning of a relationship between the two families that eventually resulted in the oldest boy enrolling in our Lutheran elementary school and the father attending the Bible information class.

The family from our congregation had a specific end in mind. They wanted nothing but the best for their new neighbors. They wanted them to know Christ as Savior. The route they used to gain a hearing for the gospel was simply to let their light shine in a quiet, unobtrusive way. The relationship between these two families never developed into a deep friendship. That doesn't always occur, nor does it have to. It did provide, however, an open door for bringing God's plan of salvation to those who did not know it.

Be genuine

By "genuine" we mean that we shouldn't pretend to be something we aren't. Christians shouldn't be afraid to admit that they, too, are weak, that they, too, face and sometimes falter under temptation. A "health and wealth" kind of Christianity, which asserts that once one becomes a Christian all of his problems disappear, besides being a patent falsehood, hinders evangelism. It promises what the Christian cannot deliver and what God himself does not promise to give.

We can look to the apostle Paul as an example here, who, even near the end of his life as a missionary, still publicly confessed, "What I do is not the good I want to do; no, the evil I do not want to do—this I keep on doing" (Romans 7:19). Paul had not achieved perfection. But what he did have—and we also have—is the Lord Jesus Christ. And through him there came to Paul and there comes to Christians today the assurance of forgiveness and power to put down the old man and let the new man take ever greater control of our lives.

Don't give up

In a certain sense, we can say that evangelism is a process, if we include all that may lead up to the time when one first has the opportunity to verbalize the way of salvation. At times, as was the case with our members in San Jose, it may take quite a while before this opportunity arises. One might be tempted to give up before the chance for witnessing presents itself. In other cases, we might be rebuffed every time we try to share our faith with a particular individual in our personal mission field. As a result, we might be tempted to discontinue our efforts to evangelize the person.

We should not be too quick to give up. If the Lord is "patient," literally, "long-suffering" (2 Peter 3:9), we will want be patient also. There is hope to the end. In Jesus' parable of the Workers in the Vineyard, some were hired at the eleventh hour. The thief on the cross, an "eleventh hour" convert, is enjoying Paradise right now (cf. Luke 23:43).

There can be eleventh-hour converts in our day also. Only God knows when a person's time of grace has ended. From our perspective, one's time of grace is one's lifetime. When we establish relationships with non-Christians within our circle of friends and neighbors, therefore, we will want to seek to maintain these relationships for the long term. Who knows when the Lord might provide the opening for us to testify about the gospel? And who knows whether the tenth or the twentieth time we've witnessed may not be the time the Holy Spirit breaks through, convicts the person of sin, and convinces him that in Jesus is forgiveness and the life that extends into an endless eternity?

Look for openings

All of this assumes, of course, that we are actively looking for opportunities to witness. Such openings present themselves more often than one might expect. A number of years back Edwin Rauff, director of the Research and Information Center for the Lutheran Council in the United States of America, conducted 180 hour-long interviews in seven diverse counties across the United States, counties that were at least 50% unchurched. He interviewed people who had not been members of a church or, if members, had not been attending for at least five years. His main question was, "What made you think of joining a church at this particular time?" The interviews resulted in an informative book entitled *Why People Join the Church.*[7] Though Rauff's book was written in 1979, his findings have a contemporary ring to them.

He broke down the responses he received from his interviewees into twelve categories. We will look briefly at each of these twelve categories to see what kinds of events and circumstances make the unchurched begin to think about spiritual things.

---

[7]Edwin A. Rauff, *Why People Join the Church* (New York: Pilgrim Press, 1979).

Family relationships and responsibilities

For some, it was the need they felt to give their children some kind of religious, moral training, or to have them baptized. It may have been the grandparents who exerted some pressure on the parents to do something about the children's spiritual training; or it may have been the children themselves who were invited to Sunday school or vacation Bible school by friends and who then urged their parents to come with them to church.

In some cases, an unchurched spouse eventually responded to invitations to a church service on the part of the Christian spouse. In other cases, marriage or family problems prompted people to look to the church for help.

Most people, including the unchurched, are interested in their children's welfare. They also want to have good marriages and happy, wholesome families. Christian friends and neighbors can take advantage of this knowledge. They can speak about the benefits of baptism. They can invite their neighbors' children to Sunday school and vacation Bible school. If their congregation sponsors a Lutheran elementary school, they can mention it to their neighbors. They can encourage a family experiencing marital or family problems to speak with their pastor. They can invite them to come to church with them if their congregation is conducting a marriage or family seminar. All of these situations can be openings that afford the opportunity to bring people the fundamental message of law and gospel.

Influence of Christian people

Some of those interviewed mentioned that they started thinking about spiritual matters when they saw the difference in the quality of life of a Christian friend, relative, neighbor, or coworker. Connecting that difference in some way to the person's religious convictions, they wanted to know more about what he or she believed.

Church members will want to be ready to point people to the divine source of the admirable qualities their neighbors observe in their lives. The apostle Peter writes, "Always be prepared to give an answer to everyone who asks you to give the reason for the hope that you have" (1 Peter 3:15).

Church visit, program, special event, or sacred act

At times it was a church service the person attended, perhaps upon invitation of a friend, or while visiting relatives, or while being visited by relatives. In some cases it was a wedding or a funeral, or the baptism or confirmation of a friend's child, or a Christmas or Easter service, that triggered in the person a desire to learn more about what he or she had observed. Or the person may have attended some special church activity—a seminar, a youth program—that aroused interest to explore further what the church had to offer.

Many unchurched adults have had some kind of childhood connection with a church or churches. Sometimes an accepted invitation to a special service or church activity is all it takes to reawaken a desire to regain what the person once had as a child. For this reason we will not want to downplay the value of "come and see" invitations.

Search for community

Some of the people Rauff interviewed spoke of their loneliness. They were looking for fellowship, so they turned to a church. Through this point of contact the church was then given the opportunity to lead the person into the deepest and most lasting fellowship of all, fellowship with Jesus and other believers in the holy Christian church.

Rauff writes, "Of the many factors that lead unchurched people to church membership, fellowship is one that seems most ripe for implementation. We can't manufacture crises in people's lives [And we wouldn't want to if we could!], nor can we easily manipulate family pressures to nudge someone closer to the church doors. But there may be ways to raise the consciousness of church members to empathize with the stranger and observe some rules of church sociability."[8] We will unfold this thought somewhat further a little later in this chapter when we look at worship from an evangelistic viewpoint.

Personal crisis

A certain number of those interviewed mentioned that they started thinking about returning to church (or attending for the first time) on the occasion of a serious illness or the death of a loved one. Some described themselves as "losing control" at such a time.

It is understandable that people might be moved to reach out for help in such circumstances. Crises alert people to the sobering truth that they are not totally in control of their lives, as they may have thought while things were going well for them. The death of a

---

[8]*Ibid.*, p. 87.

spouse or close family member, divorce, marital separation, personal injury or illness, loss of a job, moving, a change of work responsibility, trouble with children or in-laws—situations such as these can make for some very anxious moments in people's lives.

It is not true, as some maintain, that people will be more receptive *to the gospel* at such times. All unbelievers are equally unreceptive to the gospel at all times. People may well be more ready, however, to turn to a friend for counsel during such times. Once again, we see the value of the personal mission field approach to outreach. If we have identified those in our network of friends, relatives, associates, and neighbors who are not practicing Christians; if we are spending time with them and loving them; if we are letting the light of our faith shine; if our friends have observed that, though we are not free of problems, we seem somehow to be able to cope with them, then it should come as no surprise that some of them may turn to us in times of crisis. We, in turn, can point them to *the* problem, sin, that lies behind life's problems, and *the* solution, the cross, that provides the answer to life's greatest problem and enables us to cope with any smaller problems that may come our way.

End of rebellion

Some whom Rauff interviewed, when asked what led them to think about spiritual matters and about returning to church, indicated that, after some years of rebellion against what they had been taught in their youth, the time had come for them to return to their former values and principles. They recalled their childhood training and realized that it was time to "go home."

This underscores the value of not giving up on a person in our personal mission field who may have had religious training in his childhood, but whose life is now at odds with what he had been taught. It might be a wayward son or daughter, like the prodigal son in Jesus' parable. Trusting in the Lord's promise, "Train a child in the way he should go, and when he is old he will not turn from it" (Proverbs 22:6), we will want to wait patiently, praying for opportunities to fan into flame the light of faith that the Holy Spirit had once kindled in his or her heart.

Feelings of emptiness

Another frequent response Rauff received was that the person felt something was missing in his life, even though outwardly things were going well. Rauff discovered that the educational or socioeconomic level of the person made no real difference. Feelings of emptiness were not just a problem of the "bored rich."

What an opportunity this feeling of emptiness provides to fill those empty places with Jesus. Again, who has a better chance to do this than one who has come to be known and trusted by those in his or her personal mission field!

God's "kairos"

Others Rauff interviewed couldn't point to any specific person or situation that had moved them to think about becoming connected with a church. It was rather, as Rauff put it, "a conviction that God in his own time brought to fruition the seedlings that may have sprouted."[9]

God uses people, of course, to plant the seed and water and cultivate the growing plant; and the people he uses most frequently are friends, relatives, associates, and neighbors.

Influence of a pastor

Still others interviewed mentioned that a particular pastor was influential in leading them to consider coming or returning to church. It might have been the pastor's reputation, or the visit he paid them while they were in the hospital, or the help he gave them in a family crisis, or the visit he made to their home.

More often than not the pastor won't be the first person the Lord uses to bring a person into the fold. Typically, the person will be introduced to the pastor through a trusted friend, a relative, or a neighbor. This underscores once again the worth of a personal mission field approach to outreach.

Journey toward truth

Others indicated that their turn toward the spiritual aspect of life began with a reading of some Christian author or a discussion with a Christian apologist.

There is merit in seeking to discuss religious matters with a friend, to find out what "hang-ups" he might have, and then to provide some answers. It could be in the form of a book. I may respond with what I already know from the Scriptures. Or I may do some personal research or find help from someone else and then come back to my friend with the results of my inquiries. Long-term relationships

---

[9] *Ibid.*, p. 140.

with people in one's personal mission field can lead to opportunities such as these.

Response to evangelism

Some respondents to Rauff's questions told him that what brought them back to church was the evangelism work of the congregation. They were reached through the formal efforts of a congregation that initiated an evangelism thrust into the community. We will speak more of this in chapter 6, "Establishing an Evangelism Calling Program."

Reaction to guilt and fear

Finally, some of those interviewed spoke of the guilt that had been burdening them and the fear of what would happen to them when they died. They spoke of the relief they felt to be set free from a sense of guilt and to be given the security and assurance of salvation.

There are probably individuals within most people's personal mission fields who fit into this category. The unbeliever's conscience tells him that there is a holy God who sets the standards, and his conscience also informs him that he has fallen short of that standard. Hence, the guilt and the fear. If we are alert to this fact, we may find an opening to bring to someone in our circle of family and friends the good news of the "Lamb of God, who takes away the sin of the world" (John 1:29).

All of Rauff's findings through his many hours of interviews underscore the importance of establishing relationships within our personal mission fields and of looking for openings the Lord provides. It goes without saying that a congregation whose membership has such a mission mindset is in a much better position to evangelize its community than a congregation that looks primarily to the pastor or to the pastor and evangelism committee as its outreach specialists.

Communicate the gospel

We build bridges to people in our personal mission fields by establishing relationships with them. In these relationships we look for openings. Then we communicate the gospel. Though not all church members will be equally gifted in communicating the message of law and gospel, all can be taught some simple ways of verbalizing God's plan of salvation. We will look briefly at a few of these ways. A congregation might do well to spend some time in a series of Bible classes, first talking about establishing relationships and what kinds of openings to look for, and then teaching some simple ways to communicate the gospel.[10]

"Personal testimony"

Personal testimony tends to be looked down upon in Lutheran circles as being too subjective, too much "I" and not enough "Jesus." There is good reason to approach the subject of personal testimony somewhat cautiously because it can focus too much on self and not enough on the Savior. At the same time, there is biblical warrant for proper Christian testimony, for telling what Jesus means to me.

The psalmist writes, "Come and listen, all you who fear God; let me tell you what he has done for me" (Psalm 66:16). He then relates how God had listened to his prayer and not withheld his love from him. Jesus instructed the Gerasene out of whom he had just driven a legion of demons, "Go home to your family and tell them how much the Lord has done for you, and how he has had mercy on you" (Mark 5:19). What the Lord has done for me—that was to be the content of the healed demoniac's message.

The apostle Paul also did not hesitate to use a personal testimony approach. Writing to Timothy, he says, "I was once a blasphemer and a persecutor and a violent man." But, he says, "I was shown mercy because I acted in ignorance and unbelief. The grace of our Lord was poured out on me abundantly, along with the faith and love that are in Christ Jesus. Here is a trustworthy saying that deserves full acceptance: Christ Jesus came into the world to save sinners—of whom I am the worst" (1 Timothy 1:13-15). That was Paul's story: from blasphemer to believer by the mercy of God.

Why had God been so merciful to him? He explains, "I was shown mercy so that in me, the worst of sinners, Christ Jesus might display his unlimited patience as an example for those who would believe on him and receive eternal life" (verse 16). Note how Paul shines the spotlight, not on himself, but on Christ, on his "unlimited patience" and love for Paul and all sinners.[11]

Likewise, Christians today can properly respond to witnessing opportunities with personal testimony. They can tell people what they

---

[10]Cf. the Bible study course, "Always Be Ready to Give an Answer," by Paul Kelm, in the *Getting Everyone Involved* manual (NPH); also, "Witness Where You Are" by the same author, a friendship evangelism workshop outline appended to chapter 7 of the *Evangelism Handbook* (NPH).

[11]For another example of Paul's personal testimony, cf. his defense before King Agrippa in Acts 26.

once were ("I was a sinner on the way to hell"), what has happened to them ("I've been rescued from death and hell"), how this happened ("Jesus died to take my sins away"), and what this means to them ("I know my sins are forgiven and that one day I will go to heaven"). Then they can tell their friends that what Jesus did for them he has done for all people. It should not be difficult for Christians to give such brief "what Jesus means to me" personal testimonies when they have occasion to do so.

Bible stories

Another way to respond to openings is with a Bible story pertinent to the situation at hand.

- To a person who doesn't know the way of salvation one might tell the story of the nighttime conversation between Jesus and Nicodemus (John 3).
- If someone says, "I'm such a bad sinner, God will never forgive me," the stories of David's adultery, of Peter's denial, and of Saul's persecution of the church will demonstrate how the Lord forgives even the most grievous of sinners.
- A friend who once was an active Christian but has wandered away and wonders, "Will God take me back?", would benefit from hearing the parables of the Lost Sheep, the Lost Coin, and the Prodigal Son (Luke 15).
- To a friend more concerned about the things of this life than spiritual things you might relate Jesus' Parable of the Rich Fool (Luke 12) as a warning against placing one's trust in material things.
- Someone who keeps putting you off when you try to talk about spiritual matters, who says, "I'll get serious about such things later," might do well to hear Jesus' parable of the Wise and Foolish Virgins (Matthew 25), with its strong reminder that one does not know the day or the hour.

It would not be difficult to find Bible stories to fit many other situations. Members who have attended their congregation's Lutheran elementary school or who have been faithful in Sunday school will probably know most of these Bible stories already. They will appreciate help, though, perhaps through a Bible class series, on which stories fit which situations.

Scripture texts

The message of salvation can be told in just a few Bible passages that can quite easily be put to memory by most Christians. The following three passages, for example, tell everything that needs to be said:

- "All have sinned and fall short of the glory of God" (Romans 3:23)
- "The wages of sin is death" (Romans 6:23)
- "God so loved the world that he gave his one and only Son, that whoever believes in him shall not perish but have eternal life" (John 3:16)

Or, one might walk a friend through a short portion of Scripture such as Romans 3:20-24 or 2 Corinthians 5:14-21, and through this Scripture portion let the Holy Spirit speak God's law and gospel directly to the person's heart.

One could do some role-playing, utilizing passages such as these, in a Bible class on communicating the gospel to our friends and neighbors. The goal would be to assure God's people that they have the tools they need to convey to others the message of salvation. They can be led to see that it is not difficult to tell what Jesus means to me, or to use Bible stories to respond to situations arising in a friend's life, or to employ a few simple Bible passages to point their friends to God's plan of salvation.

Tracts and videos

There are also such tools as videos[12] and tracts[13] available, which can assist the church member in communicating the message of salvation to someone within his or her personal mission field. Some congregations place an inexpensive tract into every bulletin once or twice a year. In the service, members are invited to give or mail the tract to someone in their personal mission field for whom the tract would appear to have special meaning. They are encouraged to include a brief explanatory note with the tract, e.g., "I thought you might appreciate this. Maybe we'll find an opportunity to talk about it" [or: "Please read it and tell me what you think about it."]

---

[12]*Soul Search,* a 15-minute video (NPH), presents a simple law-gospel message. The video comes with specific suggestions on how to make optimum use of it.

[13]For a helpful "how to" guide on the use of tracts in evangelism, cf. "Outreach through Tracts" in the *Getting Everyone Involved* manual (NPH). Northwestern Publishing House also offers a good selection of evangelism tracts.

"Come and see"

We should not discount the value of a "come and see" approach. That is what Philip told his friend Nathanael. Then he brought him to Jesus. This resulted in Nathanael's confession, "You are the Son of God; you are the King of Israel" (cf. John 1:45-51). The woman at Jacob's well did the same. She told her fellow Samaritans, "Come, see a man who told me everything I ever did. Could this be the Christ?" The people came and many believed (cf. John 4:28-42).

There is some value in conducting Visitors' (or Friendship) Sundays on a periodic basis, thereby giving all members a special opportunity to invite those in their personal mission fields to a worship service designed especially with the unchurched in mind. Some members may feel more comfortable in doing this than in evangelizing their friend or neighbor on their own. We will have more to say about Friendship Sundays later when we speak of worship and evangelism.

A variation on the "come and see" approach used by some congregations is to distribute the pastor's calling card periodically to members with the encouragement, "If you have a friend who's experiencing problems, feel free to give him or her this card. You might introduce it with something like: 'My pastor and my church have been a big help to me when I've gone through some difficult times in my life. Why don't you give our pastor a call. His phone number is on the card.'"

In this section we have been focusing on building an every member "bridge-building" mission mindset. Before moving on to the second half of this chapter, we should mention that the process of building bridges from Christian to non-Christian, as helpful as it is for gaining a hearing for the gospel, can also be an impediment to evangelism. We can concentrate so heavily on building bridges that we neglect what's really important: *telling people about Jesus.* That would be like spending so much time planning a project that there's no time left for doing it.

Sometimes we may wait too long for the "opportune moment" to arrive. It may be possible at times to "create" such opportune moments by a well-chosen comment or question. I have had the opportunity from time to time to discuss life and death issues with people sitting next to me on a plane simply by asking them (after some introductory pleasantries), "How do you feel about your relationship with God?" Or, "If you were to die tonight, are you sure you would have eternal life?" We mention this, not to make Christians feel guilty if they don't do the same, for we all have different gifts, different skills, different personalities, as well as different opportunities. Rather, we bring it up to illustrate that sometimes, depending on the time and circumstances, the best thing may well be to get right to the point. Getting close to a person is not evangelism. Telling a person about Jesus is evangelism. Christians will rejoice whenever the Lord enables them to seize an opportunity or to create an opportunity to do so.

2—Building a Corporate Mission Mindset

In talking about developing a congregational mission mindset, it is important to work to create and sustain such a mindset, not only on the level of the individual member, but also on the part of the congregation as a whole. That is the subject of the remainder of this chapter: developing a corporate, that is, a total congregation mission mindset. The one follows closely upon the other. When the individual members of the congregation recognize and appreciate that God has called each of them to bring the gospel to those living around them, then they will also see that the entire congregation (which obviously consists of the total number of individual members) has the same mission. In what follows we will look at the congregation's program of worship, education, and fellowship activities from such an evangelistic perspective.

Worship and evangelism

It is clear from the Scriptures that God wants Christians to gather with other Christians to worship the Lord who has created and redeemed them and, through the gospel, brought them out of spiritual death into spiritual life. The question we want to consider in the section before us is this: Is there a place for the *non-Christian* in the public worship of the church? Can, or should, the church's worship be used as an evangelistic arm of the church? A look at the early history of the church indicates that, for the most part, public worship was not seen as an evangelism tool. Werner Elert observes:

> Admission was not just for anybody. . . . The gathering for worship in the early church was not a public but a closed assembly, while the celebration of the Eucharist was reserved for the saints with utmost strictness.[14]

In the first few centuries after Christ, only after instruction had begun were the non-baptized invited to the service. They were not

---

[14]Werner Elert, *Eucharist and Church Fellowship in the First Four Centuries*, translated by Norman E. Nagel (St. Louis: Concordia, 1966), pp. 75,76.

permitted to attend the whole service, however, but only the first part, from the introit to the sermon, called the "Mass of the Catechumens." Only after they were fully instructed and baptized were they allowed to be present at and participate in the communion section (referred to as the "Mass of the Faithful").

Martin Luther also did not consider the Sunday service to be the primary evangelism tool for the many in Germany who literally were non-believers. Evangelization was to be done through the catechism, the "instruction in which the heathen who want to be Christians are taught and guided in what they should believe, know, and do, and leave undone, according to the Christian faith."[15]

On the other hand, Luther did create his German service (the *Deutsche Messe*) "for the sake of the unlearned folk" so that the gospel might be "publicly preached to such people to move them to believe and become Christians."[16] Luther understood what the church has always recognized, that public worship holds what people need to become Christians. For what is the heart and center of Christian worship? Is it not the gospel? And it is through the gospel that the Holy Spirit works the miracle of conversion.

Lutheran worship is ideally suited for evangelism

A case can be made, therefore, for public worship to serve as one of the ways (although not the only or even the primary way[17]) by which the church can evangelize its community. Lutheran liturgical worship, because it is full of the gospel, offers what people need, not just to grow as Christians but to become Christians. From the opening greeting to the parting blessing the liturgy proclaims the Christ who was born, lived, died, rose, and ascended "for us and for our salvation." The full reality of full forgiveness is announced in the absolution, the sermon, and the words of institution. The cause of forgiveness, the finished work of Christ, is reviewed in the appointed lessons from the Word. The person of Christ is taught in the songs of the liturgy. It is obvious that the public worship of the church sets a full table of the gospel. And the gospel is what the Holy Spirit uses to convince and convert the lost.

---

[15]*American Edition,* Vol. 53, p. 64.

[16]*American Edition,* Vol. 53, p. 63.

[17]Unlike American Revivalism, which considers public worship to be the *primary* vehicle for outreach.

In view of the gospel-centeredness of Lutheran liturgical worship, the *Christian Worship Manual* is not overstating the case when it says,

> The final accounting of the history of the church may show that the liturgy, carefully prepared and pastorally led, has contributed as much to the growth of disciples inside and outside the church as anything the church has ever done. This is true because the liturgy showcases that which the Holy Spirit uses to make disciples: Word and sacrament.[18]

Besides its focus on the means of grace, Lutheran worship has several additional characteristics that aid the cause of reaching the lost.

Lutheran worship contains law as well as gospel. In the sermon, in the confession and absolution, it convicts as well as comforts. Therefore, Lutheran worship contains what is necessary to prepare the heart so that it might rejoice in the message of forgiveness.

Because it is built on the church calendar and its set of propers, *Lutheran worship emphasizes a single theme* each Sunday and festival. Visitors may not be able to understand everything that occurs at worship, but most will be able to leave the service with the primary focus of the day in mind.

Lutheran worship holds a proper balance of justification and sanctification. Lutheran liturgical worship imitates the balance St. Paul provides so beautifully in his epistles. Note, for example, Paul's emphases in the Letter to the Romans: "I urge you, brothers, in view of God's mercy [justification], to offer your bodies as living sacrifices [sanctification], holy and pleasing to God—this is your spiritual act of worship. Do not conform any longer to the pattern of this world, but be transformed by the renewing of your mind. Then you will be able to test and approve what God's will is—his good, pleasing and perfect will" (Romans 12:1,2). Note the emphasis, but also note the order: first justification, then sanctification; first Christ for us, then Christ in and through us. That is also the emphasis of Lutheran liturgical worship.

Lutheran worship offers a balance of proclamation and response. Luther, deploring the mostly passive participation of the congregation in his day, restored a healthy amount of congregational involvement in worship. The liturgical worship of the Lutheran church con-

---

[18]Gary Baumler and Kermit Moldenhauer, ed., *Christian Worship Manual* (Milwaukee: Northwestern Publishing House, 1993), p. 112.

tinues that emphasis. The service is not only sacramental in nature, God coming to his children in Word and sacrament; it is also sacrificial, believers going to God in confession, prayer, and praise.

Some point out that a visitor to the service, if he is not yet a Christian, is unable to truly worship God. That, of course, is true. Christian worship is a fruit of faith. On the other hand, the non-Christian who is present as a congregation of believers wholeheartedly participates in the worship may well be led to want to learn more about the Christian faith that produces such a heartfelt response. In this respect, the public worship of the church serves as a pre-evangelism tool.

Lutheran worship balances continuity and variety. People like to know where they are going, which is easier if they have been there before. This is one of the values of the repetitive nature of Lutheran liturgical worship: It gives a certain feeling of ease and comfort. The worshiper doesn't have to learn something new each week.

On the other hand, too much continuity can result in a mechanical worship, which isn't worship. There is value, therefore, in providing variety in worship within a certain continuing framework. That is another of the strengths of Lutheran liturgical worship. It anticipates, encourages, and actually insists on variety. The proper of the service, that is, the set of lessons, psalms, prayers, and hymns that changes from Sunday to Sunday, allows an infusion of a variety of texts and many musical styles and arrangements.

The liturgy of Lutheran worship allows for a balance of traditional and contemporary forms. The liturgy is an order of service the Lutheran Church has inherited from the church of western Christendom. Parts are as old as Christianity itself; in fact, the progression of lessons and psalms in the Word section of the liturgy is as old as the rite of the synagogue. While the liturgy contains some relatively recent additions (for example, the confession/absolution and the offering), most of the forms Lutherans employ in their worship are more than a thousand years old. Lutheran liturgical worship expresses the ties Lutherans have with the whole Christian church on earth. It helps to emphasize that they are not a sect. Their worship has deep roots. A service that uses that which is good from the past, that follows the way Christians have worshiped ever since Christians began to worship, demonstrates the links God's people have with believers who have gone before them.

This does not mean that there cannot be and should not be good contemporary elements in worship. To communicate properly, it is imperative that we speak to people in the idiom of our day. We are living in an urban, industrial, multi-cultural society. Our educational level is different from that of a hundred years ago. Our social and environmental problems are different. Our language has changed.

We will want to take all this into account in our hymns, prayer language, choice of Bible translation, sermons, etc. *Christian Worship: A Lutheran Hymnal,* the hymnal of the Wisconsin Evangelical Lutheran Synod, consciously seeks to balance the ancient and the contemporary. Though the liturgy may consist of ancient texts, these texts are used in fresh and understandable translations. Musical settings may be as ancient as plainchant (for example, the psalm tones) or as contemporary as the psalm refrains and the freshly-composed canticles in the Service of Word and Sacrament. The hymns in *Christian Worship* represent every age of Christendom and many musical styles.[19]

There is something in Lutheran worship for a variety of musical tastes, from the traditional to the contemporary, and this is right and proper. Visitors—to say nothing of members—come from a variety of ethnic and social backgrounds, and their tastes will obviously differ. The key issue in the selection of music for worship is almost never whether the music is traditional or contemporary. The fact is that there is bad and good traditional music just as there is bad and good contemporary music. The issue is rather, does the music—its text and style—point to Christ or detract from Christ?

Lutheran worship balances solemnity and warmth. Lutheran congregations, which properly make much of the power of the means of grace to convert the unbeliever and nurture the believer, are rightly the first to emphasize solemnity at worship. In Word and sacrament, human beings come into contact with the living Christ. Like Peter, who fell to his knees praying, "Go away from me, Lord; I am a sinful man" (Luke 5:8), Lutherans come to worship with a deep sense of awe. They reverently assent to the psalmist's directive, "The LORD is in his holy temple; let all the earth be silent before him" (Habakkuk 2:20). John Brug noted the value of solemnity in Lutheran worship when he wrote:

> The character of good liturgy is that it deemphasizes individuals and unites worshipers in corporate praise of a majestic God. It directs less attention to human feeling and to individual desires and more attention to the majesty and goodness of God. Liturgical worship recognizes that although God is our truest

---

[19]*Christian Worship: A Lutheran Hymnal* (Milwaukee: Northwestern Publishing House, 1993).

Friend, he is not our "buddy." He is a holy God, who is to be feared.[20]

Solemnity need not be achieved at the expense of warmth, however. The center of Lutheran liturgy is the gospel. The gospel is joyous, heart-warming good news. It is only natural for the people who conduct the liturgy to reflect the joy of the gospel. What C. F. W. Walther writes about the preacher applies just as well to the liturgical leader: "If you do not mingle Law with Gospel you will always mount your pulpit with joy. People will notice that you are filled with joy because you are bringing the blessed message of joy to your congregation."[21] When the person leading worship is himself imbued with the gospel and communicates a warm, comfortable, and personable style, then he will not get in the way of what the liturgy means to be: a glad and happy proclamation of the fullness of Christ's blessings.

Lutherans take a balanced approach to worship. They balance law and gospel, justification and sanctification, proclamation and response, continuity and variety, the traditional and the contemporary, solemnity and warmth. All of these are hallmarks of Lutheran liturgical worship. Such a service, with the gospel at its center, will benefit both Christian and non-Christian, member and non-member, mature believer and recent convert. It is entirely proper, therefore, to conclude that Lutheran liturgical worship can serve as a valuable part of a congregation's program of outreach. It can function well as a tool to attract and interest inquirers. It was my experience, in fact, throughout about 25 years of service in the parish ministry, all in mission-type settings, that Lutheran liturgical worship does not hinder evangelism. My experience was that worship that attracts and spiritually benefits members will also attract and spiritually benefit non-members.

Lutheran worship requires the best in preparation

Those involved in conducting Lutheran worship are going to have to work and plan if they are to achieve the balances that are the hallmarks of Lutheran worship. It deserves the best of our time and efforts.

It must be said that this very obvious truth has not always been practiced. Pastor Larry Peters, in an essay entitled "Lutheran Wor-

---

[20]John F. Brug, "Approaching a Majestic God," *Parish Leadership,* Vol. 1, No. 1, Fall 1992, p. 25.

[21]C. F. W. Walther, *The Proper Distinction between Law and Gospel,* trans. by W. H. T. Dau (St. Louis: Concordia, 1928), p. 406.

ship and Church Growth," wrote about this problem in his own Missouri Synod:

> Lutherans have generally not done a great job utilizing the resources for worship their liturgical forms provide. It is a sad truth that much Lutheran worship is dull, boring, and seemingly irrelevant. This is an abuse of the liturgical form and not a proper use of it.[22]

One of the recurring complaints voiced by some today is that visitors are "turned off" by Lutheran liturgical worship. If this observation has validity in one place or another, the question must be asked if it is the liturgy that offends or the way the liturgy is done. If we have in fact failed to put our best efforts into worship, this is a matter that needs to be addressed. There is no justification for slipshod preparation or execution of the liturgy. What Francis Rossow wrote about preaching applies also to presiding at the liturgy:

> The foolishness of preaching consists in its content, not its style. What is foolish is our message, not the manner of communicating the message. The foolishness of preaching does not necessitate foolish preaching.[23]

It is not enough for Lutherans to hide behind a book or a liturgical form expecting the unchurched to drop into the pews informed about and appreciative of the liturgy.[24] We need to work at presenting the liturgy in a way that neither confuses nor confounds the visitor or new Christian. Examine some worship bulletins and you will find an array of directions, references, and technical jargon decipherable only to the active member of long standing. We need to use common sense and carefully present the liturgy so that its use is a joy instead of a burden.

No congregation can do all things well. Choose carefully what can be done well and build upon it. A simple, spoken liturgy is better than an elaborately sung liturgy that is done poorly. If the liturgy requires too many explanations, page turns, or verbal directions, it will distract and frustrate even the informed worshiper. Especially in the

---

[22]Larry Peters, "Lutheran Worship and Church Growth," an essay prepared for and distributed by the Lutheran Church—Missouri Synod's Commission on Worship.

[23]Francis Rossow, *Preaching the Creative Gospel Creatively* (St. Louis: Concordia, 1983) p. 14.

[24]Some of the thoughts in the following few paragraphs are drawn from the previously cited essay of Larry Peters.

new mission, printing out the liturgy and hymns each week may be an important key to the success of the service. Care must be taken, however, not to infringe on copyright regulations.

We need to take special care with the music of the service, since music plays a vital part in Lutheran worship and involves the congregation directly. Choose hymns and choral music with care. Choose them for what they say, for the way they support the theme of the day, for the way the melody supports the text, and with an eye toward the musical ability of the parish musicians and congregational singers. It may be wise that, for the sake of the visitor (or recent convert, for that matter), the choice of hymns for the day include one or two hymns that are of the more familiar variety. A good place for familiar hymns is at the opening and the close of the service.

Preachers need to recognize and put into practice the difference between preaching law and gospel and merely preaching *about* law and gospel. A good sermon will not only appeal to the intellect but will also paint pictures upon the canvass of the heart. Sermons should not be directed only to the emotions, of course, but Lutheran preachers perhaps need the reminder to preach to the heart as well as to the head. Preachers also need to watch their vocabulary. Technical jargon can go over the head of many a member, not to mention a visitor to the service. Good preaching, like good liturgy, is seldom an accident. Both require hard work.

Strive for a warm and caring worship atmosphere

What the congregation *gives* to the visitor is of prime importance. How the congregation *treats* the visitor is of secondary importance. The gospel is more important than the atmosphere in which the gospel is proclaimed. Yet there is a correlation between the two. Visitors whose Sunday morning experience leaves them with the impression that no one really cared about them are less likely to return than those for whom the hour of worship was a more positive experience. We want unchurched people to come to church, and we want them to come back because we know we have what they need. A congregation that knows it exists not just for itself, but for all in the community who need to hear the message it is proclaiming, will strive to make every visitor feel welcome.

Perhaps it is beneficial to view the worship experience as a first-time visitor might perceive it:

> When we drove up to the church, I was impressed immediately by the appearance of the property. The lawn was mowed, the

shrubbery was trimmed, the paint job was new. I figured that the members of the congregation must take pride in their building because the place obviously had received a lot of tender loving care.

I knew we were going to get to the church without a whole lot of time to spare, and I was hoping I wouldn't have to park so far away that I'd be late. When I drove into the parking lot to drop off Cara and Ben (my wife and three-year-old), I was delighted to see some empty parking spaces marked "Visitors." They were located near the main entrance, right next to several spaces reserved for the handicapped. I was impressed again when I saw a ramp leading to a side entrance. My thought was, "This church thinks of everyone."

The three of us entered the main lobby and several people greeted us with handshakes and smiles. Cara asked about a nursery. One of the people who greeted us volunteered to show us the room where the nursery was already in session. It was a neat, clean room staffed by an adult and a couple of teenage girls. They were nice to us and very nice to Ben. He was actually happy to stay when we left.

An usher stood at the door of the main part of the church. He offered us a program (the pastor kept calling it a service folder) and escorted us to our seats. I was relieved the usher hadn't dragged us way up to the front, and I was impressed that the people sitting at the end of the pew didn't make us crawl over them. They moved and gave Cara and me plenty of room to sit. I noticed immediately an in-bench speaker system for the hearing impaired.

The service folder was neat, sharp, and friendly—not like some of the folders I had seen in other churches we had visited. I grabbed a hymnal out of the book rack in front of me; it looked pretty intimidating. When I took a closer look at the folder, I noticed that it gave an outline of the service and directions for using the book.

It was just 10:30 when the organ stopped playing and the pastor walked into the altar area. He welcomed everyone and announced the theme for the day's service. What he said was short and sweet and just enough to make it clear what was going to be happening.

I found some things in Lutheran worship to be different from what I had experienced in my own church. Three of the hymns were brand new to me (Cara knew one of them), but the congregation did quite well and appeared to enjoy singing. In fact, I must say, the singing really reverberated throughout the church building.

I definitely was not used to all the standing and sitting these Lutherans did. The hymnal was helpful, however, and pretty easy to follow. There were a couple of times when I wasn't at all sure where we were, but the people sitting next to us noticed that we were a little confused and quietly pointed out the right page in the book.

The thing about the service that impressed me the most was the sermon. I knew Cara was impressed, too, because she never opened her purse for a piece of gum! What I really liked was that the pastor based everything he said on the Bible; he didn't give all sorts of personal opinions. He was easy to follow and spoke in a down-to-earth way. I didn't understand everything he said, but he said a lot that made me think. In fact, I'm still thinking about it.

After the service the pastor welcomed everybody again, especially the visitors, and invited everyone to stay for a cup of coffee and some refreshments. He was very friendly when we saw him at the door. He introduced us to a young couple about our age who talked with us a little and asked us to sign a guest register. When we told them we had to pick up Ben at the nursery, they offered to walk along. They invited us for a cup of coffee and introduced us to some people who were friends of theirs. They also invited us for coffee (Lutherans are really into food!).

A few days later we received a hand-written note from the pastor and a little card from the couple we met. Neither was anything big, just a few sentences saying they were glad we could come and inviting us to come again. The pastor volunteered to stop over and answer any questions we might have. On Wednesday another couple from the congregation stopped at our house. They didn't insist on coming in (we invited them in anyway) but just wanted us to know how pleased they were that we had worshiped in their church.

A warm and caring worship atmosphere as illustrated above obviously is not the most important part of a congregation's outreach strategy. The efficacy of the gospel is not dependent on the friendliness of a congregation, the upkeep of its property, the availability of parking, a church nursery, or other such externals. It is true, however, that congregations demonstrate concern and love for visitors not only in the message they offer but in the way they offer the message. First impressions count. Negative impressions discourage visitors from returning. Positive impressions do not guarantee that a visitor will be won for Christ, of course, but they may bring a person back to hear the gospel a second time. Who can know on which visit the Holy Spirit will work his great work of conversion?

A congregation is wise, therefore, to concern itself about such things as

- appearance of the church property
- adequate parking
- directional signs
- concern for the handicapped
- church acoustics, including assistance for the hearing-impaired
- the worship folder or bulletin
- the work of the ushers and greeters
- a staffed nursery
- a system for recording the visits of newcomers
- a good system for timely follow-up
- a general congregational atmosphere that says to the visitor, "We're glad you're here and look forward to seeing you again"

The pastor and members of the evangelism committee will want to remind the members of the congregation from time to time about the importance of maintaining an evangelism mindset during the Sunday hour of worship. It's natural, for example, that members look forward to visiting with each other after the service. They may be so happy to see friends that visitors are inadvertently ignored. These problems can be addressed casually and easily at church council meetings, meetings of the various groups in the congregations, and Bible classes. Members who love the lost will appreciate the gentle reminder to keep hearts open and eyes out for visitors who come to worship.

In summary, Lutheran liturgical worship,

- when its strengths are emphasized and its balances maintained,
- when it is carefully planned and artfully executed by the congregation's leaders and enthusiastically entered upon by the congregation's members,
- when it is accompanied by a congregational mindset that opens wide its arms to the visitor to its services,

has served and can continue to serve as a good tool for congregational outreach with the gospel.

What about alternate worship forms?

In the foregoing we have brought out that Lutheran worship leaves much room for wholesome variety within the continuity of the liturgy. The propers (lessons, psalms, prayers, hymns) change from week to week. There can also be variation in the ordinary (the unchangeable parts of the service, e.g., the confession and absolution, the creed, the various songs of the liturgy).[25]

In certain situations and in certain areas, however, congregations may come to the conclusion that their evangelism program would benefit from an occasional simplified service prepared especially with the inquirer in mind. Some congregations call it a *Friendship Sunday.*

Preparation for a Friendship Sunday begins several weeks before the Sunday with an encouragement to members to bring unchurched friends to church on that particular Sunday.

The pastor might depart from the church year calendar on Friendship Sunday and preach on a simple law/gospel text that clearly sets out God's way of salvation. The hymns will be very familiar, for example "Amazing Grace" or "Beautiful Savior." The entire order of service will be printed in the service folder, including perhaps even the hymns. The liturgy will be set aside for that Sunday and be replaced by a basic progression of lessons and hymn stanzas. A sample order of service follows:

Greeting by the pastor

Opening hymn (Choose a hymn of praise here and have the congregation stand for the last stanza.)

---

[25]An entire section of hymns in *Christian Worship: A Lutheran Hymnal,* for example, is entitled "Hymns of the Liturgy" (Nos. 262-278). Worship leaders may substitute these hymns (or others) for various parts of the ordinary.

Invocation (e.g., "We worship God the Father who created us; we worship God the Son, our Lord Jesus Christ, who saved us from our sins; we worship God the Holy Spirit who causes us to believe and to live our lives for Christ.")

Responsive Psalm (spoken)

Hymn stanza (The hymn stanzas that follow the psalm and lessons need not come from the same hymn; but it might be well for them to be accompanied by the same well-known tune. Have the congregation be seated after this stanza.)

Lesson

Hymn stanza

Lesson

Hymn stanza

Gospel (Announce the reason for standing at this point. "We stand to hear the words of Jesus Christ.")

Apostles' Creed (The congregation is seated after the Creed.)

Choir anthem

Hymn (a well-known hymn)

Sermon

Offering (An announcement may be made that visitors should not feel obligated to participate in the offering, which supports the mission of the congregation.)

Responsive Prayer of the Church

Lord's Prayer (The traditional version seems the best choice here.)

Hymn (another well-known hymn)

Prayer (Have the congregation stand for the prayer, blessing, and hymn.)

Blessing (Perhaps an alternate to the Aaronic Blessing is in place.)

Closing hymn stanzas (another hymn of praise)

Announcements (invitation to a coffee hour; welcome to return)

The Friendship Sunday concept has some obvious advantages, especially for visitors. They hear a simple and clear proclamation of law and gospel. The service excludes what might be difficult for one or another guest, e.g., an unfamiliar liturgy and difficult hymns. The concept also has advantages for the members of the congregation. Especially in congregations with little past evangelism experience, the Friendship Sunday can help raise mission awareness and encourages action.

There are, however, some disadvantages to the Friendship Sunday concept. For one thing, not all barriers can be eliminated for every visitor. One guest may enjoy simple hymns; another will find the simple hymns demeaning and trite. One guest may enjoy the simple sermon; another will find it intellectually unchallenging. Some visitors may be attracted by the very basic order of service; others may find it empty.

Other disadvantages may accrue to the congregation itself. A once-a-year or twice-a-year Friendship Sunday may tend to compartmentalize evangelism efforts, as though witnessing for Christ is something a Christian does only at specific times. It may give members the idea that the only time to bring friends is on a Friendship Sunday and therefore may discourage them from "striking while the iron is hot." Finally, it may deter the development of an everyday evangelism mindset, since members may conclude that they need to work at evangelism only for certain Sundays of the year.

None of these disadvantages is implicit in the Friendship Sunday concept, but they need to be considered as the idea of a Friendship Sunday is discussed by pastors and evangelism committees.[26]

Another worship format that has evangelism in mind is the so-called Seeker Service. Popularized and propagated by Willow Creek Community Church, a large, growing congregation in suburban Chicago, the Seeker Service (although not necessarily called by that name) is the regular worship format of many of America's megachurches. Some have estimated that as many as 1,000 Lutheran congregations have adopted the concept as well.

Its detractors call the Seeker Service "entertainment evangelism." Some of its practitioners don't hesitate to use that label themselves.[27] Everything is eliminated that is liable to make one or another guest feel uncomfortable or threatened. An objective in the minds of many is to make Christianity appealing, attractive, and relevant to anyone

---

[26]A suggested resource for those contemplating or planning a Friendship Sunday: the *Friendship Witnessing Manual* (NPH).

[27]Cf. the enthusiastic endorsement of "Entertainment Evangelism" by Walther P. Kallestad in *The Lutheran,* May 23, 1990, p. 17.

disassociated from or dissatisfied with traditional Christianity. The Seeker Service seems to be especially aimed at young and middle-aged Americans from the middle and upper classes.

The Seeker Service is different from Friendship Sunday in several ways.

- The Friendship Service sets aside the liturgy but not traditional elements of Christian worship. Sermons, hymns, prayers are retained. The Seeker Service often employs non-traditional forms of communication such as drama, puppet shows, testimonials, and staged musical ensembles. The service usually consists of a series of "acts" which are "performed" for the "audience." Kallestad writes: "When people come to Community Church of Joy on Sunday morning, they have fun. We may have a stage band, comedians, clowns, dramas, mini-concerts and productions, high energy choreography, as well as many other entertainment forms."[28] The preacher delivers a religious talk rather than a text-based sermon.
- The order of service used on a Friendship Sunday remains participatory in character. Though simplified, the service involves a presiding minister as well as worshipers. The Seeker Service tends to be very one-sided. The worshipers are passive for the most part; they may become involved in a hymn or a prayer.
- The Friendship Service keeps worship within a traditional worship setting. There are pews and organ, altar and pulpit. The Seeker Service works best in an auditorium or theater setting. The ideal worship space is wide rather than long, seats are individual and comfortable, there is a stage rather than an altar, and the pastor speaks from a small podium (often made of plexiglass to avoid the "pulpit" look) dressed in a business suit rather than a liturgical vestment. Many congregations design their churches specifically for the Seeker Service concept. Some contemporary church designs are able to be adapted for either a traditional service or the Seeker Service.
- Although the Friendship Service may include religious music in a contemporary style, the Seeker Service places strong emphasis (in many cases exclusive emphasis) on Christian con-

[28] *Ibid.*

temporary music. The music is purposely in the style of the popular music preferred by young, white, middle-class Americans and is invariably performed by soloists or small ensembles accompanied by piano, guitar, flute, and drums.

The Seeker Service, as it is currently practiced in America's megachurches, fits in well with the Arminian theology most of them practice. In Arminian theology, the key to conversion is not using the means of grace to effect a change of heart (the classic Lutheran understanding) but convincing and compelling the free will to make the change itself.

Revivalism became the American manifestation of Arminianism. Charles Finney (1792–1875), the preeminent revivalist, set down revivalistic theology on the subject of conversion: "A revival is not a miracle or dependent on a miracle in any sense. It is a purely philosophic result of the right use of means."[29] Finney's most famous means for conversion was the classic tent meeting. The tent meeting concept with its fiery sermon, emotional hymns, and altar calls, originally took place in an actual tent, but eventually moved into mainline church buildings. Dwight Moody, Billy Sunday, and Billy Graham are all the spiritual descendants of Charles Finney, and all share the same theological point of view: If the mind and emotions of human beings can be touched in the right way, they will choose to add themselves to the Christian community.

Finney's revivalistic theology finds a counterpart in the Seeker Service in today's neo-evangelical churches, though in a more refined way. The gospel is proclaimed at the Seeker Service, but not as a means by which the Spirit miraculously draws people into the church. The gospel is proclaimed rather as a reasonable and reassuring thing one might be wise to believe. The accompanying ambiance, style, and enthusiasm serve primarily to make the gospel more appealing and attractive, and whatever negates the reasonable and reassuring nature of this gospel is eliminated.

It should also be noted that the gospel of neo-evangelicalism is more often the story of a moral God than a saving God. God is portrayed not so much as one who gives life through Christ's blood atonement, as one who makes life better for those who become followers of Christ. Such a "theology of glory" appeals to people living in an age of secularization, individualism, and instant gratification—a

---

[29]Michael Scott Horton, *Made In America: The Shaping of Modern American Evangelicalism* (Grand Rapids: Baker, 1991), p. 60.

mindset inimical to true worship, to say nothing of a scriptural theology of the cross.

Given these theological underpinnings, is it possible for Lutherans to adapt the Seeker Service concept or any portions thereof within the parameters of Lutheran theology? Any congregation that is giving thought to putting the concept to use must be willing to ask and answer questions such as the following:

- What barriers will have to be removed in a Lutheran Seeker Service? Is it only the external liturgical trappings that cause problems for visitors (e.g., vestments, organ music, pews, etc.) or is it doctrinal content that repels? Some assume it is the format of the Seeker Service that draws visitors to the megachurches in such amazing numbers. In fact, it may be theological emphases (and, in some cases, the lack of them, e.g., no mention of sin, condemnation, blood atonement) that so many find attractive. What confessional Lutheran congregation in an effort to attract the lost in a Seeker Service will want to sacrifice exactly what it knows converts the lost!

- Can the Seeker Service avoid trivializing the gospel? Are Kallestad's clowns and comedians the appropriate vehicle for the greatest story ever told? Lutheran musician Carl Schalk reminds us:

  > We do not come to worship to shape it to our own ends, but to be shaped by God who calls us together to hear his word and share his meal. . . . Calls for a more pragmatic consumer-oriented worship and church music are more concerned with sociology and psychology than with theology. The claim that such approaches are theologically neutral is sheer nonsense. The medium is the message; there is a close connection between what we believe and how it is expressed and celebrated, whether in word, action or music.[30]

- Since the ambiance of the Seeker Service depends a great deal on contemporary Christian music, congregations need to ask, "How much of Christian contemporary music is usable?" Much of what is available from evangelical music publishers simply does not tell the story of Christ. It speaks of wrongs but not guilt, majesty but not mercy, goodness but not grace.

---

[30]Carl Schalk, "Church Music in the '90s: Problems and Prognoses," *The Christian Century,* March 21-28, 1990, p. 308.

Proponents of this music insist that there are some good contemporary Christian texts, and they are right; but those who choose the texts must exercise careful discernment.

Space constraints prevent us from saying much about the *music* of Christian contemporary music. Suffice it to say at this point that it, too, needs to be evaluated with care. Music in Christian worship should not be drawing attention to itself. The gospel it conveys, not the music, is what needs to be brought to the heart. The critical factor in church music, therefore, is to make the text predominant and the music subservient. To put the music ahead of the message militates against the biblical means of grace theology, which insists that the Spirit works in the heart only through the means of grace.

- Does the congregation have the ability to present contemporary Christian music and dramatic presentations well? Often these means of communication take a high degree of talent and skill. A service that is nothing more than a meager imitation does nothing to attract visitors.
- How will visitors be moved from the Seeker Service into the mainstream of Lutheran worship? If guests are attracted by the non-participatory and entertainment-oriented Seeker Service, will they really be eager to attend to the "work" of Lutheran liturgical worship?
- Is the desire for a Seeker Service prompted by honest evangelistic interests or by anti-liturgical interests within the congregation itself? It is noteworthy that many evangelicals are moving away from their non-liturgical moorings. An evangelical writer, Eugene Peterson, laments regarding much of evangelical worship:

> A Freudian pleasure principle is substituted and worship is misused to harness God to human requirements. Worship is falsified into being a protective cover for self-seeking. . . . We may be entertained, warmed, diverted, or excited in such worship; we will probably not be changed, and we will not be saved.[31]

---

[31]Eugene Peterson, *Five Smooth Stones for Pastoral Work* (Richmond: John Knox Press, 1980), p. 145 (Quoted by John Pless in the article, "Liturgy As Evangelistic Outreach," in *The Confessional Lutheran Research Society Newsletter* Epiphany 1992—Letter No. 26, p. 3).

Lutherans would be well-advised to think twice before stepping in the direction of that from which some in the evangelical world are already beginning to back away.[32]

- Does a desire to conduct a Seeker Service with all of its trappings stem from a lack of confidence in the power of the means of grace? Does the congregation think that to attract and to hold newcomers it must use gimmicks, that it must entertain rather than edify through proclamation of law and gospel? Or, in genuine concern for the spiritual level of the inquirer, has the congregation made the decision to offer a service that the novice to Christianity will more readily grasp, a service that still centers on the means of grace, but in a simplified "milk" rather than "meat" format?

These are the kinds of questions that need to be openly raised and honestly answered by those Lutherans who are considering a Seeker Service for their evangelism efforts. Although it must be said that congregations may in Christian freedom utilize at least certain features of this outreach method, we are not convinced that the advantages of such a service outweigh the liabilities.

To repeat what was said earlier, we are convinced that Lutheran liturgical worship,

- when its strengths are emphasized and its balances maintained,
- when it is carefully planned and artfully executed by the congregation's leaders and enthusiastically entered by the congregation's members,
- when it is accompanied by a congregational mindset that opens wide its arms to the visitor to its services,

has served and can continue to serve as a good tool for congregational outreach with the gospel.

Education and evangelism

We want to look briefly now at two more elements of the congregation's program from an outreach perspective. A congregation with a

---

[32]Cf. also Robert Webber, *Celebrating our Faith: Evangelism Through Worship* (San Francisco: Harper and Row, 1986); and Michael Scott Horton, *Made in America: The Shaping of Modern American Evangelicalism, op. cit.*

corporate mission mindset will naturally be concerned that its educational agencies, as well as its organizations, take outreach into consideration when planning and executing their programs.

Sunday school and Sunday morning Bible class

Most people, including the unchurched, want to instill in their children some kind of values on which they can build their lives. That is one reason why they often will send their children to Sunday school, even though they themselves may not attend church. This underscores the importance of the Sunday school in a congregation's overall approach to the unchurched.

In many congregations, especially those privileged to operate a Lutheran elementary school (LES), the Sunday school tends to be somewhat neglected. The congregation's board of education often must spend a considerable amount of time discussing the affairs of the LES in its meetings, with the result that not much quality time is devoted to the Sunday school. Sometimes, because the workings of the LES demand so much time and energy, not much care is expended in choosing Sunday school teachers and providing ongoing training.

In addition, many congregations that operate an LES do not actively encourage the children of the school to attend the Sunday school. In some congregations, in fact, a strong tradition has been established over the years that LES children do not attend Sunday school. Any number of reasons are advanced for this tradition, e.g., the Sunday school simply repeats what the children have already learned in the LES, and the children of the LES, with their daily training in the Word of God, will intimidate the non-LES children in the Sunday school. Therefore, the reasoning goes, it is better for the LES children not to be in the Sunday school.

This tradition has a number of negative consequences. Among them, children of the LES do not develop the habit of coming together for study of the Word on Sunday morning, making it much more difficult to transition them into teen and adult Bible class after they graduate from the LES. In addition, if these children stay home during the Sunday school hour, it is likely that their parents will do the same, with a resultant weakening of the adult Bible study program of a congregation.

There are also some specific outreach-related ramifications:

- In some instances unchurched adults may be more inclined to accept an invitation to attend a Sunday Bible class than a church service. Obviously, members who are not participating in the Bible class themselves are not in a good position to be inviting their unchurched friends to come with them.

- More often than not, unchurched children will find their way into a congregation's Sunday school through the invitation of their friends in the neighborhood. Children of the congregation who themselves are not attending Sunday school are depriving themselves of a prime way of introducing their unchurched friends to the Savior.
- Bible class and Sunday school are also the most likely setting for training members for personal evangelism in the community.

It is worth a congregation's while to devote quality time to a vital Sunday morning program of Christian education for all ages and for all families of the congregation, whether or not the children are in the LES. Many congregations have successfully blended both non-LES and LES children in the Sunday school. Teachers can be trained and the curriculum can be coordinated to surmount the obstacles discussed above.

There is also evangelistic value in a twelve-month program of Christian education in the congregation. Many congregations slow down considerably during the summer months. Some discontinue Sunday school and Bible class by the end of May and don't start up again until the middle of September. A number of arguments are advanced in favor of such a practice. Attendance drops so drastically in the summer, it is said, that there doesn't seem to be a compelling reason to continue during this time. Proponents of closing down the congregation's program of Christian education during summer also point out that this gives the teachers some much-needed time off.

Simply from the perspective of the need for the ongoing nurture of the believer, it would not be difficult to make a good case for the value of a year-round program of Christian education. Just because the numbers are fewer due to summer vacations doesn't invalidate the worth of offering Sunday school and Bible class for those who are not on vacation. Teacher "burnout" can be addressed by engaging substitute teachers during all or a portion of the summer months.

There are also some direct outreach-related benefits in a congregation conducting a year-round program of Christian education. For one thing, if there are children in the Sunday school whose parents are still unchurched, the Sunday school is the one tie the church has to these children—and through them to their parents. Congregations that close down their Sunday school for three months will find that they lose a good percentage of such children over that time period and must start all over in fall. Second, most moving, especially of families, takes place in the summer months. Congregations with an outreach mindset will naturally be interested in reaching families new to the community and inviting them to visit their church. Again, it is not difficult to see the value of having a full-scale program in operation also during the summer to which newcomers may be invited.

There is also merit from an outreach perspective in congregations offering a Sunday morning "entry level" course designed for the inquirer. Some congregations have found it helpful to conduct their basic Bible information (pre-membership) class on Sunday morning. This may be the one time that most prospects are available in suburban America. People who attend this class, in addition to learning the fundamentals of the Christian faith, begin to develop the habit of participating in a Sunday morning Bible class. It is not a big step to move from this class to another upon completion of it. For that matter, since in most congregations there is a wide variation in knowledge of the Scriptures on the part of the members, it would be helpful to be able to offer options also for members. We will have more to say about this in the final chapter.

Vacation Bible school

A summer vacation Bible school (VBS) can be an excellent tool for reaching the unchurched children of a community. In general, the congregations that benefit most from the outreach potential of a VBS are those that intentionally aim at reaching the unchurched through their VBS.

Such congregations choose the dates for the VBS with one primary question in mind: At what time in the summer will we be most apt to attract unchurched children to our VBS? Experience has shown that often the best time is near the end of summer when children are beginning to look forward to getting back into a more structured kind of environment.

Congregations that plan to use VBS as an outreach tool will publicize it, not just within the congregation, but throughout the community or throughout the portion of the community in the neighborhood of the church. Some congregations, for example, annually blanket the homes around the church with member-distributed invitations to the VBS. The result has been a large number of unchurched children in attendance year after year.

A congregation with an outreach-oriented VBS will take special care in the selection of teachers and will seek to prepare them thoroughly. It will also provide guidance in working with the unchurched. Some congregations with Lutheran elementary schools, looking for the very best in teaching to bring the message of salvation to those who may never have heard it before, utilize the teachers of the school for their VBS.

An outreach-oriented VBS does not, or at least should not, end with the final day of VBS. Follow-up on unchurched children who attend the VBS is essential and needs to be a part of the overall plan. The best initial follow-up will generally be by the child's VBS teacher. It will be helpful to give the teachers some basic assistance in follow-up procedures as a part of their pre-VBS training.

Planning materials are available for congregations who desire to use the VBS as an outreach tool, with suggested timetables, checklists, etc.[33] As with most other congregational programs, outreach won't just happen. It needs to be consciously factored in and then carefully implemented.

Lutheran elementary school

Some congregations have found the Lutheran elementary school to be a good outreach tool. During most of the years I served as a parish pastor in San Jose, California, about one-half of the adult converts in the congregation came through contacts initiated by the LES. Our school attracted many of the unchurched people of the community because they hoped it would meet some concerns they felt were not being properly addressed in the public school. They were looking for such things as discipline, inculcation of moral values, and personal concern for students on the part of the teachers. They weren't looking for the "one thing needful," since unbelievers don't know what the "one thing needful" is. Therefore, when we enrolled their children in our school, we were able to give the children much more than the parents ever expected. And, in time, we also were able to bring that same message of forgiveness, new life, and salvation to a majority of the parents.

From our experience over the years of using the LES, not just as a nurturing, but also as a mission arm of the church, we developed a number of guidelines that can help congregations avoid some pitfalls:

---

[33]Cf. *Step by Step through VBS* (NPH).

1. *Be properly motivated.*
   It is not numbers or the financial assistance that tuition students bring that should lead a congregation to open the doors of the school to the unchurched, but rather a concern for souls who could benefit from the message of salvation the school is privileged to teach.

2. *Emphasize your philosophy, aims, and purposes.*
   Make sure that they are written in your school handbook and carefully go through them with the parents of prospective students.

3. *Present the message of salvation to the family.*
   Do this for two reasons: Out of concern for the souls of the family and to make clear to the parents the basic Bible message their children will be learning.

4. *Discuss doctrinal differences.*
   Be completely open with people so they know what their children will be learning and that we will not permit children in the classroom to argue for other home-taught views regarding baptism, creation, etc.

5. *Do careful screening.*
   Often parents seek out a private school solely because their child hasn't been able to get along anywhere else or has certain needs that require teachers with specialized training. Our schools may not be equipped to handle some of these students.

6. *Make clear the way the school operates.*
   People need to know right at the outset how our schools are administered, the place of the school board and the principal, the way to handle grievances, how children are disciplined, etc.

7. *Expect church and Sunday school attendance on the children's part.*
   Make it clear that the exhibition of little involvement in church and Sunday school is grounds for re-evaluation of enrollment for the next year.

8. *Secure agreement to participate in the Bible information class.*
   We cannot expect that all people will join upon completion of the class; but we can expect them to attend it. Failure to

do so is also grounds for re-evaluation of enrollment for the next year.

9. *Specify an annual enrollment.*
   Make it clear that all non-members' children are enrolled on an annual basis only. Possible grounds for dismissal: failure to attend the Bible information class, non-existent or extremely poor church or Sunday school attendance, or severe discipline and/or academic problems in the classroom.

10. *Take care how you advertise.*
    Don't give the impression that you need students. Make it clear that you are selective, that non-members' children may be enrolled only if they meet the criteria we set. People should clearly realize that they are not doing us a favor but that we are doing them a favor by enrolling their children in our school.

11. *Keep non-member families informed about church events.*
    A chief concern should be to attempt to draw the unchurched mission families into the congregational fellowship. Keep them informed about congregational functions (special services, etc.) through mailings, notes from school, articles in the school newsletter, etc.

12. *Maintain a close relationship with the pastor and/or evangelism committee.*
    When the principal makes calls on unchurched mission families who have applied for school enrollment, he should make sure he records a summary of his call and gets it into the hands of the pastor and/or evangelism committee who can then make follow-up calls.

13. *Remember these are souls for whom Jesus died.*
    This may be the one way that they will be brought into contact with the message of salvation. Therefore, we will want to look upon these children and their parents as wonderful opportunities the Lord places before us and do all we can to lead these children and their parents out of darkness into God's marvelous light.

Using the Lutheran elementary school as an outreach agency of the congregation provides one more opportunity for the congregation to respond to our Lord's Great Commission. In some situations the LES, within the framework of such guidelines as listed above, has been, and can be for others, a marvelous vehicle for touching the lives of children and their parents with the saving gospel of Jesus Christ.

The LES can also provide an excellent opportunity for children to be trained for personal witness. An *Evangelism Handbook for Young Christians* (NPH) has been developed for just this purpose. The handbook provides a variety of evangelism projects, devotions, Bible studies, and witness training helps for preschool through junior high children.

"Fellowship" activities and evangelism

Congregational organizations, e.g., a women's or men's group, a couples' club, a youth organization, a recreational group, or a church-sponsored home Bible study group, can serve as another avenue of outreach within the congregation. Some unchurched people who would balk at an invitation to attend church might accept an invitation to join a member in an organizational activity. For some it is a less threatening first step toward the church, a sort of side door rather than front door approach. It would be good for congregational organizations to deliberately adopt an "open door" policy toward guests, to plan some activities especially with guests in mind, and then for the participants in these organizations to actively seek to bring with them some of the unchurched within their circle of friends, relatives, associates, and neighbors. Through that first step, unchurched people can be brought into contact both with Christians and with the gospel. In time, follow-up can be made to bring these individuals into the pastor's Bible information class.

Congregations with a corporate mission mindset might also encourage each of the organizations in the congregation to adopt one outreach goal each year. For example, the choir might determine to do Christmas carolling in a rest home; the Lutheran elementary school or Sunday school might sponsor a congregational mission fair; the youth group might participate in a neighborhood religious survey; the men's group might refurbish a church sign or bulletin board in need of repair; a home Bible study group might devote time to a scriptural study of how to share one's faith with a neighbor. When organizations of the congregation take the time to set annual outreach goals, they serve the dual purpose of keeping the work of outreach before the congregation and also of fostering specific evangelism activities.

Creating and sustaining a congregational mission mindset, a zeal for evangelism on the part of the individual members and on the part of the congregation as a whole, is the basic element in a congregation's overall program of outreach with the gospel. Such a zeal is implanted by the Holy Spirit through the gospel. Congregational leaders can channel that zeal and guide it in ways we have been discussing in this chapter. Then a congregation is ready for further steps such as organizing and training for outreach.

Chapter Five: Planning and Organizing for Outreach

1—The Concept of Planning

In this chapter we are going to talk about planning. In particular, our focus will be on planning for outreach in the congregation. Planning is an orderly way to move from "now" to "then," from "the way things are" to "the way things ought to be." It is not a question of whether or not one will plan (not to plan is, in fact, a plan in itself); it is rather a question of how best to plan to carry out the mission the Lord has given his church.

Christians recognize that planning has certain limitations. They are well aware that only God knows what the future holds. It is an act of arrogance to assume that we can make absolutely definite plans for the next day, much less for the next year. The Christian will always say, "If it is the Lord's will, we will . . . do this or that" (James 4:15).

We see a properly balanced approach to planning in the ministry of the apostle Paul. On his second missionary journey, for example, Paul's plan was to travel to Ephesus. But when the Lord directed him by means of a vision to bring the gospel to Macedonia, Paul willingly changed his plans in order to walk through the door for missions God had opened for him in Europe instead of Asia.

Christians today will want to approach planning in the same humble spirit Paul exhibited. Flexibility, an openness to the Lord's leading, will be one of the "givens" in the planning process of a Christian congregation.[1]

Planning applies to every area of work the Lord has entrusted to a congregation. It addresses such key questions as:

- What is it that we are called upon to do? What is our *purpose* or mission?
- Where are we right now? What is our *assessment* of our current situation?

---

[1]It may be helpful to reread the section entitled, "What do planning, goal setting, making use of statistical studies, etc., have to do with the mission of the church?" (chapter 3, p. 138ff.).

- Where should we be going? This involves establishing *objectives* and both long- and short-range *goals.*
- How will we get there? This is the *implementation* stage of planning. Certain structures may have to be set up, policies and action plans established, and timelines settled upon.
- How can we do it better next time? *Evaluation* is also a key part of a congregation's overall planning process.

Planning is an ongoing process. Mission clarification (What is God calling us to be and do?) leads to assessment (Where are we now?). Assessment leads to goal setting (Where do we want to be?). Goal setting leads to implementation (How do we intend to get there?). Implementation, upon completion, naturally leads to evaluation (To what degree did we achieve our objectives and goals? How can we do it better next time?). Evaluation leads us back to mission clarification, since we will want to make sure everything we do furthers the mission of the church. And so the cycle begins again.

Management experts speak about four basic management functions: planning, organizing, leading, and controlling.

Planning involves

- estimating the future (forecasting)
- establishing objectives and goals (the end results to be accomplished)
- programming (establishing action steps needed to reach the objectives and goals)
- developing policies (standing decisions that apply to recurrent questions)
- establishing procedures (standardized methods of performing specific work)
- scheduling (time sequencing the programming steps)
- budgeting

Organizing includes developing an organizational structure, clarifying and assigning work, and establishing relationships (who is responsible to whom).

Leading involves decision making, communicating, motivating, and selecting (recruiting) and developing (training) people.

Controlling includes establishing performance standards (position descriptions), performance measuring (by comparison with the position description), performance evaluating (by comparison with overall objectives and goals), and performance correcting (helping to see that certain things are done better the next time around).

In this and the next chapter, "Training for Outreach," we will touch upon most aspects of these four functions, all of which apply in some measure to every kind of organization, including a Christian congregation. In this chapter we will present seven steps for congregations to consider as they plan and organize themselves for congregational outreach. We do this under the assumption that the congregation, as it is being nourished regularly by the gospel in Word and sacrament, desires to reach out to its community with the gospel. We are assuming that this desire is already expressing itself to a greater or lesser degree in ways discussed in the previous chapter, e.g., the members have identified their own personal mission fields and are practicing friendship, bridge-building evangelism within these mission fields, and the congregation as a whole is intent on utilizing its worship, educational agencies, and fellowship activities not just for nurturing the believer but also for evangelizing the unbeliever.

2—The Process of Planning

The seven steps that follow are not the only way by which a congregation can plan and organize itself for the work of outreach. They have proved, however, to be beneficial to congregations. They have helped them to sharpen their focus on what needs to be done and how to go about doing it. The steps are chronological, following the planning cycle outlined above. They start with a study of the congregation's reason for existence (mission clarification). They move from there to an assessment of the congregation's current situation. They proceed to establishing objectives and goals and from there to action plans to implement what the congregation has determined to do.

Step 1: Prepare a congregational mission statement

Function and form

A mission statement is a statement of function. Function has to do with why an organization exists. An understanding of its mission is thus basic to everything a congregation does.

We need to distinguish between function and form. Form has to do with structure, with how we go about doing our work. Function, therefore, must precede form. "What" and "why" come before "how." You need to know where you are going and why you want to go there before you try to figure out how to get there.

Following his resurrection, our Lord clearly set forth the function he intended his church to serve. He did this not just once, but five times. Each of the Gospels ends with a statement of the church's function, and the book of Acts begins with one. Each is spoken directly by Jesus. "Go and make disciples of all nations, baptizing them in the name of the Father and of the Son and of the Holy Spirit, and teaching them to obey everything I have commanded you" (Matthew 28:19,20). "Go into all the world and preach the good news to all creation" (Mark 16:15). "Repentance and forgiveness of sins will be preached in his name to all nations, beginning at Jerusalem" (Luke 24:47). "As the Father has sent me, I am sending you. . . . If you forgive anyone his sins, they are forgiven; if you do not forgive them, they are not forgiven (John 20:21,23). "You will be my witnesses in Jerusalem, and in all Judea and Samaria, and to the ends of the earth" (Acts 1:8). Knowing what they were called to do, the believers of the early church could then determine how to go about doing it. Function precedes form.

A second principle: function is more important than form. Another way of putting it: mission is more important than method. What one is doing and why one is doing it is more important than how one goes about accomplishing it.

The prophet Micah recognized this truth. He writes, "With what shall I come before the LORD and bow down before the exalted God? Shall I come before him with burnt offerings, with calves a year old? Will the LORD be pleased with thousands of rams, with ten thousand rivers of oil? Shall I offer my firstborn for my transgression, the fruit of my body for the sin of my soul? He has showed you, O man, what is good. And what does the LORD require of you? To act justly and to love mercy and to walk humbly with your God" (Micah 6:6-8). Israel had reversed the proper order. The form, the outward sacrifices, had become more important than the function, true worship of God from the heart. In New Testament times, the Pharisees did the same. They felt compelled to defend the structure of the Jewish worship of the day, but they had lost sight of its purpose. For them, too, form had become more important than function, while just the opposite is true.

Third, function must be served by form, not the other way around. Structure is meant to serve mission. When one has determined from Scripture the mission the Lord has assigned to his church, then one seeks to establish forms and structure that will serve the mission.

The account in Acts 6 is a good example of this principle at work. In their love for one another, the early Christians had established a "food pantry" through which the poor in their midst, especially the widows, could be supported. A dispute arose, however, between the foreign-born, Greek-speaking widows and the native, Aramaic-speaking widows. The Greek-speaking widows complained that they were being overlooked in the daily distribution of food. In their response to the problem, the apostles revealed their understanding of the principle that function needs to be served by form. Waiting on tables was getting in the way of the church's mission of proclaiming the soul-saving gospel. So the apostles recommended that godly men be chosen to superintend the distribution of food while they continued to give their attention "to prayer and the ministry of the word" (v. 4). Thus, the apostles set up a structure, a form, that would serve the function of the church. It worked. The account closes with the words, "So the word of God spread. The number of disciples in Jerusalem increased rapidly, and a large number of priests became obedient to the faith" (v. 7). Function is served by form, not vice versa.

A fourth guiding principle: function is changeless, while form needs to be flexible. Three of Paul's mission messages have been preserved for us in the book of Acts: his sermon at Antioch in Pisidia (Acts 13), his message to the Lycaonians in Lystra (Acts 14), and his address to the philosophers in Athens (Acts 17). Because of the differing circumstances, the form of his presentation varied from place to place. Yet the heart of the message did not vary. He was Christ's "chosen instrument" to carry Christ's name before the Gentiles (Acts 9:15). That was his function. That could not change. What could and should change was the form, if failure to do so hindered fulfillment of the function.

A statement of function such as a congregational mission statement will be rooted in the never-changing truths of Scripture about God's mission for his church. It will be a clear, precise, biblical delineation of what God is calling his people to do. Forms established to carry out that mission will vary from age to age and from place to place.

Value of a mission statement

Several factors underscore the value of a congregational mission statement:

Without a clear sense of mission

- it is difficult to know where you are going. The church goes about its business as usual, but may be unclear as to what its business is. When there is no clear sense of mission, forms, traditions, and structures tend to be preserved for their own sake. People need to know and agree on what they are trying to do or they will tend to do little, or even at times find themselves working at cross purposes.

- it is difficult to plan. The important keeps getting overshadowed by the urgent. The significant tends to be replaced by the pressing need of the moment, with the result that the important keeps getting relegated to a "to do when we finally have time" list.
- it is difficult to evaluate. How do you know whether or not you have arrived, if you haven't figured out where you are going? Busyness is not always an indication that a congregation is progressing well in the Lord's business.
- it is difficult to maintain momentum in a congregation. It is difficult to become and remain excited about the ministry of one's congregation if that ministry hasn't been clearly defined. Many a congregation has experienced a dramatic drop of zeal and enthusiasm following a church building program. In part, at least, this may be attributable to a failure of the congregation to articulate a clear sense of mission. If the mission is to build a church building, then, when the building is completed, the mission is also completed. If the mission is to build the Church with the gospel in Word and sacrament, then constructing a sanctuary is seen as just a step along the way in achieving the mission. The building may be completed, but the mission continues.
- it is difficult to maintain congregational morale. Every little setback tends to be viewed as a major defeat. A feeling of pessimism begins to set in. The congregation can easily become defensive, develop a "siege mentality," and, like a turtle, retreat into its shell.

On the other hand, with a clear, scriptural sense of mission

- the congregation understands its reason for existence. A mission statement serves as a constant reminder to a congregation as to what it is all about and why.
- the congregation is more likely to be positive than negative in its outlook, proactive rather than reactive, people-oriented rather than program-preoccupied. It sees its mission, not as being against something, but as being *for* the Lord, his Word, his work, his people.

- congregational priorities can more easily be established. When a potential new program is being discussed, or a program of long standing is being evaluated, either can be measured against the congregation's mission statement. The question will always be, "How does this relate to our mission?"
- temporary setbacks can more easily be weathered. If a congregation has a long-range view, any crisis is then only a small obstacle, a momentary problem that the Lord will enable his people to overcome as they pursue the mission he has given them.
- the congregation is more likely to be future-oriented. Instead of looking back to the "good old days," the congregation will tend to focus its vision on the present and future to see how it can best accomplish its mission in its particular time and place.
- the congregation tends to be drawn together. A common mission of which each member sees himself or herself as a vital part helps to bind members more closely into a unified group. A sense of teamwork is experienced, as together, each using his or her own Spirit-granted gifts, the whole congregation seeks to forge ahead with the Lord's work.

Constructing a mission statement

How does a congregation go about constructing a mission statement? There is only one place to begin, with a study of the Scriptures. It is good to involve as many members as possible, since all of God's people in the congregation are a vital part of the nurture and outreach mission of the church. They are more likely to see this if they themselves grapple with the question, "Why do we exist as a congregation?" A Sunday morning Bible class series on the mission and ministry of the church would be a good way to inaugurate the process of forming a congregational mission statement.[2]

After thorough Bible study, it would be good to assign to a small group the responsibility of constructing the statement. One way to begin is to write a series of paragraphs, no matter how long, that say all the committee thinks needs to be said about why their congregation

---

[2]A suggested Bible study aid: "So I Have Sent You—A Bible Study of the Church's Mission and Ministry," by Paul Kelm, in the *Gearing Up for Evangelism* manual (NPH).

exists. These paragraphs should reflect the results of the Bible study, the input from congregational members who participated in the Bible study, and the uniqueness of the congregation. In general, all congregations will have the same mission, as passages such as those quoted above (Matthew 28:19,20; Mark 16:15, etc.) bring out. Yet no two congregations are exactly alike. The age, economic, educational, and social level of the members and of the community; the location of the congregation; even the gifts of the members, will have a part to play in the particular mission of a specific congregation. The mission statement of a congregation located in a retirement community, for example, will probably be worded somewhat differently from that of a congregation in a suburb consisting largely of young families.

When the series of paragraphs are completed, the next step is to prioritize them (which is #1, #2, etc.). Then boil each paragraph down to a few summarizing sentences. A mission statement ideally should be short and succinct.[3] Possibly the statement could be distilled into a brief, memorable phrase or sentence for use on church stationery, bulletins, banners, etc.

Then test the statement by asking such questions as: Is it biblical? This, of course, is the first and most important consideration. Does the statement summarize properly the mission the Lord has assigned to his church?

Is it clear? Does it state precisely what you want it to say in such a way that others too will clearly understand it?

Is it pointed and personalized? Does it establish parameters for your congregation's ministry, specifically identifying the mission of your congregation in your time and place?

Is it realistic? Does the statement describe what the congregation, under God, is able to accomplish?

The statement should be formally adopted by the congregation and then publicized and used. If a large number of members of the congregation were involved in the original Bible study and a good cross-section was chosen to draft the statement, it should not be difficult for the congregation as a whole to assume ownership of it. Ideally, the statement should be the measure of all plans the congregation makes and the basis for all congregational actions.

---

[3]The mission statement of the Wisconsin Evangelical Lutheran Synod, for example, is one sentence: "As men, women, and children united in faith and worship by the Word of God, the Wisconsin Evangelical Lutheran Synod exists to make disciples throughout the world for time and for eternity, using the gospel to win the lost for Christ and to nurture believers for lives of Christian service, all to the glory of God."

It is good for each board, committee, and organization in the congregation to review its program annually in light of the congregation's mission statement. The mission statement, too, should be evaluated periodically, as to its clarity and relevance to the situation of the congregation, and revised as necessary. Again the assumption, which hardly needs to be said, is that congregations will not tamper with the biblical mandate Christ has given his church. Any revisions will be in the area of how that mandate can best be carried out by a particular congregation with its particular members in its particular community.

Step 2: Conduct a congregational self-study

A self-study is an assessment of where a congregation is at the present time. It assesses congregational strengths and weaknesses. It looks at opportunities that lie before the congregation to fulfill its mission as well as obstacles that threaten the fulfillment of its mission.[4] The intent of such a careful self-analysis is to determine where a congregation stands at the present time in relation to its mission. This is also the place for a congregation to develop a community profile to help it better understand the community it is seeking to reach with the gospel.

Useful in assisting congregations in this phase of planning for outreach is *An Instrument for Congregational Self-Study* (NPH), a set of nine pamphlets that cover every area of congregational work. Part Six of this self-study instrument is on Evangelism. Other helps: "A Tool for Congregational Self-Study" and "Preparing a Community Profile."[5]

Step 3: Draw up a statement of purpose for the congregation's evangelism committee

We are assuming here that the congregation already has an evangelism committee or that the work of leading the congregation's evangelism efforts has been clearly delegated to some group within the congregation. If the congregation's structure at present does not include such provisions for evangelism leadership, that would need to be put into place before proceeding with the following steps.

Many congregations have separate evangelism committees that are directly represented on the church council.[6] In this way the work

---

[4]One approach has been called a S.W.O.T. analysis (**S**trengths, **W**eaknesses, **O**pportunities, and **T**hreats).

[5]Found in the *Gearing Up for Evangelism* manual (NPH).

[6]Cf. the Model Constitution and Bylaws for Congregations of the Wisconsin Evangelical Lutheran Synod (Milwaukee: Northwestern Publishing House, 1981).

of outreach can be kept constantly before the rest of the congregation. *The Evangelism Handbook* (NPH) contains a sample congregational structure which coordinates evangelism with other areas of congregational ministry.[7]

For a congregational evangelism committee to function properly, it needs to clearly articulate its purpose. Purpose answers the question, "Why do we exist?" The purpose of an evangelism committee, as well as every board, committee, or organization of the congregation, should flow out of the congregation's mission statement. If it does, then the work carried out under the leadership of the evangelism committee will help to fulfill the mission of the congregation.

The purpose of the evangelism committee might be stated somewhat as follows:

> The continuing purpose of the evangelism committee of ____________________ Lutheran Church is to make disciples through the power of the Spirit by identifying the lost in our community and proclaiming to them the saving gospel of Jesus Christ.

The above is only an example of what a committee might formulate. As with a congregation's mission statement, an evangelism committee's statement of purpose should not be imposed on the committee but be developed cooperatively with all members of the committee. Again, as in the case of a mission statement, the best way to begin the process is through a joint study of the Scriptures on the part of the committee.

Step 4: Determine your objectives

Once the evangelism committee has formulated a statement of purpose, then it is ready to establish its objectives. Objectives flow out of purpose. Objectives are what are required for an organization, in this case the evangelism committee, to accomplish its purpose. Objectives are long-range targets. Generally, they will be qualitative rather than quantitative, that is, they will state the kinds of things the committee will work at without going into specific detail. Objectives offer a broad-scale answer to the question, "What shall we do to accomplish our purpose?"

By way of example, we offer the following as possible objectives of a congregation's evangelism committee:

---

[7]Cf. appendix 1 of chapter 2, "Structuring the Evangelism Board or Committee."

The objectives of the evangelism committee shall be

1. To develop and maintain an evangelism mindset in our congregation
2. To search out the unchurched, especially in the congregation's "area of responsibility," in order to gain them for Christ and the church
3. To provide opportunity for all members to receive basic training in witnessing and friendship evangelism
4. To train some members for evangelism calling and through them maintain an ongoing program of evangelism visitation
5. To establish and maintain evangelism record files
6. To provide for a meaningful reception, orientation, and assimilation of new members into the congregation
7. To work closely with the board of elders in follow-up of inactive members
8. To project a positive image in the community
9. To engage in regular study of methods, programs, etc., that could benefit the congregation's program of evangelism

Step 5: Establish your goals

Goals are those achievements that help an organization carry out its objectives. If objectives answer the question, "What should we be doing to fulfill our mission?", goals answer the question, "What should we be doing to fulfill our objectives?"

Unlike objectives, goals will be quantitative and measurable. They will be narrow rather than broad in scope, specific rather than general. Setting annual goals directly related to its objectives and purpose will help the congregation's evangelism committee concentrate on a certain, manageable (and meaningful) number of activities during the course of the year. If the committee does not establish goals for itself, if it does not plan what it seeks under God to do during the year ahead, it will tend to "spin its wheels." A goal-less, plan-less committee can easily become demoralized and begin to question its reason for existence.

As stated previously (cf. chapter 3, p. 138f.), the committee needs to take care to establish goals that are in keeping with its sphere of responsibility. The committee can, and probably should, set *ministry* goals, i.e., action it intends to take; but it will not want to establish goals in terms of results, which is the province of God.

For example, the committee can plan two major visitations in the coming year of all the families on its prospect list, to be carried out immediately before the start of each of the two annual Bible information classes. It can set a goal of reaching X number of families with X number of callers. A part of the goal, however, cannot be that as a result of this concerted effort, X number of people will be brought to faith and into the fellowship of the Lutheran church. That is the work of God the Holy Spirit through the means of grace. Goals should be formulated within our God-given sphere of responsibility. Properly done, goal-setting can help give direction and momentum to the committee as it seeks to carry out its purpose and objectives.

Some practical hints for those unaccustomed to setting goals: To be most helpful, goals should be stated in terms of end results rather than in terms of the process or activities required to get to the end result. They should be achievable in a specified period of time. They should be definite rather than vague. A goal such as "in the coming year we are going to make more calls on the unchurched," does not provide much direction to the committee. Ideally, goals will be challenging, encouraging God's people to stretch a bit in the use of their time and their gifts, yet reachable. It is also good that goals be established cooperatively by the whole committee rather than dictated by the committee chairman, the pastor, or any other individual or group. Cooperatively established goals are much more likely to be "owned" by each of those involved in setting them.

Some have found it helpful to think of the acronym S.M.A.R.T. when establishing goals. S.M.A.R.T. goals are

S pecific—rather than general

M easurable—that is, quantitative rather than qualitative

A cceptable—they fit the situation both theologically and practically (people will "own" them)

R ealistic—challenging, yet achievable

T imed—subject to both intermediate and final deadlines

If, for example, an objective of the congregation's evangelism committee is to train some members for evangelism calling and through them maintain an ongoing program of evangelism visitation, a S.M.A.R.T. goal of the evangelism committee might be:

To offer ____ times within the next twelve months a training course in (name here a specific law-gospel presentation) in which at least ____ people will be enrolled.

Note that this goal is specific. It is measurable. It is timed. It is realistic, provided that the committee, drawing on past experience and present potential, inserts numbers that appear to be attainable. It is theologically acceptable; and, if a mission mindset has been established in the congregation, it will also be accepted and owned by the members.

The evangelism committee (as well as the rest of the boards and committees of the congregation) will find it helpful to think in terms of setting two kinds of goals, long-range and annual goals.

Establishing long-range goals, sometimes called strategic planning, helps the committee look at the broad picture. It is good for a congregation, and likewise its boards and committees, to ask and answer the question, "Where would we like to be, under God, five years from now?" and then to begin to take specific steps to achieve that goal.

At the same time, it is helpful for the evangelism committee to establish annual goals under the various objectives of the committee. The number of goals a committee establishes needs to be realistic, however. Setting too few goals may not challenge the congregation sufficiently in terms of expenditure of time and gifts and energy in grateful service of their Lord. On the other hand, setting too many goals can be counter-productive. It produces frustration when a committee plans to do much more than a person or group of people can accomplish in a given time.

Step 6: Develop your action plans

Action plans are the steps that need to be taken to fulfill a specific goal. The evangelism committee's statement of purpose explains *why* the committee exists. Its objectives and goals state *what* the committee proposes to do to fulfill its purpose. Action plans have to do with *how* the committee plans to bring specific goals to completion. A goal looks to the end, while action plans have to do with what needs to be done to reach that end.

An action plan needs to be put into place for every goal. Resolutions to do something (goal setting) are ineffective, obviously, unless they are carried out. For them to be accomplished, the committee needs to determine such things as, Who is going to do it? When will it be done? What resources (including funds) are needed to get it done? That is the purpose of action plans. For a simple task, the action required may be quite simple in terms of the number of people, the time, and the resources needed to fulfill it. More complex tasks, of course, will require a more complex plan of action. We list below what needs to be taken into consideration in developing an action plan:

1. *Determine the steps that need to be taken to achieve the goal.* This can often best be done by a process of brainstorming, involving everyone on the committee. Gather the committee and ask, "What has to happen before we reach this goal?" It is helpful to list all the responses on a chalkboard or flipchart. After everyone has had a chance to give input, arrive at consensus on the best path to your goal. Then arrange the steps in a time sequence. Often it is beneficial to begin with the target date, the date when everything needs to be finished, and to work back from there. That helps to determine when you need to begin if you want to be finished by the due date.

2. *Fix responsibilities.* Groups that fail to clearly delineate who is responsible for what quickly learn the truth of the old adage, "Everyone's responsibility is no one's responsibility."

3. *Anticipate obstacles and plan how to overcome them.* You probably won't catch them all, but you can catch some. When you foresee potential obstacles and therefore plan for them, you create a smoother path to the ultimate goal. The most critical obstacles tend to be on the personal level: Whom must we convince? What fears must be answered? What objections may be raised? Plans to meet and overcome such obstacles should be formulated in advance.

   In planning, it is good to anticipate even minor obstacles. For example, in most parts of our country a congregation planning an outdoor church picnic should anticipate the possibility of rain and therefore have Plan B in the wings. Or, if the evangelism committee has invited a missionary to give a slide presentation to help heighten the congregation's mission awareness, it will want to anticipate that the projector bulb may burn out and therefore have a spare on hand.

4. *Determine costs and sources of funding.* It is likely that in most congregations the costs of the planned annual programs for each board, committee, and organization are a part of the annual budget. Sometimes, however, unanticipated expenses arise. If, in seeking to implement a particular goal, e.g., plac-

ing newspaper advertisements a certain number of times a year, it is discovered that the rates have gone up since church budget time, adjustments will have to be made. Either the number or size of the advertisements will have to be reduced or additional funds will have to come from some source. At times financial considerations help to determine if a goal is truly realistic.

5. *Determine what other resources will be needed.* If, for example, a goal of the evangelism committee is to present a one-day seminar on the subject of friendship evangelism, it needs to make sure that proper facilities and equipment (e.g., overhead projector and screen, a sufficient number of tables and chairs, possibly refreshments and baby-sitting) will be available on the day of the seminar. It will also have to determine who will see to it that these resources and materials are on hand.

6. *Set target dates.* For major projects that will take some time to complete, e.g., an outreach-oriented vacation Bible school, it is wise to set, not just the final date, but several intermediate dates as well. These serve as checkpoints along the way to make sure the work is progressing well toward the completion of the goal. Intermediate checkpoints help prevent last-minute panic that can occur on the eve of the event if a number of vital items have not been completed.

7. *Establish reporting responsibilities.* Lines of accountability should be clear. Who has the overall responsibility for the project? How will he know that the work is being done? Does everyone involved report directly to him? Or are certain individuals asked to take responsibility for certain parts of the total project, including the recruitment of people to help them? Will these individuals, then, have the responsibility to keep the project leader informed about progress in their particular area of work?

8. *Develop criteria for evaluation.* How will we know if we have done what we set out to do? Clearly stated, S.M.A.R.T. goals based on carefully crafted objectives will provide such criteria.

9. *Determine follow-up procedures.* With some projects the job is not done when it appears to be done. The target date for an outreach-oriented vacation Bible school, for example, will be

the day when the vacation Bible school begins. Everything has to be ready by that date. Yet, when the vacation Bible school comes to an end, vital work still remains. Who will follow up on unchurched families who sent their children to the vacation Bible school? When will they do it? What training do they need to receive? Who will train them? What materials need to be prepared for them to take along on their visit? What will we do about the families our visitors fail to reach? Do we telephone them? Put them on a mailing list? Who will phone them? By when? When should they receive mailings? From whom? Who is responsible for getting it done? It may well require another set of action plans to assure that the goal to follow up on these families is achieved.

Another example: What happens after people, upon completion of a Bible information course, publicly confess their faith and are received into the fellowship of the congregation? What steps might, perhaps should, be taken to help assure that those who have been introduced to the basics of Christianity now continue to "grow in the grace and knowledge of [their] Lord and Savior Jesus Christ" (2 Peter 3:18)? What kind of classes might the church offer to them? How soon after their reception into membership? When will the classes be taught? Sunday mornings? A week night? A weekend seminar? What materials do we need? Who will see to it that the proper amount of material is on hand? Who will teach the classes? Who is responsible for inviting the new members to the classes? What, if anything, do we do about those who do not attend the follow-up classes? Once again, we see the value of an action plan, this time for organizing and operating a program of nurture for the new Christian in the congregation.

A person might be inclined to think that following the preceding nine steps for every goal the evangelism committee establishes is too time-consuming. "Just do it," some might say. Up to a point that is good advice. People can spend so much time planning to do something that they hardly have time to do what they planned for. On the other hand, knowing what you are going to do before you begin to do it, knowing who is going to do it, knowing if you have sufficient resources (both people and funds) to get the job done, anticipating and perhaps overcoming problems before they happen, sequencing the steps required to finish the work, determining who is responsible to whom—all of this can actually save valuable time. It's something like constructing an outline before you begin to write a paper. It provides a clear sense of direction and helps you on your way to a finished product.

Planning—establishing goals and action plans to accomplish the goals—is work, often hard work (although it does get easier and quicker after the first few times through it). It is a part, though, of an evangelism committee's doing what it can to assist the congregation in its God-given mission of reaching out to the community with the gospel.

Step 7: Develop policies and procedures

Policies are standing guidelines under which an organization operates to carry out its objectives. They are similar to goals in that they help to fulfill objectives and require action plans to carry them out. They are different from goals in that they recur automatically until such time as the group determines to change them. We might call policies, then, recurring goals. The recurring action plans required to carry out policies are sometimes called procedures. Procedures are simply a standardized way of performing certain repetitive work. For example, a congregation that conducts an annual outreach-oriented vacation Bible school would be wise to develop a set of procedures that can be followed from year to year.

The congregation's evangelism committee will find it helpful to establish certain policies under each of its stated objectives. Generally, policies will be established over a period of time. When the committee finds that a particular activity has helped to further the congregation's extension of the gospel to the community, e.g., a community religious survey, it may decide to repeat that activity annually. To conduct an annual community religious survey then becomes one of the policies of the evangelism committee.

Policies should be written and kept in a place where they are readily accessible—both for implementation and review. Writing policies down helps to assure that they are not forgotten or overlooked. Written policies also serve as a time-saver. To use the example cited in the previous paragraph, until the committee decides otherwise, it will conduct a community religious survey each year. This does not eliminate the need for annual planning and goal-setting, but it does cover those areas of work that are not likely to change from year to year.

It should be added, though, that all policies and procedures should be reviewed each year to see how well they are contributing to the achievement of the committee's purpose and objectives. Some policies and procedures may have to be revised or eliminated; others perhaps should be added. The evangelism committee may want to arrange them by the month in which they are implemented. It may also want to break itself down into sub-committees and assign each sub-committee the implementation of certain policies.

At the risk of being overly prescriptive, we list below an example of policies that might fit under the above-stated objectives of a congregational evangelism committee. The assumption is that policies such as the following will be established by the committee as a whole. What follows can serve as thought-starters for the committee.

Objective 1: To develop and maintain an evangelism awareness in our congregation.

It shall be the policy of the evangelism committee

1. to produce one article per month on evangelism for the Sunday bulletin and one article per quarter for the monthly newsletter
2. to develop and maintain greeter teams to serve before and after each regular worship service
3. to request annually that each organization in the congregation adopt one evangelism-related goal for itself
4. to develop and maintain a congregational tract rack and promote the use of tracts as a witnessing tool for members
5. to promote an annual evangelism Sunday

Objective 2: To search out the unchurched, especially in the congregation's "area of responsibility," to gain them for Christ and the church.

It shall be the policy of the evangelism committee

1. to consider the area bounded by ______ to be the congregation's prime "area of responsibility"
2. to conduct a religious survey ______ times a year that covers ______ % of the congregation's area of responsibility in order to cover the entire area every ______ years (A telephone survey could be a variation of this)
3. to organize a ________-a-year door-to-door literature distribution (e.g., before vacation Bible school and before Easter) within the congregation's area of responsibility that covers ______ % of the area in order to cover the entire area every

_____ years (A variation of this could be a bulk mailing program a certain number of times a year covering a certain percentage of the congregation's area of responsibility)

4. to utilize every possible means to determine when newcomers move into the congregation's area of responsibility
5. to send a letter of welcome to each newcomer
6. to assign an evangelism caller to visit each new family

Objective 3: To provide opportunity for all members to receive basic training in witnessing and friendship evangelism.

It shall be the policy of the evangelism committee

1. to offer annually a ____ -lesson course on basic witnessing and friendship evangelism with the goal of eventually training every family in the congregation
2. to provide all new members with a one-session course on basic witnessing and friendship evangelism

Objective 4: To train some members for evangelism calling and through them maintain an ongoing program of evangelism visitation.

It shall be the policy of the evangelism committee

1. to offer _____ evangelism training course(s) per year
2. to seek to involve _____ % of the congregation's membership in one of these courses
3. to incorporate on-the-job training as an integral part of the evangelism training course
4. to conduct ongoing evangelism visitations throughout the year to visitors to services, member referrals, and such other current prospects the pastor may put into the hands of the evangelism committee
5. to send early in the week a personal welcoming letter over the signature of the pastor to every visitor to a church service
6. to visit or arrange to visit every visitor to a church service within one week of attendance at the service
7. to conduct an intense visitation program in the weeks prior to each new Bible information class

Objective 5: To establish and maintain evangelism record files.

It shall be the policy of the evangelism committee

1. to record and file all contacts with the unchurched on the part of the evangelism callers and the pastor
2. to make periodic mailings (e.g., before the beginning of a new Bible information class, a new Sunday school term, vacation Bible school) to all families in the evangelism "prospect" file[8]
3. to assist evangelism callers with timed reminders that a prospect should be contacted
4. to keep people on the congregation's "soul responsibility list" until they have joined the congregation, joined another congregation, moved away, died, or explicitly requested that they do not want to be on it any longer

Objective 6: To provide for a meaningful reception, orientation, and assimilation of new members into the congregation.

It shall be the policy of the evangelism committee

1. to prepare a new member welcoming packet that will provide for each new member an introduction to the life and work of the congregation
2. to arrange a public reception into membership for all new members (confirmation, profession of faith, transfer)
3. to arrange for periodic new member welcoming dinners
4. to provide sponsors for each new member or new member family who will help to assimilate the new member into the life and work of the congregation
5. to evaluate periodically the congregation's group life to determine if there are a sufficient number and variety of groups to enable the new member to find his or her place in one or more of them

Objective 7: To work closely with the board of elders in follow-up of inactive members.

It shall be the policy of the evangelism committee

---

[8]A prospect newsletter service is available from the WELS Evangelism Office, 2929 N. Mayfair Rd., Milwaukee, WI 53222-4398.

1. to make through its evangelism callers such calls as the board of elders requests it to make on members who are neglecting the means of grace
2. to use in such calls basically the same approach as used when visiting the unchurched

Objective 8: To project a positive image in the community.

It shall be the policy of the evangelism committee to publicize the congregation and its work (e.g., submit to the newspaper accounts of newsworthy congregational events, newspaper advertising, radio and television spots).

Objective 9: To engage in regular study of methods, programs, etc., that could benefit the congregation's program of evangelism.

It shall be the policy of the evangelism committee

1. to secure copies of all material produced under the auspices of the Synod's Commission on Evangelism for study with a view to its possible use in the congregation's program of evangelism
2. to solicit from the pastor for study and possible use materials and books produced by other sources that may be of help in the congregation's program of outreach
3. to develop as necessary material that fits the specific needs of the congregation
4. to make an annual review of the objectives and policies of the evangelism committee and to make revisions as required by changing circumstances
5. to include in this review detailed goal setting for the year ahead as well as more general goals for the next five years

Throughout this chapter we have been talking about the work of the congregation's evangelism committee (or board of outreach, or whatever title the congregation has given to the group responsible for leading the congregation in the work of evangelism). We have spoken of the value of this group being directly represented on the church council, and we have stressed throughout the importance of taking the time to plan.

What we have not mentioned, though it has been an assumption all along, is that the evangelism committee is not the only group that does evangelism in the congregation. Its purpose is to provide leadership, ideas, and direction for the entire congregation. One of its primary functions will be to keep the work of gospel outreach constantly before the eyes of all of the members of the congregation. It will want to involve as many as possible in this vital work. It will seek to provide opportunities for training for the whole congregation in basic "friendship evangelism" techniques. It will also endeavor to identify those with a special gift for evangelism and offer them more intensive training for evangelism visitations on behalf of the congregation. That is the subject of the next chapter.

Chapter Six:
Establishing an Evangelism Calling Program

In chapter 4, "Creating a Congregational Mission Mindset," we talked about the value of offering a certain amount of training, especially in the area of "friendship evangelism," to all the members of the congregation, training to help Christians "build bridges" to those within their own personal mission fields.

That is one level of congregational outreach training. There is a second level: a more intensive evangelism training program for those members of the congregation who may have a special gift for evangelism. There are a number of reasons for a congregation to involve more than just the pastor in its formal program of evangelism visitation. For one thing, there is the principle of multiplication. One pastor can do the work of one man. If a pastor takes the time to train even one other member in evangelism calling, the number of qualified callers in the congregation is doubled. One reason Christ gives leaders such as pastors to his church is to train members for serving their Lord according to their gifts (cf. Ephesians 4:11,12).

Second, experience teaches that lay people can often be more effective evangelists among their peers than pastors in the sense that some people are more willing to listen to a lay person, who in their mind represents the "satisfied customer," than a pastor, whom some look upon as the "salesman." The gospel is no more and no less powerful if it comes from the mouth of a lay person or a pastor, of course. The difference lies in the willingness of the unchurched person to listen to what either a pastor or a lay person has to say.

One further reason to involve lay people in the congregation's formal program of outreach with the gospel is that some members may have a special gift for this kind of work. It is good to give such individuals the opportunity to put this gift to work in the congregation.

In what follows we will talk about recruiting people to be trained for evangelism visitation in the congregation. We will inquire first about what qualifications to look for in prospective evangelism callers. Then we will look at the recruitment process. After that we will discuss how to train lay evangelists, looking both at methodology and material that might be used. We will turn then to a description of the evangelism visitation itself. Following that, we will discuss how to locate people to call on and how to keep appropriate records. Finally, we will look at two different kinds of congregational evangelism visitation programs.

1—Recruiting Workers

Qualifications to look for

What qualifications should be sought in prospective evangelism callers? Another way of putting it: What are some distinguishing marks of those who may have a gift for evangelism calling?

Spirit-filled

Most important, of course, are *spiritual* qualifications. When the apostles suggested that the Jerusalem church choose some men to help them with the distribution of food to the widows, they did not say, "Look for men with organizational skills." First of all, they should be men "who are known to be full of the Spirit and wisdom" (Acts 6:3). We cannot see the Spirit, but we can see the effects of the Spirit's work. People filled with the Spirit are people who hunger for Word and sacrament. People filled with the Spirit are people in whom the luscious fruit of the Spirit is blossoming—love, joy, peace, patience, kindness, goodness, faithfulness, gentleness, and self-control (cf. Galatians 5:22,23). Look, then, for people whose lives reflect the indwelling of the Spirit, for people who are faithful in worship and Bible study.

There are also some practical qualities to look for:

A demonstrated ability to listen

Evangelism per se is telling; listening, however, is important in that it helps a person know when and how to approach someone with the saving gospel. Listening also tends to earn a respectful and attentive audience.

A heart for people

One who has difficulty relating to people will have difficulty in establishing an atmosphere conducive to verbalizing God's plan of salvation. This does not mean the individual needs to have a gregarious, outgoing personality. It is helpful, though, if the person's personality is such that he or she can relate to people on a one-to-one basis and finds it relatively easy to relate even to strangers.

A non-judgmental attitude

By non-judgmental we do not mean that the evangelist doesn't care about the truth, but that he or she recognizes that an unbeliever is bound to have opinions that do not stand the test of God's Word. One has to have the Spirit to understand the things of the Spirit. The evangelism caller may have to refuse to let himself be drawn into an argument. He may have to permit some unscriptural ideas expressed to go unchallenged—for the time being—in the interest of the more critical mission of bringing to the person the basic message of law and gospel.

Teachable

Prospective evangelism trainees do not have to be above average in intelligence, but they should be willing to learn. There are some people who find it difficult to accept instruction, who already have their minds made up about the best way of doing things. It is not easy to teach such people. The congregation should be confident that those serving as congregational evangelism callers have been taught and will use what they have been taught in their calls.

New converts?

Should the congregation use recent converts for evangelism calling? In certain respects this is desirable. A new convert may have the kind of enthusiasm for sharing the gospel we don't always see in those who have been Christians for many years, perhaps all their lives. Further, a new Christian may understand and relate to a non-Christian better than a lifelong Christian. On the other hand, new Christians still have a long way to go in their understanding of the Scriptures and may not be able to answer the kinds of questions raised on an evangelism call. Perhaps the best of both worlds would be to pair a more mature Christian with a more recent convert and send them out together on calls.

Women?

Is it possible for a woman to serve as a congregational evangelism caller? There appears to be no cogent reason not to include women among those making evangelism calls in the name of and on behalf of the congregation. They go out, not as ones with authority over the man, but as ones with a message to share. There is nothing in the Scriptures to indicate that a woman is restricted to sharing the good news of Jesus Christ only with another woman—even in the name of the congregation. Both Priscilla and Aquila were involved in explaining the Word of God to the Alexandrian Jew, Apollos (cf. Acts 18:24-26).

Nor do the Scriptures forbid women to engage in public ministry, that is, ministry of the gospel conducted in the name of and on behalf of the congregation. Rather, the Scriptures make it clear that, if a woman is asked to serve in some form of public ministry, she must not be in a position of authority over the man (cf. 1 Timothy 2:11,12).

The recruitment process

In general, it is best not simply to ask for volunteers when seeking to build up a corps of evangelism callers in the congregation. Those who volunteer will not necessarily be those with the gifts needed for the work. Conversely, there may well be some in the congregation with the appropriate gifts who hesitate to volunteer themselves for the job. Just as our Lord did not call for volunteers, but *appointed* the Twelve, it is probably wise for a congregation to do the same.

It is helpful to follow a two-step recruitment process. The first step consists of a personal letter to the nominee, the second of a personal visit.

Send a personal letter

The first thing you will want to do in the letter is to describe the work to be done. Here is one reason for establishing job descriptions. A copy of the job description for a congregational evangelism caller will make it clear what activities and time commitment are expected of the person. Congregations that have not established job descriptions could begin in the following fashion: Ask the present holder of the job, e.g., the one who is at present making evangelism calls on behalf of the congregation, to write up all that he or she is doing as an evangelism caller. It will be helpful to give the person a format to follow. You might use or adapt the following one:

Position Title:

Purpose:

Responsibilities:

Accountable to:

Term of commitment:

Time required:

Additional comments:

After the person has prepared the job description in light of what he or she is presently doing, it should be returned to the pastor or committee chairman for review and possible revision. If it is revised, it should be returned to the present job holder for his or her reactions to the revisions. Once both the chairman and/or pastor and the job holder agree on the wording, then bring it to the church council for adoption. Many congregations keep all of their job descriptions in a loose-leaf book, thus easily permitting revisions from time to time. In general, it is helpful never to give a job to a person in the congregation without also giving him or her a description of what the work entails.

A letter to a nominee should not only describe the work to be done, it will also want to show how that work fits into the big picture, that is, how it relates to the mission of the congregation. If the congregation has drawn up a mission statement, it would be good to include a copy of it in the letter and to state in a sentence or two how serving as one of the congregation's evangelism callers relates to the congregation's mission.

Third, in the letter you will want to explain why you are asking that particular person to be trained for serving as an evangelism caller. You will want to explain that those who nominated him or her for the position are of the opinion that the person possesses the gifts needed for the work. Just as a congregation takes care in choosing other workers, it will want to do the same when choosing those who will be trained for calling on the unchurched. Not all Christians have the same gifts. Though all Christians are called upon to teach one another (cf. Colossians 3:16), for example, to some Christians the Spirit has given the special ability to teach. In the same way, though Christ calls upon all believers to tell others the good news of redemption, to some Christians the Spirit gives a special aptitude for bringing the gospel to those who do not yet know Christ.

The apostle Paul talks about the subject of spiritual gifts in 1 Corinthians 12 (also Romans 12:1-8). In 1 Corinthians 12 he compares the Church with the human body. Just as there are many different parts in the human body, each with a different function to perform, so it is in the Body of Christ, the church. "To each one [each member of the Body] the manifestation of the Spirit [spiritual gifts] is given for the common good" (verse 7). The Spirit gives these gifts "to each one, just as he determines" (verse 11). It is not a question of the gospel being more or less powerful in the hands of a gifted or a non-gifted person, of course, just as the Word taught to believers is equally powerful whether or not the one teaching it fits the biblical criterion of being "able to teach" (1 Timothy 3:2). But just as we seek to choose as teachers in the church those who have the special gift of being able to teach, so we will want to seek to utilize as evangelism callers those who appear to have a gift for presenting the gospel especially to those who are not yet a part of the Body of Christ.

How might a congregation discover such persons? One suggestion that some congregations have found helpful is to conduct a series of evangelism training meetings open to all. Advertise these sessions as an opportunity to take a somewhat in-depth look at ways of presenting the basic message of salvation to those who do not yet know Jesus as their Savior. Then draw out of that group for further training individuals who may have given some evidence of an aptitude for this kind of work.

During my years in the parish ministry, I would issue an invitation to those attending the classes to accompany me on some evangelism calls. I would make these calls each evening upon conclusion of the class. Usually, some responded positively to that invitation. Abilities that surfaced during the class and interest exhibited in joining me on some calls uncovered certain individuals who, upon further training, were able to serve as evangelism callers.

Pay a personal visit

Sending a letter with the above information beforehand gives the person a chance to prayerfully think through what is being asked of him or her. A personal visit, step two of a suggested two-step recruitment process, provides an opportunity for the nominee to ask questions. The visitor, who could be either the pastor or the evangelism committee chairman, will want to review the contents of the letter and be ready to answer questions. He will want to assure the person that training will be provided to help qualify him for what he is being asked to do.

He will not want to manipulate the person through faulty motivational tactics, such as motivating by guilt ("Many people in our neighborhood will go to hell if we don't get people to call on them"; or, "After all that Jesus did for you, I'm sure you can't say no to this"); or by appealing to loyalty to the organization ("You can't let your church down") or to pride ("You're the only one I can count on"). There is one proper motivation: what God has done for us in Christ. "Christ's love compels us" (2 Corinthians 5:14), writes the apostle Paul. "In view of God's mercy," says Paul in another place, "offer your bodies as living sacrifices, holy and pleasing to God—which is your spiritual act of worship" (Romans 12:1,2). God's great mercy as evidenced in giving his Son as the sacrifice for my sins—that is what properly motivates the Christian to be willing to offer himself or herself in sacrificial service to God.

There are some secondary factors that those calling on nominees should be aware of as they encourage individuals to accept the nomination to be trained for service as evangelism callers:

People want to do work that is meaningful. That is why it is important to relate what the person is being asked to do to the congregation's mission statement.

People want to do work that is challenging. It is neither honest nor helpful to downplay the amount of work involved. It should not be surprising that a nominee who is told, "There's nothing to it," might respond, "Then why are you asking me to do it?"

People want to do work they are able to do. That underscores the importance of seeking to match gifts with task and also of assuring sufficient training.

People want to know how much time is involved—both the term of commitment and the amount of time required weekly (or monthly) during that period of time. Here we see the value of a job description that states both term and time requirements.

People want to have a feeling of achievement. Clear, measurable goals on the part of the committee can help people see that their service will make a difference.

2—Training Workers

Number of trainees

If a congregation is just beginning to train members to serve as congregational evangelism callers, we recommend it start small. Two trainees are probably enough to begin with. Preferably, the trainer will be the pastor himself. After people are trained, they can then not only make calls on their own but assist the pastor in training others. This is in accord with Paul's words to Timothy: "The things you have heard me say . . . entrust to reliable men who will also be qualified to teach others" (2 Timothy 2:2).

Materials

We strongly recommend the utilization of one basic law-gospel witnessing outline to train congregational lay evangelists. Trainees should be taught to reproduce this basic outline from memory, including key Bible verses and suitable illustrations, and then gradually to flesh it out in their own words.

Some contend that it is not helpful to teach a specific law-gospel witnessing outline to people. Some of the most commonly-heard arguments include the following:

- The claim that using a prepared presentation sounds too much like a "canned speech." This is possible, of course, just as a pastor's memorized sermon can sound "canned." Neither a memorized sermon nor a memorized law-gospel evangelism presentation has to sound "canned," however, and it won't if it is spoken from one heart to another heart. In my evangelism calling over the years, I utilized for the most part just one simple law-gospel presentation. Even though I used it hundreds of times, it never in any way felt to me like a canned speech, nor do I believe that it was perceived in that way by those on whom I called. Each time it was fresh and new because it was being spoken to a person who had never heard it before, a person who, I knew, needed to hear the message.
- The claim that evangelism will occur spontaneously when people are properly motivated and, therefore, that a specific method is unnecessary. The shepherds, for example, upon leaving Bethlehem's manger, spread the good news without benefit of any training. On the other hand, Jesus spent the better part of two years teaching his disciples before he sent them out on their own for the first time. During these two years, they were learning by listening to what Jesus said and by observing what Jesus did. There is a place for both in the church: for spontaneous witnessing without benefit of any training other than that received through the regular preaching and teaching of the Word and also for witnessing that follows more intensive instruction in what to say, how to say it, how to overcome people's objections, etc.
- The claim that training congregational evangelists could create an elite, and thus potentially divisive group, consisting of those who have learned a special technique to which others have not been introduced. The possibility of that happening seems to be as remote as that of Sunday school teachers becoming an elitist group within the congregation. When a congregation has a proper understanding of spiritu-

al gifts, it will rejoice to see people serving in various areas in accordance with their gifts.

- The claim that having a trained corps of evangelism callers in the congregation will discourage the rest of the members from involving themselves in witnessing. There is such a danger, of course, whenever certain people are chosen to carry out a certain task. People might think, "That's their job," and dismiss it from their minds. When congregations utilize "greeters" before and after the Sunday service, for example, some might conclude that the greeters, and they alone, are responsible for making the visitor feel welcome. Or, when elders are trained for calling on members who have begun to absent themselves from the means of grace, the tendency of some might be to conclude that care for the straying member is the job of the elders.

  Such does not have to be the case, though. If, while a congregation is training lay evangelists, it is also actively promoting the "personal mission field" concept described in chapter 4, this will help to keep before the mind of each member that we're all in this vital work of outreach together.

  Also, having trained evangelism callers in the congregation does not preclude the use of others. For example, after visiting a prospect, an evangelist might ask a member who lives nearby to follow up with an informal "friendly neighbor" contact as a further indicator of the congregation's care for the person.

There are some strong arguments in favor of teaching certain members of the congregation a specific law-gospel witnessing outline. Among them:

- A prepared law-gospel presentation, learned well before visiting the unchurched, is a good confidence builder. Often people hesitate to become involved in a congregational calling program on the unchurched because they feel they do not know what to say. Training in a specific approach can help to overcome that barrier.

- It serves as a helpful training tool. In what follows we are going to suggest that an ideal way for training lay evangelists is for them to accompany someone experienced in calling on the unchurched—to listen and observe before they are asked to make such calls on their own. If they hear the same basic law-gospel outline again and again, this will help them in the learning process. In time they will be able to reproduce quite well what they have heard on many occasions.

- Training evangelism callers in one specific law-gospel presentation helps to assure "quality control" among evangelism callers. After training, they will be going out on their own, entrusted with the awesome responsibility of bringing the Word of life to people. It is good for the congregation whom they represent to know that those newly-trained in evangelism calling will be communicating the same message as their pastor and others previously trained in calling.
- Learning in advance a basic law-gospel witnessing outline helps to control the direction of an evangelism visitation. In the early years of my ministry, prior to learning such a basic presentation of law and gospel, my calls on the unchurched tended to be directionless. Often I left the home without having proclaimed the good news of salvation. Once I had a basic witnessing outline in my mind, one that I had learned well, this had a dramatic effect on my calls on the unchurched. Now, almost without exception, if I was able to get into a home, I did not leave without having brought to the people the message of God's law and God's gospel contained in the witnessing outline I had committed to memory. Utilization of such a specific witnessing outline obviously does not mean that one should never deviate from it. It is not meant to be a confining straitjacket; but it does serve well as a general guide to help give direction to an evangelism call.

What materials should one use? This will have to be determined by the pastor and/or evangelism committee. It goes without saying that the material must be doctrinally sound, that it correctly present law and gospel. Ideally, it will be built on a framework of Scripture passages to impress on the hearer that the caller isn't presenting his own ideas, but the message of the Bible. It should be logical in the sense that the hearer is able to discern a progression of thought from step to step. The outline should also be "transferable," that is, it should be clear and simple enough that members being trained for evangelism calling are able to learn it.

Two such outlines, both of which include complete training manuals, are *Talk About the Savior*[1] and *God's Great Exchange.*[2] Martin Luther talked about God's "gracious exchange," my sin and sorrow for Jesus' holiness and righteousness.[3] That is the heart of the God's Great Exchange presentation. God put the sins of the world upon Jesus and in return credited to the world the righteousness of Jesus —"a great exchange indeed! / Could Jesus' love do more for me / To help me in my need?"[4]

God's Great Exchange follows a five-point outline:

What God Demands:	Holiness and no sin
What God Sees:	Sin and no holiness
Man-made Remedies:	Try harder
	Balance your bad deeds with good deeds
	Compare yourself with others
God's Remedy:	His Great Exchange
God's Promise:	"Believe in the Lord Jesus and you will be saved"

The presentation is built around the framework of this outline and about a dozen simple Bible passages.[5]

Training methodology

Just as it is important that no person be asked to do something in the congregation without telling him or her what is involved (job description), so no one should be asked to begin a task without proper

---

[1]Written by my father, Wilmer M. Valleskey.

[2]Developed by my colleague in the parish ministry, Robert Hochmuth, for teaching the doctrine of justification to youth confirmation classes. I adapted his outline for use as a law-gospel evangelism presentation. Both manuals are available from Northwestern Publishing House.

[3]*Weimar Edition,* 2, 749, 33.

[4]Hymn 41, stanza 5, in *Christian Worship* (Milwaukee: Northwestern Publishing House, 1993). Nikolaus Herman, the hymn's author and composer, was a contemporary of Luther.

[5]A set of three training videotapes that includes a role play of a *God's Great Exchange* presentation is available from Northwestern Publishing House, as is also an eight-page *God's Great Exchange* brochure that may be used as an aid in giving a law-gospel witness or be left as a reinforcement tool.

training. In some cases, the training may simply consist of a one-time walk through the task. In the case of evangelism calling in the name of the congregation, which is a little more complex task than some, more training is desirable. What follows is a training process that many have found to be helpful. We present these suggestions under the assumption that, while each congregation will probably want to establish its own training methodology, it is helpful to be able to work from something. It is usually easier to adapt than to invent.

We suggest that training of members in evangelism calling consist of three elements, all of which are occurring simultaneously. The three elements are home preparation, class study and discussion, and "on-the-job" participation in evangelism calls in company with a more experienced caller. We also suggest, as mentioned earlier, that a congregation start small, that the pastor thoroughly train one, or perhaps two, persons over a period of several months before attempting to bring others into the program.[6]

Home preparation would consist first of memorization of a law-gospel witnessing outline and the Bible passages that are part of the outline. It would then proceed to a "fleshing out" of the outline, putting into one's own words (within the framework of the outline) the Bible's message of sin and grace. Specific assignments should be given for preparation prior to each meeting.[7]

Ideally, the class study, discussion, and the evangelism call will occur on the same evening. During the class session, perhaps 45 minutes in length, the trainer will review the assigned material with the trainee(s). Reviewing can be done through role playing once the basic outline and passages are learned and the trainee is beginning to flesh out the outline. Following this time of review, the trainer will present the new material and make an assignment for home study. Then the trainer and trainee(s) will go out together on an evangelism call. During this time the trainee can learn by observing a more experienced caller in action.

We suggest that the training of congregational evangelism callers include some sessions on handling objections. Christians frequently express the fear that they won't know how to respond when someone

[6]*God's Great Exchange* envisions a minimum of a 15-week training program. In the author's experience, if a person accompanies the pastor on calls for six months to a year, this is not excessive.

[7]Training manuals such as *God's Great Exchange* and *Talk About the Savior* provide such assignments.

raises an objection to what they say. Appended to this chapter (Appendix A) is a brief outline, "Handling Objections, or 'What to Say If They Say . . .'", developed by Pastor Paul Kelm.[8] Its "Five Principles for Handling Objections" can serve well as a training tool to help people overcome their fear of not knowing how to respond when someone raises an objection.[9]

Also appended to the chapter (Appendix B) is a practical list of "Dos and Don'ts of an Evangelism Call." It would be good for the trainer to work through this list prior to taking a trainee out with him on a call.

3—The Evangelism Call

As mentioned above, it is good that an evangelism call follow directly upon the class session, if possible. There are two reasons for this: It helps to reinforce immediately what was taught that night, and it also requires only one night of both the trainer and trainees' time per week rather than two.

Number of callers

How many should go out on a call? We are assuming that there would be at least two, the trainee and a more experienced caller. Can there be more than two? Many, including the author, have found that it is possible for three people (but generally not three men) to make a visitation—two trainees and one trainer. The obvious advantage in this is that it helps to increase more quickly the number of trained callers in the congregation. Congregations will have to determine for themselves what works best.

Advance appointments?

Should advance appointments be made? There are pros and cons. In favor:

- Making appointments in advance is a good time saver. You don't have to travel to several places before you get into a home.

---

[8]Kelm adapts Donald Abdon's "Four-Step Method for Handling Objections" *(Training and Equipping the Saints)* [Indianapolis: Parish Leadership Seminars, 1977], pp. 230-244.

[9]A more detailed treatment of the same subject is found in the manual accompanying the video *Soul Search* (NPH).

- People will tend to be ready for you, e.g., they will be done with dinner; perhaps they will have prepared their little children for bed.

Arguments against making appointments in advance:

- It is easier for people to decline over the phone someone's offer to pay them a visit than it is at the door. As a result, you may miss out on getting into homes you otherwise might have been able to reach with the gospel.

- Setting appointments in advance gives some people a reason for not being home. There are people who have difficulty saying no, but who do so simply by making sure to be somewhere else at the agreed upon appointment time.

The degree of interest exhibited (Have they visited church? been referred by a member? inquired about some congregational program?) is a prime indicator of whether or not an appointment should be made. Interested people will welcome an appointment.

Local conditions may also play in. People in a large metropolitan area, for example, may have to travel an hour or more one way to and from work. Often they arrive home well into the evening and don't eat until quite late. Under such circumstances, an advance appointment is a good idea.

Either way, someone must have the responsibility for arranging the calls. In a number of congregations it has worked to have the pastor or evangelism committee chairman provide the names and a volunteer appointment secretary organize the calls, arranging them by geographical area, providing directions, if necessary, and making appointments, if that is desired.

In the home

We might break down the evangelism visitation into three parts: pre-evangelism, presentation of law and gospel, and closing the visit.

We are using the term "pre-evangelism" to describe the opening moments of an evangelism call. This is the time to get to know the person, to demonstrate your interest in the individual as a person, not simply as a "prospect" for church membership. It is also a time to deal briefly with objections the person may raise about Christ and/or the church. To accomplish this, it is vital to do two things: ask questions and listen.

I have found it helpful to move gradually from the most general and least personal to the more specific and personal. One might, for example, make comments or ask questions about *things* he has observed (e.g., a finely landscaped yard, some trophies on the mantle), and then proceed from there to questions about the *people* themselves (e.g., their family, their jobs). The next step would be to inquire about their *church* background. By that point you have begun to bridge the gap between the secular and the sacred and are ready to share with the people God's plan of salvation.

These early moments of an evangelism call and the "small talk" you engage in are an integral element of an evangelism call. You will tend to learn things about the people that will be helpful in your witnessing to them. And, by showing yourself to be genuinely interested in them, you will be earning the right, so to speak, to ask more personal questions of a spiritual nature.

The heart of the call, of course, will be the presentation of law and gospel. For the sake of the person(s) being trained in making an evangelism call, the evangelist should follow the outline the trainees are learning. He will make it clear beforehand to the trainee(s), however, that he will not subordinate the needs of the people they are visiting to the needs of the trainee(s). If the occasion seems to demand a different approach, he will use it. Experience has shown, however, that usually one will be able to use the approach the trainees have been learning, modifying it as the situation warrants.

Training manuals such as *God's Great Exchange* give suggestions for gradually involving the trainees in the law-gospel presentation as the training progresses. The goal is for the trainees to be able in time to conduct the whole call, with the trainer largely in the role of an observer. Eventually, God willing, such trainees will be able to conduct calls on their own. They can then take along another person or persons who can learn by observing just as the former trainee did. In that way, little by little, the number of trained evangelists in the congregation grows.

The final element of an evangelism call is the close of the visit. The three "dos" and "don'ts" under "Closing the Visit" in Appendix B of this chapter summarize this part of the call:

- Don't remain too long after the law-gospel presentation. Let your message of sin and grace be what lingers in the person's mind and heart.

- Do seek a commitment from the person. The kind of commitment we are speaking of has nothing to do with a decision to believe in Jesus. Faith is the Holy Spirit's work through the gospel, and is not in any way brought about by a self-willed decision.[10] We are referring to something even unbelievers can do, that is, to commit themselves to some kind of action that will keep the person in contact with the Word. It might be a promise to attend church, Bible class, or a Bible information class. If we believe that faith comes from hearing the Word of God, it stands to reason that we will want to do what we can to assure that the person is kept in touch with the Word on an ongoing basis. Especially valuable is a commitment to attend the Bible information class where the truths of the Word are systematically unfolded for a newcomer to the Christian faith or to the Lutheran Church.
- Do leave appropriate study and informational material. Study material may consist of a law-gospel tract or perhaps a New Testament. It may be helpful to mark certain key passages and to direct the person to these passages. Informational material will include such basics as church service and Bible class times, information about the Bible information class, Sunday school, etc.

After the call

It is important to take the time that very evening to write up a summary of the call. The summary may be brief, yet it should be detailed enough to include any information that may be helpful for a subsequent call, whether it be by the same people or a different group. Congregations will want to develop a method of "rating" prospects to help determine when the next call should be made.[11]

There is some value in the evangelism callers' mailing a brief, handwritten note to the people on whom they have called. In the note they could express appreciation that the people opened up their homes to them. They could also mention that they look forward to seeing them again, e.g., at church, Bible class, the Bible information class, or another visit to their home.

Quite often another call on the family will be required. That is the third thing to remember following a call. Don't only write up the re-

---

[10]For a discussion about the place of talking about faith in an evangelism call, cf. chapter 3, pp. 88-91.

[11]We will discuss record keeping a little later in this chapter.

sults of the call and send a note to the people, but determine when another call should be made, who should make it, and what the subject of the call should be. If the ultimate goal of evangelism is to give the Holy Spirit the opportunity to make disciples through the gospel,[12] then we will not be satisfied with a one-time proclamation of the gospel. We will keep working with people, applying the means of grace the Lord has given us as often as we can. We will not give up on people unless they have made it very clear that they no longer desire to listen to us. Even then we will want to keep them in our prayers. And we will want to include them in occasional mailings in the hope that in time an opportunity will again present itself for further visitations.[13]

4—The Prospect File

Sources for the prospect file

In talking about recruiting and training congregational evangelists, we are assuming that there will be people for them to call on. This is not an unrealistic assumption. Most congregations in most areas should have no difficulty in compiling a list of unchurched people in their community for their "prospect" file. Generally speaking, however, this list will tend to remain relatively short unless intentional effort is exerted to increase its size.

A relatively large prospect file is helpful for at least two practical reasons. For one thing, postal regulations permit bulk mailings at a greatly reduced rate provided that the mailing goes out to a minimum number of addresses.[14] With a bulk mailing permit, a congregation can regularly send out such items as "prospect newsletters" and announcements of special services and events to all on their list. Such ongoing contact helps to keep the congregation in touch with all "prospects," even those it may not be able to visit personally for a time.

Second, most prospect lists will include a significant number of those who for one reason or another have indicated they don't want a member coming to their home. A relatively large prospect list is thus required to yield a sufficient number of names of people open to an

---

[12]Cf. "Is the mission of the church to preach the gospel or to make disciples?" in chapter 3, p. 134.

[13]For specific recommendations pertaining to sequencing of calls cf. "Survey and Listening Visits" in the *Locating the Lost* manual (NPH).

[14]At present that minimum number is 200.

evangelism call.[15] In its desire to bring to as many as possible the message of sin and grace, the congregation will want to build as large a prospect list as it can.

We list below a number of sources the congregation will not want to overlook in locating people who need to hear the one message that gives life now and forever.

Visitors to services

This is a prime source of "prospects" for follow-up. More often than not, those who visit a service are open to a visit from someone in the congregation. This underscores the importance of seeking to build a mission mindset on the part of all the members in the congregation (cf. chapter 4). If a large number of members are involved in a Philip-like "come and see" ministry (cf. John 1:43ff.) and are bringing their friends to church, the result will be a large number of people for the congregation's evangelism callers to visit.

To that end, a congregation may want to promote and conduct periodic "Friendship Sundays" that utilize a somewhat simplified liturgy and the simpler, more familiar hymns.[16]

To gain a greater amount of useful information from the visitor, we would also suggest that a congregation utilize guest cards or a pew register rather than (or in addition to) the traditional guestbook. A sample guest card is found in Appendix C. One side of the card is for members, the other for visitors. Congregations utilizing such cards ask all worshipers to fill out a card, often during the time of the offering. The cards are then gathered during or following the completion of the offering.

Families of Sunday school and vacation Bible school enrollees

This source of prospects can be maximized by intentionally using the Sunday school and vacation Bible school as mission arms of the church. The congregation might undertake a neighborhood canvass each fall with the specific intent of discovering children who are not attending Sunday school. The same can be done each year in the weeks prior to the annual vacation Bible school. Besides the obvious blessing the children will receive through their participation in the

---

[15]About 20 percent of the average prospect list consists of "active" prospects, those who are open to visitation by congregational evangelism callers.

[16]Cf. chapter 4, p. 197ff., for a discussion of the Friendship Sunday concept.

Sunday school and/or vacation Bible school, this provides an excellent point of contact with the parents.[17]

Lutheran elementary school inquirers

Refer to chapter 4, p. 208ff., for a discussion on using the Lutheran elementary school as an outreach arm of the church.

People requesting pastoral acts

Non-members who contact the church regarding baptism of a child or a marriage, for example, can be added to the church's prospect list. When the pastor visits with them, not only can he provide information about the congregation's procedures, but he can share with them the Bible's message of sin and grace and urge attendance at a Bible information class. These people can then be put on the congregation's prospect list for follow-up calls.

Member referrals

From time to time the evangelism committee might place into the Sunday service folder an insert such as the sample in Appendix D. This can be especially helpful in the weeks immediately prior to the formation of a new Bible information class. At the very least, those whose names are referred by members can receive a personal letter and a follow-up phone call inviting them to the class.

Bible information class referrals

Names for future Bible information class members can be obtained from those who are presently attending the class. They tend to be enthusiastic about the class, thankful for what they are receiving week after week. When you are close to the end of the course, it is good to solicit from class members names of those whom they feel might benefit from the class. A form such as found in Appendix D could be distributed to every member of the class. In addition, the pastor might want to encourage class members not just to invite a friend to the next series of classes but to come along with him or her the first few times. To alleviate misgivings, it is wise to tell members what will be done with the names and what kind of contact their friend(s) will receive.

---

[17]Cf. chapter 4, p. 205ff., for more on this subject.

Unchurched spouses of members

In most congregations there will be a number of families in which only the husband or, as is more often the case, only the wife belongs to the church. Pastors and evangelism committees, recognizing the unchurched spouse to be a potential evangelism prospect, will want to look for opportunities to maintain contact with him or her. Periodic friendly visits and invitations to the Bible information class—by letter or phone call or at times by a personal visit—will continue to demonstrate to the unchurched spouse that the church is interested in him or her as a person. Inviting a non-member spouse to join in social or recreational activities of the congregation is another way of keeping contact and can help to develop in him or her positive impressions about Christians. Many a time, often after several years of such low-key contact, the spouse does agree to attend the Bible information class and is brought by the Holy Spirit into a saving relationship with Jesus Christ.

Prospects uncovered in religious surveys

The most natural kind of evangelism is that which goes on spontaneously in the workplace, the family, the neighborhood, where Christians develop relationships with the unchurched people with whom they regularly rub shoulders (cf. chapter 4, "Creating a Congregational Mission Mindset"). There are many, however, who do not number any Christians among their friends or whose Christian friends do not see themselves as missionaries in their own right. Religious surveys, either door-to-door or by phone, can uncover such people. Much helpful material is available to assist congregations in organizing religious surveys and evaluating their results. In particular we recommend Appendices X through XVII of chapter 4 ("Locating Prospects") in the *Evangelism Handbook* (NPH). These appendices contain guidelines for a religious telephone survey; a simple, religious fact-finding survey; and a religious canvass-witness survey. The appendices also include a canvass survey sheet for use by canvassers; two religious opinion survey forms; and an explanation of a so-called farming method of religious survey (which involves repeated low-key friendly visits by the same people to the same homes in their neighborhoods).[18]

---

[18]The section entitled "Tele-Touch: A Phone Outreach Strategy" in the *Locating the Lost* manual (NPH) is also helpful.

Responses to newspaper advertising or articles

For helpful guidelines, refer to chapter 3, "Publicizing the Church and Its Message," in the *Evangelism Handbook* (NPH).[19]

Guests of church organizations

Refer to chapter 4, pp. 211,212, for a look at congregational organizations from an evangelistic perspective.

New residents

Appendix IV of chapter 4, "Locating Prospects," in the *Evangelism Handbook* (NPH) offers guidelines for new resident outreach.

Inactive members

The congregation's board of elders may well appreciate assistance in visiting those who have begun to stray from the means of grace. In many cases, such people are in need of hearing the same elementary law-gospel message the congregational evangelism callers are bringing to the unchurched in the community.

The above is not meant to be an exhaustive list, but rather to be suggestive of the wide range of possibilities from which to assemble a congregational prospect list.[20]

Managing the prospect file

It stands to reason that some sort of system needs to be set up to organize and manage a growing list of names assembled through the various avenues mentioned above. A well-organized, properly utilized prospect file serves a number of valuable purposes.[21]

Purpose of the file

1. The prospect file can assist the congregation in a *regular* program of visitation. The visit that seemed only yesterday may have actually taken place months ago. Chronological

---

[19]Further assistance is available through the Mass Media Office of the WELS Commission on Evangelism, 2929 N. Mayfair Rd., Milwaukee, WI 53222-4398.

[20]For more suggestions, cf. chapter 4, "Locating Prospects," in the *Evangelism Handbook* (NPH).

[21]The ten purposes listed below, along with the concluding, summarizing statement, are taken (slightly abridged) from chapter 5, "Cultivating Prospects," of the *Evangelism Handbook* (NPH).

filing or regularly scanning the cards (calling up information from the computer) can stress the urgency of another contact. Careful notation will direct the appropriate nature and focus of the next call.

2. The prospect file can assist the congregation and pastor in giving special attention to certain prospects. Times of crisis should be met by more frequent contact. Special needs on the comment section of the card can be shared with the evangelism committee, board of elders, or members whose loving care can win an audience for the gospel.
3. The comment section on the prospect card may even include seemingly insignificant details that can be used later to establish rapport with the prospect. One little comment referring to a previous conversation can build a bridge that could lead to an opportunity to present the Word of God. Jesus opened the door to the Samaritan woman with a request for a drink of water.
4. The prospect list can be used for sending personalized invitations to a prospect. A form letter entered into a computer can be personalized for each individual. Letters can be sent to announce a new Bible information class, VBS, start of Sunday school, picnic, potluck, special services, school plays, concerts, etc.
5. The prospect file allows for an appropriate distribution of Christian literature. Notes should record what tract or devotional literature was left with or mailed to the prospect.
6. The prospect list can be used for the intensive cultivating that takes place two months before the next Bible information class begins. Prospects with mild interest can be revisited. Perhaps a door will open at this visit. Letters and brochures can highlight the personal and spiritual blessings such a course will mean to the person's life.
7. The prospect list allows the pastor to systematically pray for people. St. Paul asked people to pray that doors of opportunity might open for the gospel. A pastor and the evangelism committee can pray over specific needs of people and ask the Lord to open the door.
8. The prospect file will assist the pastor by taking some of the responsibility for prospects off his shoulders and transfer-

ring it to other members of the congregation. The shared concern for souls will become evident and infectious. More names for the prospect file will then come from the people.

9. The prospect file will assist the opening of "side doors" to the congregation. By looking at a list, you can encourage certain members with similar interests to take a prospect under their wing. Invite prospects to groups open to nonmembers, such as singles, seniors, college age, marriage enriching programs, school functions, or fellowship gatherings in the congregation.

10. The prospect file allows you to focus on the children and invite them to Sunday school, VBS, youth activities, Pioneers, or the Lutheran elementary school. The concern you have for the children will become apparent to the parents. Often a child will lead them.

Persistent and frequent contact is the key to cultivating prospects. The prospect file is the key to appropriate contact, whether by phone, by mail, or by personal visitation.

Organization and use of the file

It stands to reason that if a prospect file is to fill such purposes, it needs to be carefully organized. Some suggest establishing a four-level filing system.[22]

- ***Level One:*** *The address of every residence in the congregation's target area.*
  Depending on the size of the community, it could be the whole community or a portion thereof. Generally, a radius of 1-5 miles (a reasonable driving distance from the church) and about 5,000 homes is as much as a congregation can handle. These addresses can be obtained from direct mail services (Yellow Pages—Advertising: Direct Mail) or from a street index phone directory (available from the public library) and be typed or scanned into the church's computer. Or, direct mail services will provide mailing labels covering the church's target area. This level one list is used for occasional general

[22]We are summarizing in what follows the chapter entitled "The Prospect File" in the *Prospect and Witness Nurture* manual (NPH). The reader may want to look to this chapter for further detail.

mailings (addressed to "Occupant") to invite people to special services or special events, e.g., the Easter service or vacation Bible school. A variation of this level one list is to subscribe to a service that provides a monthly list of new residents (or mailing labels for all new residents).[23] Still another variation is to mobilize a large number of people in the congregation once or twice a year to blanket their parish area with printed invitations to special services or events.

- ***Level Two:*** *The names and addresses of every identified unchurched family in the church's target area, plus the names and addresses of unchurched families outside the target area that have come to the congregation's attention.*
  Such a listing is developed by door-to-door and/or phone canvassing as well as by the many methods of locating prospects mentioned earlier. The list can be kept current through a newcomer contact program. Those on the level two list would receive more frequent mailings (preferably personally addressed). Mailings with "address correction requested" help to keep this list up-to-date. A periodic phone call (or personal visit) to all on this list does the same.[24]

- ***Level Three:*** *A listing of every unchurched family where face-to-face contact has been made and there is sufficient reason to include them in the mailing of a monthly prospect newsletter.*
  In addition to regular mailings, the evangelism committee will want to plan personal follow-up calls on the families in this level. (The names in level three will be a selection of names from level two, just as the names in level four below will be a selection from those in level three. Prospects will "move" from one level to another according to the level of the interest they have expressed. They should not be removed from the file unless the family moves out of the area or joins another church.) A master file should be made for every family in the third level and arranged alphabetically, geographically, by the calendar (date of last or next call), by interest

---

[23]Cf. Appendix 4 of chapter 4, "Locating Prospects," in the *Evangelism Handbook* (NPH).

[24]Cf. the section entitled "Assessing Future Service to Prospects" in "The Prospect File," *Prospect Witness and Nurture* manual (NPH).

demonstrated, or by a combination of the above (should not be difficult to do with a computer data-base program).[25]

- ***Level Four:*** *The active prospect list.*
  It is with this list of "better" prospects that the pastor and evangelism callers will work most regularly. It will generally consist of 20-40% of the prospect newsletter mailing list (mailed to all level three prospects). These are the families that are receiving regular personal follow-up calls. Their names should be kept in a "tickler," or calendar file, so that it is always clear when the next contact is scheduled.

It is helpful for the pastor and evangelism committee chairman to select someone to serve as the prospect file coordinator. This person would be responsible for such things as

- keeping the master file up to date
- providing pertinent files (or file printouts from the computer) to those making evangelism visits
- relocating files as directed by the pastor and/or evangelism committee chairman into the appropriate interest-level section of the file
- transcribing onto the master file new information gained by evangelism callers
- assisting the pastor in preparing and mailing a prospect newsletter
- keeping the "resource file" up to date (tracts, articles, and clippings of a spiritual nature that could be included in mailings to those on the prospect list)

The pastor (or evangelism committee chairman) would be responsible for

- overseeing the work of the prospect file coordinator
- reviewing names with the prospect file coordinator periodically to determine their correct placement in the file
- determining the priority for visitations and assigning visits

---

[25]Sample evangelism file forms can be found among the appendices of chapter 5, "Cultivating Prospects," in the *Evangelism Manual* (NPH).

- authoring the prospect newsletter
- locating nurturing resources and giving them to the file coordinator for filing

It will require some time to put into practice something similar to the above suggestions on organizing and using a prospect file; but it is time well spent when one remembers that each name represents a soul for whom Christ died. It is good to ask, How can we as a congregation best utilize our particular resources of people, materials, and funds to bring the gospel to these people? Organizing and categorizing a prospect list helps a congregation exercise good stewardship in its evangelism calling. In time, if a congregation is working at building up a prospect list, the list likely will grow to such a size that decisions will have to be made as to who on the list receives a regular personal call, who receives an occasional call, who receives only a regular mailing (e.g., a monthly prospect newsletter), and who receives just an occasional mailing. The above suggestions are not meant to be prescriptive, of course (each congregation has to assess its own situation); but they may be helpful to congregations as they seek to be good stewards in their outreach with the gospel.

5—Short-term or Ongoing Calling Programs?

The assumption throughout this chapter has been that the congregation, through its pastor and evangelism committee, will be actively working at recruiting and training people in the congregation for calling on the unchurched in the community. We have not yet dealt with the question: How often should members of the congregation go out on evangelism calls? Weekly? Twice a month? Monthly? Ultimately, each congregation will have to decide, since there are a number of variables involved, e.g., the number of people to call on, the number of trained evangelism callers in the congregation, as well as the amount of time the pastor and evangelism callers are able to devote to calling.

Our suggestion is that congregations think in terms of two kinds of evangelism calling programs: short-term and ongoing. The idea behind a *short-term* calling program is to mobilize a relatively large number of people for a relatively short period of time to accomplish a specific short-range goal. Such a program may be utilized before a new Bible information class, immediately after an outreach-oriented vacation Bible school, or following a telephone or door-to-door religious survey or a Friendship Sunday.

Those asked to become involved in a short-term evangelism calling program will need to receive training for this work, but not nearly as much as those engaged in ongoing, week-to-week law-gospel calls on the unchurched. Generally speaking, the purpose of their calls will be either to get some preliminary feedback that will assist those who will later make more in-depth calls, or to invite people to participate in some specific congregational activity. A short-term evangelism calling program might be used for initial calls after a religious survey to help determine that people should be listed as level three or level four prospects and should receive a follow-up call by the pastor or another evangelism caller. Or a short-term evangelism calling program could be used to issue, in a short, prescribed period of time a large number of personal invitations to the pastor's new Bible information class.

Whenever it is critical for many people to be reached in quick order, short-term evangelism calling programs fill that need. Such programs are helpful for another reason. Every congregation has capable members whose schedule makes them reluctant to commit themselves to formal congregational service on an ongoing basis, but who would be willing to serve once or twice a year for a brief period of time to accomplish a specific task.

A congregation also needs an *ongoing,* year-round calling program, in which callers are going out each week on evangelism calls (or semi-monthly or monthly, if weekly is impossible). An ongoing calling program is necessary for timely visits to those who attend church or enroll their children in Sunday school, for following up on "good" prospects uncovered in telephone or door-to-door religious surveys, for calling on newcomers to the neighborhood, etc. The congregation may not need a large number of callers to be engaged in the ongoing calling program of the church, but it will benefit greatly from a solid corps of trained callers. We suggest that the evangelism committee enlist these ongoing callers for one year of service at a time, with opportunity to re-enlist. Open-ended commitments are difficult for most people to make.

+ + + + + + +

Earlier in this book we mentioned that evangelism is quite simple. All that is needed is the gospel, one who has come to believe the gospel, and someone who needs to hear the gospel. This chapter has centered on the second and third parts of this equation: training evangelists (who have the gospel) and locating the unchurched (who do not have the gospel). When these two are brought together and the evangelist is able to verbalize the gospel, God assures us of his blessing. He promises that his Word will not return to him empty.

In brief, we might summarize this chapter on training for evangelism with the following nine points:

- Personally recruit
- Start small
- Utilize one law-gospel outline in training
- Employ on-the-job training
- Sequence calls
- Seek to funnel "prospects" into the Bible information class
- Keep working at building the prospect list
- Carefully organize and wisely use the prospect file
- Maintain both short-term and ongoing calling programs

May the Lord bless the propagation of the means of grace through those whom congregations train and send out with the gospel!

Appendix A: Handling Objections or "What To Say If They Say . . ."

A. Remember

1. You don't have to answer every question or objection to bring people to faith by the gospel.
2. You don't have to handle a question or objection on the spot. Use your resources: pastor, other Christians, Bible helps. You can always get an answer and get back to your friend.
3. Objections or "tough answers" are usually a ploy by which a person is trying to avoid the big question: How do I stand with God? Love for another person requires that we respectfully hear him out, respond only as we are able, but keep returning to the main issue—sin and grace.

B. Five Principles for Handling Objections

1. LISTEN . . . what's the stated objection or problem . . . what may be the real issue . . . what is the mood: angry? defiant? hurt? confused? frustrated?
2. ACCEPT the objection . . . which means that you acknowledge it as a genuine concern, that you'll try to understand, and that you grant him the right to his opinion. This does not mean that you agree, only that you wish to keep communication open. Some response-introducers:
   a. "I'm sure a lot of people feel that way . . ."
   b. "I can understand how you came to think that . . ."
   c. "I can see that this really bothers you . . ."
   d. "That's an interesting observation . . ."
   e. "I'm glad to hear you say that . . ."
   f. "I'm sorry to hear you say that . . ."
   g. "I used to think, too, that . . ."
3. Catch the KEY WORD or PHRASE in the objection, and use that word to turn the subject back to sin and grace, whether by
   a. limited agreement which leads to a different conclusion as you work back to the point of your visit; or
   b. looking at the key word or phrase from a different, perhaps totally opposite, perspective because of what the truth in Jesus does to a viewpoint; or

c. using a key word or phrase of your own that focuses the issue differently and allows you to bring the discussion around to more important things.

4. Always GET BACK to biblical ground. A discussion that sets only your opinion against someone else's is a stalemate. Arguing is always losing. And "majoring in minors" (spending too much time on secondary or insignificant issues) is not witnessing. "Thus says the Lord" is not arguable; and "sin and grace" is the religious issue worth spending time to elaborate with a non-Christian. Without faith in Jesus, all other religious issues can't be understood properly.

5. SET THE ISSUE ASIDE if you can't lay it to rest by

a. promising to return with a better biblical answer; or

b. encouraging attendance at your church's Bible information class; or

c. arranging a visit with the pastor.

Remember that our objective is to expose a person to as much of God's Word over as much time as possible. Inability to answer an objection is, therefore, to your advantage. If the person refuses to continue the discussion later, he would be saying that he wasn't serious about his question or that he'd rather remain a spiritual bigot than hear a biblical answer.

C. A Simple Approach: "FEEL, FELT, FOUND"

To an objection, the evangelist replies: "I can see how you might *feel* that way. Others have *felt* the same thing, I know (or: "I once felt that way myself"). But what I've *found* is . . ." (Here the evangelist takes the conversation back to sin and grace by the most natural means possible.)

D. For difficult objections ("I don't believe in a God . . . the Bible . . . heaven or hell") it may be best to simply say: "That's interesting. Most people believe in a God (respect the Bible, believe in a hereafter). You must have thought about this quite a bit to arrive at that conviction. Would you mind telling me how you came to that opinion?"

After politely listening, you will have earned the right to respond, "I guess I can see how you might conclude what you have about . . . I've considered the same evidence (issues, questions) but I've come to a different conclusion. Let me tell you what I believe about . . ."

Only the gospel works faith; so we seek only an opportunity to share that gospel.

E. A final option is to respond to an objection with: "Since that's the case (you feel that way), how has this affected your view of spiritual issues? For example, do you feel certain that if you died today, you'd have eternal life with God? . . ."

Appendix B:
Dos and Don'ts of an Evangelism Call

Before the call

Do learn well an evangelism presentation.

Do go to the Lord in prayer.

Do watch your grooming and manner of dress.

Do instruct evangelism trainees to look at the speaker, not at the one being spoken to (it can be intimidating to be stared at by others while someone else is talking to you).

Do encourage evangelism trainees to join in the opening conversation but to be silent during the law-gospel presentation (until such a time as they are ready to participate).

At the door

Do carefully identify yourself (who you are, your connection with the person you're visiting, your purpose for coming).

Do smile.

Don't carry a big Bible, for it may be somewhat intimidating (rather carry a smaller Bible you can fit into your pocket).

Getting started

Do try to sit where you can easily speak to each person.

Don't, as a general rule, accept an alcoholic drink.

Do ask that the television be turned down, if necessary.

Do ask questions.

Do listen.

Do address people by name.

Do avoid proselytizing.

Do handle objections briefly (try to focus your visit on the basic message of sin and grace).

Don't argue (you might well win the argument but in the process lose the person).

Don't put down other churches (the Bible information class is the right time for in-depth discussion of the doctrines of other churches).

Presenting sin and grace

Do ask for permission to proceed from time to time.

Do explain terminology (in general, seek to avoid the use of religious terminology that requires a lot of explanation).

Don't as a rule quote chapter and verse (even the book, for that matter) of a Bible passage (but do know the reference in case the person desires to see where that is said in the Bible).

Do use the phrase, "The Bible says. . . ." in preference to "Scripture says. . . ." (the term "Scripture" is not understood by all), or "The Word of God says. . . ." (this is not the time to be inviting a debate as to whether or not the Bible is the Word of God; let the Holy Spirit do the convincing through the message you proclaim).

Don't minimize the importance of the law.

Do present the gospel in all its beauty.

Do conclude with a "no strings attached" promise of God, e.g., John 3:16.

Closing the visit

Do seek a commitment from the person that keeps him or her in contact with the Word (a promise to attend church, Bible class, a Bible information class).

Don't remain too long after the law-gospel presentation (let it be what lingers in the person's mind and heart).

Do leave appropriate study and informational material.

After the call

Do take the time that night to record a summary of the call.

Do continue in prayer for the person(s) on whom you have called.

Do be sure to follow up on your call.

Do be prepared for "failures" as well as "successes" (in Jesus' Parable of the Sower and the Seed only some seed fell on good ground and sprouted, grew, and produced fruit).

Do remember there is joy in heaven over even one sinner who repents.[26]

[26]I amplify these "dos" and "don'ts" in one of the three *God's Great Exchange* video training tapes, available from the WELS Commission on Evangelism, 2929 N. Mayfair Rd., Milwaukee, WI 53222-4398.

Appendix C

[Front side of card]

WELCOME WORSHIPER!
VISITOR

Please help us to serve you by filling in the information requested below.

Date: ______________

☐ Mr. ______________________________
☐ Mrs. ______________________________
☐ Miss ______________________________
Street ______________________________
City ________________ State _____ ZIP __________
Phone ______________________________

☐ First Visit
☐ No Church at Present
☐ Visiting Area Temporarily
☐ Recently Moved into Area
☐ Children for Sunday School
☐ Interested in Lutheran Elementary School
☐ Desire Pastoral Call
☐ Desire Membership Information

Member of ______________________________ Church

in ____________________

Guest, Relative, or Friend of

____

\+ + + + + + +

[Back side of card]

WELCOME WORSHIPER!

MEMBER

Family Name ______________________ Date ____________

First Name(s) ______________________ ❑

______________________ ❑

______________________ ❑

______________________ ❑

______________________ ❑

Please indicate attendance at the Lord's Supper by checking the box by the name.

❑ Desire Pastoral Call

Comments and Address/Phone Changes:

____

____

____

____

____

Appendix D

ANY NAMES TO SHARE?

We will soon be starting another Bible information class. This class, as you may know, is designed primarily for non-members, unchurched individuals, interested in learning what our church teaches. We ask for your help in suggesting names of people who may be interested in these classes. If you know of anyone who might be interested, please fill out as much of the following as you can regarding the person. Then give this slip to the pastor or an usher, or mail it to the church.

Name of prospect ______________________________

Address ______________________________

Age ________ Married? _____ Yes _____ No

Number of children ______ Ages ______________________

Church background, if any ______________________

Place of employment ______________________

___ Relative ___ Acquaintance

___ Friend ___ Asked to see a pastor

___ Neighbor ___ Unchurched

___ Work associate ___ Non-attending

___ Student ___ Member of church outside area

Additional comments:

____

____

____

____

____

(Signed) ______________________________

___ You may use my name. ___ Please do not use my name.

Chapter Seven: Assimilating the New Member

The subject matter of the chapter before us follows logically on that of the previous one. As congregational evangelism callers bring the message of law and gospel to people, some of them will be brought into the Bible information class. Having completed that class, some will be led by the Spirit to publicly confess their faith in Christ and their agreement with the teachings of the evangelical Lutheran church. The congregation will receive such persons into its fellowship through the rite of confirmation.

Then what? God is not finished with people once they have been brought to faith in Christ. It is God's will that Christians grow in their faith (cf. 2 Peter 3:18); that they experience the joy of serving him in accordance with their Spirit-bestowed gifts (cf. Romans 12:1-8; 1 Corinthians 12); and that they "stand firm" in faith "to the end" (Matthew 24:13). That, too, is the work of the Holy Spirit. The same means of grace the Holy Spirit employed to bring about the miracle of conversion he also uses to sanctify and keep the new believer in the faith.

This underscores the importance of keeping the new convert under the influence of the means of grace. To put it briefly, that is the reason for talking about the subject of *assimilation* of members in a text on evangelism. Assimilation has to do with keeping people within the fellowship of the congregation where they might grow in faith through Word and sacrament, serve their Lord with their gifts, and continue in faith until the Lord calls them home. This is in accord with the will of Christ, who wants his church to be "teaching them [those who have become disciples by the means of grace] to obey *everything* I have commanded you" (Matthew 28:20).

1—"Backdoor" Losses

Many studies have been made on the subject of so-called backdoor losses. People join a congregation and then—at times within a relatively short period of time—fall away. Why does this happen? With his parable of the Sower and the Seed, Jesus indicated that we should not be surprised if some do fall away. The one who received the seed that fell "on rocky places," Jesus said, "is the man who hears the word and at once receives it with joy. But since he has no root, he lasts only a short time. When trouble or persecution comes because of the word, he quickly falls away." Then there is the seed that fell among thorns, "the man who hears the word, but the worries of this life and the deceitfulness of wealth choke it, making it unfruitful" (Matthew 13:20-22). Behind it all is Satan. If he cannot immediately snatch away the seed before it takes root (as he did with the seed sown along the path, Matthew 13:19), he will do what he can to uproot the growing plant. There have been, and there will continue to be many casualties along the way. Pastors, elders, and other church leaders should not become guilt-laden or despondent if they find some members drifting away from the means of grace in spite of dedicated efforts to keep them close to their Savior.

The fact that some will fall away, however, does not mean that a congregation will not expend every effort to keep the sheep of the flock in the fold where they can feast on the spiritual food that both gives and sustains life. To that end, it is helpful for congregations to seek to determine the kinds of tactics Satan uses to draw people away from the Christian fellowship. They can then devise ways of countering Satan's stratagems.

From a series of intensive interviews with people who had recently returned to church after an absence of at least five years, Edwin Rauff lists the reasons the people gave for having dropped out. Among them: lack of encouragement from family; marriage to an unbeliever; rebellion against being pushed by parents as a child; change of pastorate; moved and neglected to search for a new church; failure of the church to change with the times; perceived hypocrisy in the church; failure of the church to meet their spiritual needs; little fellowship or spirit of community in the church; unfriendliness of the church; work pressures (working or too tired on Sundays); disagreement with the church's doctrine; anger at God in time of tragedy; church perceived as too dull.[1]

Though these interviews were conducted a number of years ago, they have a contemporary ring to them. Satan hasn't come up with many new tactics in the intervening years. A study conducted between May 1988 and April 1990 by a committee appointed by the Commission on Evangelism of the Wisconsin Evangelical Lutheran Synod (WELS) confirms this conclusion. The committee was asked to made a study of backdoor losses within the WELS. Answers given by former members to the question "Why did you leave the church?" fell into six general categories:

---

[1]Edwin A. Rauff, *Why People Join the Church* (New York: Pilgrim Press, 1979).

1. Non-church-related reasons, including relocation—6%.
2. Relationship with others (conflicts with pastor, teachers, members)—13%.
3. Unhappiness with congregational programs and services (worship, educational, fellowship, counseling)—3%.
4. Church-related concerns (perceived lack of care on the part of the pastor, teachers, and/or congregation)—6%.
5. Personal issues (personal and family problems, job and leisure interests, apathy, health, transportation)—32%.
6. Disagreement with church teachings (specific doctrines and practices)—40%.[2]

The above responses, given directly by former members, are quite similar to the perception of the pastors of the WELS. In their opinion,

> of ten persons who leave our congregations by the back door, one leaves because he moves out of town for a job, enters retirement, or goes to school; two leave because they are unhappy in the congregation; three leave because they disagree with the teachings or practice of the congregation; and four leave because of a personal or family issue: they marry someone from another church, they are divorced, they are ill, or they become more interested in other activities.[3]

The text properly states that "a congregation does not have unlimited options in trying to deal with many of these reasons." For example, "we can not change scriptural teachings to keep members from leaving our congregations." There are some things we can do, however:

> We can facilitate and encourage a transfer to another congregation in the case of those whose job requires them to relocate. . . . For those who leave for personal reasons, we can and should improve our counsel and support in the interest of better family life, while recognizing that frequently these persons are not easily helped and at the same time often do not want help. Congregations can also take steps to deal with those persons who are unhappy with something or someone in the congregation.[4]

---

[2]Norman W. Berg, ed., *My Brothers' Keeper* (Milwaukee: Northwestern Publishing House, 1991), p. 21.

[3]*Ibid.*, p. 15.

[4]*Ibid.*

That brings us to the point of this chapter, which has to do with preventing backdoor losses through a process of assimilating members into the congregation. Literally, the word assimilate means to make similar to. One of the dictionary meanings of assimilation is "the process whereby a group, as of minority or immigrant peoples, gradually adopts the characteristics of another culture." An assimilated person is a person who "fits in," who does not feel like an outsider but rather an integral part of the group.

An assimilated member is a member who feels a sense of belonging, who thinks of the congregation not as *your* church or *their* church, but as *my* church. An assimilated member does not perceive himself or herself as standing on the outside looking in but as an integral part of the congregation and its God-given mission. An assimilated member shares a oneness of faith and purpose with the other members of the congregation. An assimilated member is a "satisfied customer," growing through a solid diet of God's sound Word and sacrament and living and working closely together with other members, attached to them by the Holy Spirit in the bond of Christian fellowship.

A congregation that is aware of Satan's ploys to draw people away from the means of grace and the fellowship of believers will seek to practice preventive medicine, to close the back door, so to speak. That is what assimilation is all about. In what follows we will take note of and amplify on a number of practical ways to help assimilate members into the life and work of the congregation, where they can be living, growing, and serving, kept in the faith until the end by the Spirit of God through the gospel in Word and sacrament.

2—Ways to Help Assimilate New Members into the Congregation

One: Offer discipleship training before membership on the privileges and responsibilities of church membership.

Lutheran pre-membership instruction, whether it be on the adult or youth level, properly emphasizes the doctrine of justification. Above all, we want people to be sure of where they stand with God. That certainty can come only through a Spirit-produced heart-knowledge of the finished work of Jesus on their behalf. For that reason, the message of justification, God's "not guilty verdict" pronounced over the entire world because of the perfect life and willing death of the world's Substitute, must occupy center stage in any Lutheran adult or youth confirmation course. That is the way by which the Holy Spirit assimilates people into "the Holy Christian Church, the communion of saints."

A pre-membership course of instruction will also want to concern itself, however, with assimilating people, young and old, into the local congregation where they can grow in their faith and serve their Lord in accordance with their gifts. To that end, we suggest that time be set aside in a pre-membership course for elementary instruction in the following:

How to study the Bible

The Scriptures speak highly of the believer whose "delight is in the law of the Lord," who "meditates day and night" on God's precious Word (Psalm 1:2). In a course aimed at young or new Christians, it is good to take time to give some practical instruction on personal study of the Holy Scriptures. It would be well to include at least the following in this instruction:

- *Basic principles of Bible interpretation*
  Faulty principles of interpretation produce faulty understanding of the Scriptures and are the source of many false doctrines. If, on the other hand, people learn such principles as the need to be guided by the context, both immediate and broad; the need to let the simple, oft-stated truths shed light on more difficult and obscure passages; the need to determine whether the writer is speaking literally or figuratively, they will be well on their way to a profitable study of the Scriptures.

- *An overview of Bible history*
  Time constraints in a pre-membership class would require such an overview to be brief, of course. One thing that should be stressed in this overview, though, however brief it may be, is the "red line" of the Savior-promise all the way from Genesis through Revelation. "The Scriptures . . . testify about me," said Jesus (John 5:39). As people see Christ in the Scriptures, their understanding will grow as will also their desire to continue to immerse themselves in the Word.

- *Practical hints*
  As people are encouraged to search the Scriptures on their own, they will appreciate guidance on such matters as what translation(s) to use, where to begin, what to look for, how to use such Bible study helps as parallel passages and cross ref-

erences. They will also welcome suggestions on materials to use for personal as well as family devotions.

A bare exhortation to new believers to study the Bible without accompanying practical assistance in getting started could result in wounded consciences. People tend to fear to start something they feel they don't know how to do. A few simple guidelines as outlined above can help set new members onto a path of regular, fruitful personal study of the Holy Scriptures.

Understanding Lutheran worship

Lutheran worship reflects the gospel-centered nature of Lutheran, scriptural theology. While it is true that people can and will benefit from a church service without much understanding of its structure, the worship of a believer will be enhanced by a grasp of the basic elements of Lutheran worship. A brief walk along the path of Lutheran worship and the historical church year is a most desirable feature of pre-membership instruction. This could be done in connection with a study of the Third Commandment.

The purpose and practice of prayer

The Scriptures urge God's people to "pray continually" (1 Thessalonians 5:17). One of the chief parts of Luther's Small Catechism is the Lord's Prayer, given by Jesus in response to his disciples' request that he teach them to pray. With Jesus' disciples, new Christians will appreciate not just being *encouraged* to pray, but being *taught* to pray. Certainly they will want to learn the prayer our Lord taught us; but it will also be good for them to receive some guidance on prayer in general, e.g.: May I address any person of the Trinity in prayer? Must I pray all prayers "in Jesus' name"? May I bring to God personal requests for material things? Must I always say, "Your will be done"? Does God always answer every prayer of a believer? Is it important for me to fold my hands and bow my head? Should I kneel? Are prayers "from the heart" better than prayers from a prayer book? What if I don't know what I should pray for? Or what if I don't know how to say it properly? Should I pray anyway? These are the kinds of questions new Christians may well have on their minds and which can readily be answered during pre-membership instruction.

Biblical principles of the stewardship of possessions

The mindset of Christians is 180 degrees different from that of non-Christians. The non-Christian maintains, "What is mine is mine."

Christians, on the other hand, acknowledge that God is the owner of everything and that they are but stewards, or managers, of what God entrusts to their care. Out of love for their Savior who loved them first, they want to serve God, not self, with their material possessions.

One way Christians please God with their possessions is by the offerings they bring for the work of spreading the gospel. Though a good percentage of congregations conduct an annual stewardship program, which generally includes instruction in biblical principles of giving, it is helpful to offer some basic, fundamental guidance in giving as a part of a pre-membership class. It will assist new Christians in getting a good start in this area of their lives of sanctification. It is well, therefore, to spend some time talking about the proper motivation for giving and about how the Scriptures encourage Christians to give willing, proportionate, regular, first-fruit, and worshipful offerings. This might be done as an application in the study of the Seventh Commandment. At this time the pastor can also explain the purpose for and mechanics of the congregation's annual stewardship program, including its budget and its system of offering pledges, if it employs such a system.

Use of spiritual gifts

Stewardship is often thought of as serving God with one's time, talents, and treasures. It would be good to find time somewhere in a pre-membership course for a brief study of 1 Corinthians 12 and Romans 12:1-8. These chapters speak of serving God in accordance with one's Spirit-granted gifts. A study of these chapters will help show prospective new members that there is a place for them and their gifts within the congregation. The church as the body of Christ metaphor in 1 Corinthians 12 is especially helpful in bringing out the biblical truth that the one body of Christ, the church, consists of many parts, each with his or her distinctive gifts. Having "different gifts, according to the grace given us" (Romans 12:6), Christians are encouraged to use these gifts to serve others and to give glory to God (cf. 1 Peter 4:10,11). Combining a study of spiritual gifts with an opportunity for using these gifts in the congregation (many congregations use some kind of "time and talent" form for this) can help new members to see that they, too, can make a contribution to the Lord's work with their unique set of Spirit-bestowed gifts.

Basic training in evangelism

In a previous chapter we spoke of the value of giving all members of the congregation opportunity for basic instruction in communicating the gospel. A good time to do this is right at the time people are ready to be taken into membership, that is, near the conclusion of a youth or adult confirmation course. The reader may want to review pages 181-185, which speak of various simple ways of communicating the gospel, e.g., the "personal testimony" approach, the Bible story approach, the Scripture text approach, and the "come and see" approach. New Christians are often quite eager to share with others the good news of Jesus that has given them peace and joy and hope. A little practical "how to" guidance can help them feel more confident in following through on the desire of their hearts.[5]

Two: Provide a memorable entrance into the congregation.

Most life-long Lutherans will recall the day of their confirmation when they were formally received as communicant members of the evangelical Lutheran church and vowed lifelong faithfulness to their Savior. Making the reception of *adults* into communicant membership a memorable event—whether by confirmation, transfer, or profession of faith—is also desirable. It serves as a second step in assimilating new members into the congregation, telling them right at the outset that the congregation is most happy to welcome them into its fellowship and looks forward to worshiping and working with them in the future.

In what follows, we list by way of suggestion some ways to make entrance into the congregation a memorable event for new members.

Public reception into membership for all new members

Some congregations handle all receptions of members, with the exception of youth and usually also adult confirmations, solely within the board of elders or church council and ultimately the voters' assembly. At most, a note may appear in the Sunday bulletin or monthly newsletter with the names of the new members.

We suggest a *public* reception of *all* new members—whether by confirmation, profession of faith, or transfer—to give the entire congregation the opportunity to be able to identify, welcome, and inter-

---

[5]An adult Bible information course that offers training on the privileges and responsibilities of church membership as described in the preceding section: *New Life in Christ* by Forrest L. Bivens and David J. Valleskey (Milwaukee: Northwestern, 1986). A two-year youth confirmation course that is similarly structured: *Confirmed in the Faith* (Second Edition, 1993) by the same authors, available from Oshkosh Church Supply, 258 W. 8th Ave., Oshkosh, WI 54901.

act with the brothers and sisters who are new to the congregational fellowship. This might be done on a quarterly basis. In some congregations, depending on the number of new members received in a year, it could be done semi-annually. On this Sunday, special seating can be reserved for the new members and their families. There could be a receiving line after the service followed by a brief reception. Someone could be designated to take photos of each new family for a bulletin board display. Some congregations keep these photos on the bulletin board until the next group of new members is brought in.

"Getting to know you" newsletter article

As a way of further introducing the families to the congregation, a member can be designated to interview them and then write up a few paragraphs for inclusion in the monthly newsletter. The article could include such information about the new members as what or who brought them to the congregation, their background, their family, their work, their hobbies and interests, etc.

New member dinner

Some congregations have an annual new member dinner. It may be better, however, to do this more frequently than once a year. Perhaps, depending on the number of new members, it could be held quarterly. In some congregations, this dinner is sponsored by the members of the church council and their wives with the intent of giving the new members and the current leadership of the congregation the opportunity to become acquainted with each other. It is also a good time for congregational leaders to explain to the new members the particular part of the congregational program with which they are involved. This enables the new members to get a clearer picture of the inner workings of the congregation.

New member visitation

Members of adult confirmation classes tend to develop a rather close relationship with the pastor over the several months the class is convening. It is not good for such contact suddenly to be terminated upon completion of the class and reception into congregational membership. It is helpful for assimilation if the pastor takes the time to visit the new member within the first few months of membership.

In some congregations elders are responsible for assisting the pastor in "shepherding" members, with each elder having responsibility for a specific group of members arranged by geographic zones or some other way. The elders will naturally also want to pay a visit to the new members assigned to them and not wait too long before doing this. It would be most helpful if this were done within the first month of membership.

In addition, a number of congregations have adopted a new member sponsor program. Members of the congregation are matched with new members according to age, personal interest, etc. They meet personally with the new members within the first month, introducing themselves as their "sponsors" for the year. They offer to explain anything about the congregation and its ministry that may be unfamiliar to the new family; they invite them to congregational activities; they introduce them to other members, in general doing whatever they can to help the new family feel truly a part of the congregation. The reason for suggesting a one-year sponsorship is that in a year's time the sponsor is able to introduce the new member to the whole annual cycle of the congregation's program.

Three: Make available sufficient opportunities for spiritual growth after a person becomes a member.

This thesis is directed especially to pastors of congregations and serves as a reminder of the need for balance in one's ministry. As important as it is to go out to the unchurched with the gospel, it is equally important for the pastor to spend quality time at his desk in personal study of the Word and in preparation of sermons and Bible studies.

Three areas in particular require nothing but the pastor's best: preparation for the Sunday service, preparation of his sermon, and preparation for Bible class(es). As we noted at the beginning of this chapter, some people leave the church because in their estimation the church has failed to meet their spiritual needs. Others leave because they consider the church and its worship to be "too dull." Still others turn away because of disagreement with the church's doctrine.[6]

There is no way a pastor and congregation will be able to successfully counteract all objections along such lines. People can and people will close their ears to the truth. Some will set up their own agenda as to what they perceive they need, whether or not it is in line with God's will for his people. Some will come to be entertained on Sunday morning rather than to worship. A pastor will not be able to please all the people all the time. If he is pleasing his Lord by faithfully

[6]Rauff, *op. cit.*

preaching and teaching the truth, that is the all-important thing (cf. 1 Corinthians 4:2-4).

On the other hand, the pastor will want to prepare diligently for each Sunday service. He will want to make sure he understands the theme of the Sunday and then he will want to bring out this theme in his choice of hymns, prayers, etc. He will want to encourage the organist and choir to choose music that enhances the theme of the Sunday. He will want to make sure that his sermon also contributes to the overall theme of the day and that he clearly expounds the text and makes life-related applications. He will take care that the gospel predominates in his message. With the psalmist, his fervent prayer will be that all of God's people will rejoice to have been able to come to the house of the Lord that day (cf. Psalm 122:1).

Bible class preparation also deserves priority time and sufficient time on a pastor's schedule. If some people leave because of disagreement with the church's doctrine, it should not be because a particular doctrine has never been clearly and lovingly expounded in a setting such as a Bible class, where questions and comments from the class are invited.

The congregation may also want to think in terms of multiple Bible class offerings per week on different levels. This would be beneficial for new Christians, some of whom may have difficulty participating in a Bible class designed for those with considerably more Bible knowledge.

Involving new members in carefully prepared Bible classes, covering such varied subjects as Bible books, Bible doctrines, the Lutheran Confessions, as well as contemporary spiritual issues—marriage, family, Christian ethics—is a big part of assimilating the new member into the heart and center of the congregation. To grow in faith through the means of grace and to be preserved in that faith till the end—that is one of the prime reasons for a person to affiliate with a congregation.

Four: Provide a sufficient number of service opportunities through which the new member can become involved in and identify with the life and work of the congregation.

These opportunities for service may be in the form of an officially appointed or elected position. A person might be asked to serve on a board or committee, to serve as an usher, to teach Sunday school, etc. Or the service opportunities may be more specific task-oriented, e.g., helping to mail out the monthly newsletter, participating in an annual religious survey of the neighborhood, helping out on a monthly workday, and the like.

Such service opportunities give new members the chance to use their gifts to the glory of God in service to their congregation. This helps them to feel more a part of the fellowship of believers at that particular place. It turns "*their* church" or "*your* church" into "*my* church."

Congregations will want to maximize opportunities for new members to serve. Some ways to accomplish this:

Limit terms of office

A constitution that permits unlimited terms of office can result in an entrenched group of congregational leaders with very little opportunity for newcomers to serve. Limiting terms of office opens the door to more service opportunities for more people. This also has the often wholesome effect of bringing in fresh ideas.

Expand board / committee membership

A helpful bylaw provision is one that permits boards and committees to increase in size as the situation warrants. Some congregational bylaws, for example, simply state that the board or committee shall consist of three or more members. As the congregation grows and more people are available to serve in certain areas of need, the committee or board can simply expand to fill the need and in the process give more people the opportunity to serve.

Make use of the gifts of the whole congregation

We are thinking here especially about three groups that tend to be overlooked, at least in certain areas of congregational work: youth, retirees, and women. Most congregations have difficulty retaining their youth after confirmation. The reasons for this are varied and often quite complex. One reason may well be that, in general, we do not do a very good job of assimilating our youth into the life and work of the congregation. We are not claiming that getting youth involved in service within the congregation will solve the problem of our newly-confirmed young people drifting away from Word and sacrament. That is too simplistic a solution for a complex problem. Providing opportunities for the youth of the congregation to become more personally involved in serving within the congregation, however, might well be one way to stem the drift.

Congregations might give thought to utilizing some teenagers as advisory members of certain boards. The board of elders, for example, might consider using some teens to help call on fellow teenagers who have begun to drift away from church. Teens could also serve as full members of congregational working committees, e.g., a youth committee, that are called upon to carry out the policies and programs established by the church council and voters' assembly.

Retirees also are in many instances a largely untapped reservoir of potential service in the congregation. Their number is growing. There are more people in the United States over the age of 65 than there are teenagers. In addition, people are living longer. A large percentage of retirees remain vigorous and in good health for a number of years following retirement. Americans tend to put a premium on youth and to relegate the old to the background, and thus lose out on their mature wisdom and common sense. Older members can be a good source of service within the congregation. Giving them opportunities to serve helps them continue to feel (and rightly so) that they are an integral part of the congregation.

Our congregations have always used women in service of their Lord within the congregation. Women serve as teachers in our Lutheran elementary schools, Sunday schools, and vacation Bible schools. Women serve as organists and choir directors. They prepare the elements for the Lord's Supper. They decorate the chancel with flowers. They serve at various church functions. They provide assistance in the church office. Women also serve on a whole host of what are traditionally women-staffed committees in the congregation.

There may well be other committees on which women might serve in accordance with their gifts, committees that traditionally have been comprised only of men, e.g., stewardship, evangelism, property, youth. The Scriptures clearly teach that the woman should not have authority over the man (cf. 1 Timothy 2:11,12). It would have to be clear, therefore, that any congregational committee on which a woman sits functions as an *advisory, service* committee, not as a *legislative* board. Nor should a woman serve as chairperson of a committee consisting of both men and women. With these clear scriptural principles understood and adhered to, it may be well for women of the congregation to be given the opportunity to serve in a broader capacity than has been customary over the years.

We must add one note to the subject of congregational service, however. We dare not measure the level of a member's sanctification by how much or how little he or she is involved in serving within the congregation. Service within the congregation is not the only way by which Christians serve God with their gifts. As spiritual priests, Christians are called to use their gifts wherever the Lord places them. In some cases, e.g., sickness or infirmity, people may be unable to serve in some capacity within the congregation; in other cases, e.g., a mother at home with a number of young children, it may be inadvisable for a person to be spending hours working at the church. Yet it is good for congregations to make available sufficient opportunities for congregational service so that people who are able to serve are given the chance to do so.

Five: Provide sufficient opportunities for developing close fellowship ties with others in the congregation through involvement in the congregation's group life.

Human beings, by God's design, are social creatures. The Scriptures, Proverbs especially, speak much about the joys of friendship. They speak of "the pleasantness of one's friend" (Proverbs 27:9). Proverbs describes a true friend as one who "sticks closer than a brother" (18:24). A friend "loves at all times" (17:17). What joy it must have brought to the apostles' hearts to hear Jesus tell them, "I have called you friends" (John 15:15). Friends get to know one another on a deeper level than casual acquaintances. They share one another's joys and sorrows, hopes and fears. Friends are thus in an advantageous position to encourage, strengthen, and, if necessary, admonish one another.

A Christian congregation can provide a good opportunity for the formation of close *Christian* friendships, through which believers can help each other keep their eyes fixed on Jesus, the author and finisher of their faith (cf. Hebrews 12:2). Many people who join a church are, in fact, looking for such friendship. Not all find it, as Edwin Rauff points out in the reasons people gave for dropping out of church. Some felt that the church was unfriendly, that there was little fellowship or sense of community in the church.[7]

It is not always the congregation's fault that people do not find friends in the church. For that matter, the church is not in the *social* friendship-making business. Through its gospel ministry, it makes and keeps people friends of God and thus also *spiritual* friends of each other in the holy Christian church. On the other hand, social friendships among those who have become spiritual brothers and sisters can, and often do, provide good opportunities for Christians to help and encourage one another in the faith.

The larger the congregation, the more difficult it may be for a newcomer to meet and make friends. That is where involvement in the

---

[7]*Op. cit.*

congregation's group life comes in. It provides opportunities for more person-to-person, face-to-face encounters than the Sunday morning service offers.

We might think of three different kinds of congregational groups: group events and activities, service groups and committees, and small groups formed for Bible study or other purposes.

Group events and activities

The congregation might sponsor regular (perhaps monthly) congregational fellowship nights where members of the congregation come together on an informal basis for an evening of Christian fellowship. Some service group would be responsible for setting up the program for the evening. A variation on this in a very large congregation would be for such fellowship nights to be organized for the various geographic zones of the congregation. Other suggestions: a vacation Bible school for children and adults; a weekend retreat (such a retreat could be structured for families, for adults only, for married couples, or for the youth of the congregation); or a Christian parenting seminar.

It may be well for a congregation to also include some purely recreational activities in its total program, activities that informally bring together members of the congregation, e.g., a picnic, a theater or concert outing, a sight-seeing trip, a sports night (such as a once a week open night in the school gym).

Events and activities such as the above enable new members to make Christian friends without having to formally "join" anything beyond the congregation itself.

Service groups and committees

Service groups and committees, besides assisting the congregation in its work, provide another occasion for person-to-person, face-to-face interaction of a segment of the congregation's membership. Leaders of such groups, e.g., choir, Sunday school teachers, youth groups, ladies' and men's service groups, will want to be actively recruiting new members, especially from the ranks of those who have recently joined the congregation. The leadership of the congregation would be well-advised to evaluate the various groups in the congregation on a regular basis, both as to how useful they are to the congregation in carrying out its mission and as to how well they are doing in drawing in new members. It could be that some should be discontinued and/or that new ones should be formed. Typically, new groups attract new people.

Small groups

The formation of small groups is another way to assist the assimilation process in the congregation. It provides a natural opportunity for Christians to interact on a person-to-person, face-to-face basis. You are not so likely to feel lost in a crowd when you are a member of a small group.

Small groups can take a number of different forms. Some are organized as mutual support groups, e.g., for single parents or for people recovering from substance abuse. Others are based on common interests such as quilting or discussing good books.

Still other small groups are formed primarily for Bible study. Small home Bible study groups tend to be looked upon with some suspicion by evangelical Lutherans largely because of the way they were misused during the age of Pietism (late 1600s). At that time they became a divisive force, a church within a church, a reaction against the supposed "dead orthodoxy" of a congregation and its pastor. But today, as David Kuske explained in a *Wisconsin Lutheran Quarterly* article, "Home Bible Study Groups in the 1990s," "the reason for having home Bible study in small groups seems to have shifted from the Pietists' . . . goal of creating cells of people who will reform the church to having small groups as an integral part of a congregation's work."[8] Kuske further brings out:

> There is one common thread that seems to run through all contemporary home Bible study groups. These groups are started for fellowship purposes as well as for spiritual nurture. . . . Call it a support group, call it having a sense of community, call it friendship, call it being able to spend some time with others who care about you. In any case small groups of Christians gathered for the purpose of studying God's Word together supply the fellowship for which a growing number of people hunger, living as they do in an increasingly impersonal and pagan society. This is an additional reason given by many, if not most, of the congregations in our day . . . [for] organizing home Bible study groups as part of their adult education program.[9]

In this same article Kuske warns that sometimes people form small home Bible study groups as a reaction to certain things they

---

[8]Volume 91, Number 2, Spring 1994, p. 127.

[9]*Ibid.*, pp. 127,128.

don't like about the pastor or congregation. Because of their reason for existence, they often want to operate independent of any congregational guidance. Such groups must be rejected. They have no place in the church. They have become the Pietists' "church within a church." On the other hand, as Kuske writes,

> if the home Bible study group is formed as a part of the congregation's nurturing program and its goals are the same as those of the congregation, . . . the group will welcome the guidance of pastor and church council or board of education. It will welcome materials supplied by the congregation and ongoing training of the group leader or coordinator.[10]

If a congregation forms small home Bible study groups for the reasons mentioned above, such groups can help in assimilating new members. It is of paramount importance, however, that each group has a qualified and trained leader and that it uses dependable study material. Some congregations may not have the leadership needed for developing such a program. Others may determine to use its leadership in different ways. Each congregation will have to choose for itself.[11]

In talking about getting people involved in the congregation's group life, we need to add this disclaimer: All church members will not have the same desire to become a part of some congregational group, whether large group or small. They should not be pressured to do so. One's relationship with God and with his church is not dependent on belonging to any congregational group. What Kuske says about inviting people to join a home Bible study group applies to any congregational group:

> People in each home Bible study group will naturally extend friendly invitations to others to join them (especially if the groups are organized on an area basis or if new members join the congregation, etc.). But they need to be warned not to use any pressure in the form of guilt or put downs to get someone to accept the invitation.[12]

---

[10]*Ibid.*, p. 129.

[11]For more on this topic, the reader is directed to the entire Kuske article referred to above.

[12]*Ibid.*, p. 130.

Six: Provide an ongoing flow of information about the congregation's life and work.

In a communication-saturated age, churches need to find and utilize multiple avenues for getting their message across.

New member orientation packet

We suggest that the process of providing an ongoing flow of information to the members of the congregation begin already at the time of reception into membership. Congregations would do well to put together an attractive new member orientation packet and then to have someone, the pastor or a member of the stewardship committee, work through each item in the packet with the new member. We list below the kinds of materials that congregations may want to include in such a new member packet:

1. An up-to-date brochure describing the various congregational programs. The brochure would include information on whom to call for further details.
2. A current church membership directory, preferably a pictorial directory, to help new members to be able to attach faces to names.
3. Information from the parent church body. Congregations of WELS, for example, might want to distribute and explain the purpose of such items as the official synodical periodical, the *Northwestern Lutheran;* the brief doctrinal statement, *This We Believe;* and such devotional periodicals as *Meditations* and *Wellspring.*
4. The last annual report of the congregation.
5. The current church newsletter and monthly calendar.
6. Congregational stewardship material. At this point the pastor or stewardship committee member might briefly review biblical principles of giving and explain the congregation's program of stewardship.
7. Membership information, e.g., an application for communicant membership, a copy of the congregation's constitution and bylaws, an organizational chart of the congregation, and a copy of the form that will be used in the public reception of new members.

Ongoing congregational and synodical communication

As an ongoing follow-up to such a new member informational packet, the congregation would do well to publish a monthly newsletter, as well as written quarterly reports from all the boards, committees, and organizations of the congregation. Since every member shares in the mission of the congregation, it is vital that every member be kept informed about that mission and what the congregation is doing to fulfill it. Communication—from the voters' assembly, from the church council, from organizations, from the pastor, from the Lutheran elementary school principal, from boards and committees—helps to keep the work of the church before the eyes and in the hearts of the members of the congregation.

Nor should we forget the value of communication from the parent church body. Information the church body supplies via videos, brochures, bulletin inserts, etc., helps to broaden the vision of the congregation. It reminds the members that, in fellowship with other congregations who share a common faith and mission, it is spreading the gospel not just in its own community but throughout the nation and the world.

Seven: Provide opportunity for all to have input into the congregation's program.

As an application of the biblical principle that a woman should not have authority over a man (cf. 1 Timothy 2:11,12), the highest legislative body (the voters' assembly) of WELS and other like-minded congregations consists of the men of the congregation. In some cases, a woman can be represented by her husband at the voters' assembly meeting. There are, however, many women within a typical congregation who do not have a husband to represent them. There are single women, widows, and women whose husbands are not members of the congregation.

Information about what is going on can be disseminated to all via newsletters and printed quarterly and annual reports. But what about the opportunity for all to provide some input? If we don't want a sizable number of members to have the feeling that they are standing on the outside looking in (a mark of a non-assimilated member), some kind of communication vehicle for those who do not qualify as voting members of the congregation will be helpful.

Pastor visitation

One way of obtaining such input is from pastoral visitation of the families of the congregation. If he is able to maintain a regular visitation of all the families, the pastor will tend to have his finger on the pulse of the congregation. In his visits, he can also bring up specific issues concerning which the elders or church council would appreciate some feedback.

Elder visitation

Some congregations assign every family to an elder and specifically invite those who are not voting members to make their concerns and opinions known to their elder. The elder, in turn, communicates to the church council and/or voters' assembly what he has learned.

Opinion polls

There are congregations that conduct periodic opinion polls to solicit the views of all the members on one or more issues. Often these polls are in the form of bulletin inserts. Members are asked to take a moment to fill out the form and give it to an usher. The results of such polls are taken into account by those who are called upon to make decisions on behalf of the congregation.

Congregational forums

Another option utilized by some congregations is to conduct congregational forums periodically to which all members are invited. Some congregations conduct a forum a week or so prior to each voters' assembly meeting. Board and committee chairmen give their reports and invite discussion from all present. A few weeks later the voters' assembly meets as the decision-making body of the congregation. Other congregations conduct forums on a more irregular basis, at such a time as it may be helpful to receive whole-congregational input on a specific issue or issues.

Two-way stewardship programs

Yet another way of giving all members a chance to express their views is through what might be called a two-way stewardship program. Congregational stewardship programs generally tend to be more in the way of one-way communication. The leadership of the congregation informs members about what the congregation hopes to be able to accomplish under God in the year to come. A two-way stewardship program adds another dimension. It gives ample time for members to respond, to share their hopes and dreams for the congregation, as well as their concerns. Congregations that have structured their stewardship programs in this way often are blessed to receive many helpful ideas, some of which find their way into the congregation's program of nurture and outreach. In the process, all members rightly sense that they are looked upon as a vital part of the congregation and its work.

Eight: Develop a training program for all members to assist them in understanding and responding to the needs of new members.

In chapter four we spoke about the importance of creating a congregational mission mindset, a concern for reaching out into the community with the gospel. It is also good for members of the congregation to be alerted to the importance of displaying love and care for those who have been brought into the fellowship of the congregation. To help members in understanding and responding to the needs of new members, congregations might want to utilize a Bible study by the author, "Forging Our Church into a Caring Community." It is a five-part study:

- God's Direction for a Christian Congregation
- The Christian—Cared For
- The Christian—Caring
- Caring for the Visitor
- Caring for Our Fellow Members[13]

Nine: Establish a "member care" structure for quick follow-up on the beginning stages of inactivity.

In spite of all the efforts to assimilate members into the life and work of the congregation, some will still begin to wander away from Word and sacrament and the strengthening fellowship of believers. Recognizing this fact, congregations will want to do two things: to develop and utilize a structure for detecting early signs of such inactivity and, secondly, to develop and utilize a method for immediate response to these early signs.

Detect early signs of inactivity

It is important to reach people at the earliest signs of their drifting away from the congregational fellowship, to determine what precipi-

---

[13]The Bible study is found in the *Member Assimilation and Retention* manual (NPH).

tated this drift, and then to take steps to restore the wandering sheep to the fold. Earlier in this chapter we listed reasons people gave for leaving the church. They included such factors as conflicts with the pastor, teachers, or members; unhappiness with congregational programs and services; perceived lack of care on the part of the pastor and/or congregation; personal issues such as health and family problems; and disagreement with certain teachings. In some cases these problems can be resolved, but it usually will take a face-to-face meeting or a series of meetings. The longer problems are left unattended, the more opportunity Satan has to turn people's hearts away from the Lord and his Word; and thus, the more difficult it will be to resolve them. That is why it is important to detect the earliest outward signs of straying from the fold. Norman Berg writes:

> Early intervention is the most effective way to retard the tendency to stray. . . . Studies show that we have a four to six week "window" of maximum opportunity for effective retention efforts in reaching members before they slip into inactivity. To delay a loving inquiry contact much longer than that tends to confirm the opinion of the absentee that the church does not really care for him/her personally.[14]

Except in very small congregations, however, unless a congregation develops some kind of structure for detecting early signs of inactivity, people's absence from worship can go unnoticed for some time. Congregations, therefore, need to develop some kind of soul accountability "early detection mechanism."

Some congregations utilize a Sunday "friendship register." At a certain time in the service, usually during the offering, all worshipers, members and visitors alike, are asked to fill out a form, often in a book that is passed down the pew. Members are invited to note such things as prayer requests, a desire for a pastoral call, or a change of address or phone number.

Other congregations have separate "mail boxes" in the narthex for every family in the congregation. This can save considerable money in postage and at the same time help a congregation to detect families that perhaps should be visited. When the monthly newsletter and calendar and other communications from the congregation are not being picked up, it is a possible sign of a spiritual problem. Someone can then visit the family and bring them whatever exhortation and encouragement from the Word they may need.

---

[14]*Op. cit.*, p. 41.

Still other congregations have assigned directly to their elders the responsibility for monitoring members' attendance at worship. Following the service, the elders run through the entire communicant membership and take note of those who were not present, with the pastor picking up the names they may have missed. This may not be feasible in a very large congregation, since the elders probably will not be able to recognize all the members, but it can be done in a small to moderate size congregation. The purpose, of course, is not to put fear into people's hearts that the church is checking up on them. The purpose rather is to be able to know, and to know as soon as possible, which people might be in need of some special one-to-one shepherding on the part of the pastor, elder, or other member. Membership in a Christian congregation includes such a mutual concern for one another's spiritual health.

Finally, we might note that congregations that have been able to establish a small group structure as described earlier in this chapter have with this structure a built-in way to detect early signs of inactivity. The very size of a small Bible study group of perhaps 10-12 members makes it highly unlikely that a member of the group will gradually drift away from the fellowship of believers without anyone noticing his or her absence.

Respond to early signs of inactivity

A congregation needs to develop and utilize a method for immediate response to early signs of inactivity. This is normally the work of the congregation's board of elders, although they may be assisted by others. Those assigned to make calls on straying sheep should be given adequate training prior to their being sent out. This training would include such components as the use of law and gospel in ministering to the inactive; developing listening skills; and training in dealing with conflict.[15]

We would suggest that, just as on-the-job training is an invaluable component of training congregational evangelism callers, so it is with the training of those asked to call on inactive members. Let the pastor or an experienced elder take a newly-elected elder along on a number of calls where he can see in action how law and gospel are applied to specific life situations. He will learn much from such

---

[15]It is beyond the scope of this book to suggest specific agendas for the training of elders. The reader is directed to the Board for Parish Services of the WELS (2929 N. Mayfair Rd., Milwaukee, WI 53222-4398) for information about materials for training elders and other members in visitation ministry.

observation and through it become equipped to do the same in his calling.

Visitation of the straying sheep of the congregation is difficult, often thankless, work. It does not always result in people coming back to a regular use of the means of grace. Those who do the visiting, though, can do so fortified by the promise of the Lord that his Word will not return to him empty (cf. Isaiah 55:11) and that there is joy in heaven when even one sinner is restored to the family of God (cf. Jesus' parables of the Lost Sheep, the Lost Coin, and the Lost Son in Luke 15).

At the beginning of this chapter we stated that assimilation has to do with keeping people within the fellowship of the congregation where they might grow in faith through Word and sacrament, serve their Lord with their gifts, and continue in faith until the Lord calls them home. That goal makes assimilation of members an important part of the congregation's overall work of evangelism. God's will and ours for those we evangelize is not only that they confess faith in Jesus as their Savior, but that they continue in that confession until the end.

Considering the importance of the whole process of assimilation of members, it is vital that leadership in this work be assigned to a specific group within the congregation. Three possibilities come to mind: the evangelism committee, the stewardship committee, or the board of elders. It does not matter which group receives this assignment. What does matter is that it be assigned; for everybody's business tends to become nobody's business.

+ + + + + + +

We believe. God has given to his church the great treasure of the gospel and the promise of life it contains. Evangelical Lutherans thank God for preserving his gospel in their midst in all of its priceless beauty.

Therefore we speak. We cannot keep to ourselves what God has given us (cf. Acts 4:20). We speak spontaneously of the hope that is within us. And we seek to mobilize the whole congregation for this most blessed work. We want each person in our little corner of the world to know: in Christ you have been reconciled to God.

To God alone be the glory!

Study Questions

for

We Believe— Therefore We Speak

Study Questions for WE BELIEVE—THEREFORE WE SPEAK

The Theology and Practice of Evangelism

Introduction

1. How would you define evangelism?
2. Agree or disagree? Living a Christian life is evangelism.

Chapter One: We Believe in One God, the Father, the Almighty, Maker of Heaven and Earth

1—Natural Knowledge of God

3. Compare Paul's approach to the people of Lystra with his approach to the Athenians. What were the similarities? What were the differences?
4. In Romans 1 and 2, of what two "natural" evidences for the existence of God does Paul speak?
5. What are the limitations of the natural knowledge of God?
6. Of what use is the doctrine of the natural knowledge of God in evangelism?

2—Revealed Knowledge of God

The Holy Scriptures

7. What is a key purpose of natural knowledge of God?
8. What implications for evangelism can one draw from the following?
   - The Scriptures are the inspired, inerrant Word of God
   - The Scriptures are sufficient
   - The Scriptures are powerful
   - The Scriptures are clear

9. Evangelism, stripped to its bare essentials, requires just three things. What are they?

10. Agree or disagree? The place to begin in evangelism is to convince a person that the Bible is the inspired Word of God.

The Triune God

11. The triune God is the only saving God. What implications does that truth have for evangelism?

12. What does universalism do to evangelism?

13. Agree or disagree? People must be taught the doctrine of the Trinity to be saved.

14. The triune God earnestly desires the world's salvation. What encouragement for evangelism does that fact offer?

Creation

15. How could the basic evangelism message be arranged around the concept of the image of God?

16. In what ways does the theory of evolution impact the church's work of evangelism?

17. Agree or disagree? A major task of the evangelist is to prove that evolution is false and that the Bible's teaching about creation is true.

The Fall

18. What are two consequences of the fall for all mankind?

19. What are two major implications of the fall for evangelism?

Chapter Two: We Believe in One Lord, Jesus Christ, the Only Son of God

1. How does Luther define "grace"?

1—The Person of Christ

2. What was the "dilemma" God faced as a result of the fall?

3. How do human beings attempt to solve this "dilemma"?

4. How does the doctrine of the person of Christ truly solve the "dilemma"?

5. What are the evangelism implications of the doctrine of the person of Christ?

2—The Work of Christ

6. Explain briefly—as you might to one who never heard it—the doctrine of the vicarious atonement, including Christ's passive and active obedience.

7. Why must we insist that the vicarious atonement is more than an "atonement theory"?

8. What is the value of spending time reviewing the doctrine of the vicarious atonement in an evangelism textbook?

9. Why will an evangelist want to include Christ's resurrection in his presentation of sin and grace?

10. Of what benefit is it for the evangelist to know that the ascended Christ still functions as High Priest? as Prophet? as King?

11. Agree or disagree? Knowledge that the Last Day is quickly approaching is what motivates Christians to do the work of evangelism.

3—The Result of Christ's Work: Justification

12. With what can justification be equated?

13. What are the implications of the following for evangelism?
    - *Sola gratia* justification
    - Universal justification
    - Objective justification

14. How is the Bible's doctrine of *sola gratia*, universal, objective justification emptied of its full meaning
    - by Calvinism?
    - by Arminianism?
    - by Roman Catholicism?

15. What makes the doctrine of justification "the central message of Scripture upon which the very existence of the church depends"?

Chapter Three: We Believe in the Holy Spirit, the Lord, the Giver of Life

1—Justification by Faith

1. Agree or disagree? When I die, I will go to heaven because I believe in Jesus.
2. In what sense can we define faith as knowledge, assent, and trust?
3. Agree or disagree? Some people are more receptive than others.
4. What is the result
   - if *contrition* is made to be a part of justification?
   - if *the works that follow* are made to be a part of justification?
5. What are some reasons for speaking about faith in an evangelism call?
6. Agree or disagree? One should discuss the new life of sanctification in connection with the presentation of the evangelism message.

2—The Means of Grace

7. Define the term "means of grace."
8. What is the place of the law in evangelism?
9. What place do the means of grace have
   - in the theology of Roman Catholicism?
   - in the theology of Calvinism?
   - in the theology of Arminianism?
10. Why is it important to have a good grasp both of what the Scriptures and Confessions affirm about the means of grace and what they reject as distortions of the truth?
11. Agree or disagree? Prayer has no place in an evangelism call.

12. Agree or disagree? If a person gives no evidence of true repentance, the evangelist should withhold the gospel from him.
13. What does it mean for evangelists to be "as wise as serpents" and "as innocent as doves"?
14. Agree or disagree? Apologetics and evangelism don't mix.
15. What evangelistic value is there in cultivating a relationship with a non-Christian?

    What are some caveats to beware of?
16. How might "friendship evangelism" be carried out on a congregational or church body level?

3—The Church

17. Why is it necessary for the evangelist to keep clear the distinction between church in the sense of the Una Sancta and in the sense of a gathering of people around the means of grace?
18. Agree or disagree? The evangelist will not be concerned with getting people to join his church.
19. Harmonize these two statements:

    The mission of the church is to make disciples of all nations (cf. Matthew 28:19).

    The mission of the church is to preach the gospel to all creation (cf. Mark 16:15).
20. What is the relationship between nurture and evangelism?
21. What role can planning and goal setting play in the mission of the church?

    Summarize Koester's word of caution.
22. What doctrines does proselytizing violate?
23. What is the responsibility of orthodox churches and church members over against members of heterodox churches?

4—The Ministry

24. What is the one office Christ has instituted in his church?
25. What is the significance for evangelism of the doctrine of the priesthood of all believers?

26. How do God's priests carry out their personal ministry of declaring God's praises?

27. What evangelism implications can be found in what the Scriptures teach about the public (representative) ministry?

28. Agree or disagree? Women have no place in the public ministry of the church.

29. Agree or disagree? The pastor's role as shepherd (nurturer) is more important than his role as coach (equipper).

30. In what ways can a pastor provide evangelism leadership in the congregation?

31. How does a pastor find time for outreach with the gospel in addition to his other duties of nurturing the flock, nurturing himself, and equipping believers for serving their Savior?

32. What two groups in the congregation will the pastor want to be equipping for outreach with the gospel?

5—Preservation

33. What are some primary reasons for a congregation to work at assimilating members?

Chapter Four: Creating a Congregational Mission Mindset

1. Why is it vital that a congregation take some conscious, deliberate steps to incorporate outreach to the community as a part of its overall program?

1—Building an Every Member Mission Mindset

2. What assumptions underlie the importance of seeking to create a mission mindset on the part of every member?

3. Why is simply inviting an unchurched person to come to church not always the best way to connect the person with the message of salvation?

4. What are three important steps in "bridge-building" evangelism?

5. Under the section "Establish Relationships," be ready to discuss the significance to evangelism of each of the following concepts:

- Identify your personal mission field
- Take time with people
- Let your light shine
- Be genuine
- Don't give up

6. Agree or disagree? Evangelism is a process.
7. Examine the twelve categories of responses Edwin Rauff received from his interviews, as listed in the section "Look for Openings." How might each be used to "build bridges" in one's "personal mission field"?
   - Family relationships and responsibilities
   - Influence of Christian people
   - Church visit, program, special event, or sacred act
   - Search for community
   - Personal crisis
   - End of rebellion
   - Feelings of emptiness
   - God's "kairos"
   - Influence of a pastor
   - Journey toward truth
   - Response to evangelism
   - Reaction to guilt and fear
8. What are the pluses and minuses of personal testimony?
9. What is the value of using Bible stories and/or a series of Scripture texts to communicate the way of salvation to those in one's "personal mission field"?
10. What use might tracts and videos have in a Christian's "personal mission field"?
11. What is the value of "come and see" invitations?
12. When might "bridge-building" be an impediment to evangelism?

2—Building a Corporate Mission Mindset

13. Harmonize these two statements:

    Lutheran worship is primarily for believers.

    Lutheran worship is ideally suited for evangelism.

14. Apply the statement of Francis Rossow to leading the liturgy: "The foolishness of preaching consists in its content, not style. What is foolish is our message, not the manner of communicating the message. The foolishness of preaching does not necessitate foolish preaching."

15. Examine the eleven-item list on p. 196 that describes a warm and caring worship atmosphere. Any items that strike you as more important than others? less important? Any that should not be on the list? Any that should be added?

16. What are the pros and cons of conducting occasional *Friendship Sundays*?

17. What are the differences between a *Friendship Sunday* and a *Seeker Service*?

18. In what ways does a typical Evangelical *Seeker Service* reflect the Arminian theology of the Evangelicals?

19. What questions must a Lutheran congregation considering instituting a *Seeker Service* or variation thereof seriously ponder?

20. What is the evangelistic value of whole family Sunday school?

    What difficulties present themselves?

    How might we overcome them?

21. What is the evangelistic value of year-round Sunday school?

    What difficulties present themselves?

    How might we overcome them?

22. What is the evangelistic value of offering multiple Bible class options?

    What difficulties present themselves?

    How might we overcome them?

23. To what will a congregation want to pay special attention if it desires to utilize its vacation Bible school as an outreach arm of the congregation?

24. In what ways can a congregation's Lutheran elementary school serve the cause of evangelism?

    Why is it important to establish guidelines if the school is to be used as an evangelism agency of the church?

25. What are ways by which congregational organizations can serve outreach roles?

Chapter Five: Planning and Organizing for Outreach

1—The Concept of Planning

1. What is planning?
2. What is the value of planning?
3. What are the limitations of planning?
4. In what sense is it helpful to think in terms of a planning cycle?

2—The Process of Planning

5. Distinguish between "function" and "form."

   Why must function precede form?

   What happens if form becomes more important than function?

   Why must function be changeless and form be flexible?

6. What is a *mission statement*?
7. Describe briefly the value of a mission statement.
8. If a congregation does not have a mission statement, what are the steps one might follow in constructing it?
9. What is the purpose of a congregational *self-study*?
10. Which should come first, construction of a mission statement or a self-study?
11. What is the value of a congregation's evangelism committee having direct representation on the church council?

12. Why should a congregation's evangelism committee have a *statement of purpose*?
13. Distinguish between *objectives* and *goals*.
14. What is meant by *strategic planning*?
15. Why is it important to follow all nine steps when developing an *action plan* to accomplish a goal?
16. How does the establishment of *policies* and *procedures* fit into a congregation's overall program of evangelism?

Chapter Six: Establishing an Evangelism Calling Program

1. List several reasons why a congregation should involve more than just the pastor in its formal program of evangelism.

1—Recruiting Workers

2. Of the qualifications for callers listed in this section, which would you consider to be the most important? the least important?
3. Why is it ordinarily best not to ask for volunteers for training as evangelism callers?
4. Of what value is a two-step recruitment process, i.e., sending the nominee a personal letter and making a personal visit?
5. Where does a job description fit into the process of recruiting workers?

   Where does the congregation's mission statement fit in?

   Where do spiritual gifts fit in?
6. Agree or disagree? Why the nominee agrees to serve is more important than the service itself.

2—Training Workers

7. Why is it helpful for a congregation to start an evangelism training program with just a few people?
8. Agree or disagree? The arguments advanced in favor of utilizing a specific evangelism outline in outreach work outweigh those advanced against such a use.

9. What factors should be taken into account when choosing materials to be used for training congregational evangelists?
10. What advantages do you see in an evangelism caller training methodology that centers on on-the-job training?

3—The Evangelism Call

11. Agree or disagree? It is best if an evangelism calling team consists of three people.
12. Agree or disagree? One should make advance appointments for evangelism calls.
13. What are the three elements of an in-home evangelism visitation?
14. What constitutes a "successful" evangelism call?
15. Which, in general, is preferable: seeking a commitment from a person to attend church or to attend the Bible information class?
16. What needs to be done after the call?

4—The Prospect File

17. What is the value of assembling and maintaining a relatively large prospect file?
18. Agree or disagree? Some pastors serve in locations where there are no unchurched people to call on.
19. Summarize the content and purpose of each of the suggested four levels of a congregation's evangelism prospect file.
20. Agree or disagree? There comes a time when a person's name should be removed from the prospect file.

5—Short-term or Ongoing Calling Programs?

21. Of what value is it for a congregation's calling program to be both short-term and ongoing?

Chapter Seven: Assimilating the New Member

1. What is the rationale for a chapter on new member assimilation in a textbook on evangelism?

1—"Backdoor" Losses

2. Agree or disagree? Congregations can prevent backdoor losses.
3. Describe a person who could be called an assimilated member.

2—Ways to Help Assimilate New Members into the Congregation

4. How can the Bible information class be used to begin the assimilation process?
5. How does providing a memorable entrance into the congregation assist with the assimilation process?
6. What does a pastor's preparation time for the Sunday service, his sermon, and his Bible class have to do with assimilation?
7. What are the implications of the following for assimilation?
   - Limiting terms of office
   - Expanding board/committee size
   - Making use of the gifts of the whole congregation
8. What does the congregation's group life have to do with assimilation?

   Agree or disagree? A congregation would be wise to inaugurate a program of small home Bible study groups.
9. Explain the connection between congregational communication and assimilation. When should this communication begin?
10. How can a congregation ensure that all its members have the opportunity for input into the congregation's program?
11. In what sense are the needs of new members the same as that of visitors?
12. Evaluate the various ways of detecting early signs of inactivity.

    Who should be assigned the responsibility for assimilating members?